HISTORIC
SHIPS

"FOR TO SEE THE MARVELS OF THE OCEAN."

*—The Chevalier Antonio Pigafetta
who sailed with Magellan.*

From the fiords sailed daring sea rovers
in their dragon-prowed ships

HISTORIC SHIPS

BY
RUPERT SARGENT HOLLAND

Illustrated by MANNING DeV LEE

GROSSET · & · DUNLAP
PUBLISHERS · NEW YORK

CL
Manufactured in the United States of America

To
CHARLES AND MARY HYDE
IN REMEMBRANCE OF MANY SUMMERS
ON THE COAST OF MAINE

PREFACE

Ships have played a part in the history of almost all nations and the literature that deals with them is vast and fascinating. The author of this book is indebted to many writers, but he owes special acknowledgment to the following works: The Discovery of America, by John Fiske; The Barbary Corsairs, by Stanley Lane-Poole; The History of Portugal, by H. Morse Stephens; Venice, by Alethea Wiel; Salve Venetia, by F. Marion Crawford; The History of England from the Fall of Wolsey to the Defeat of the Spanish Armada, by James Anthony Froude; The *Mayflower* and Her Log, edited by Azel Ames; The History of the United States, by George Bancroft; The Life of Nelson, by Captain A. T. Mahan; Charleston, by Mrs. St. Julien Ravenel; The Book of Old Ships, by Henry B. Culver; The Maritime History of Massachusetts, by Samuel Eliot Morison; Ships of the Seven Seas, by Hawthorne Daniels; Down to the Sea in Ships, by Irvin Anthony; Our Naval Heritage, by Fitzhugh Green; The Mercantile Marine, by E.

Keble Chatterton; and The Tale of Our Merchant Ships, by Charles E. Cartwright.

The illustrations in full color by Manning de V. Lee are from paintings made for the Year Book of the Class of 1926 of the Naval Academy at Annapolis. The decorations are by Edward Shenton.

CONTENTS

ILLUSTRATIONS

11

CHAPTER I

SHIPS OF THE
ANCIENT WORLD

I

SHIPS OF THE ANCIENT WORLD

FROM the time of Noah's Ark, and doubtless long before that, there have been ships, for men are by nature rovers, explorers and traders, and rivers, lakes and oceans offer tempting thoroughfares. Let a group of boys play by the water and see how soon they will be devising some craft to ride the waves or journey alongshore. A similar instinct led primitive man to cut a log in the forest, launch it on a stream, and sitting astride his first boat propel himself by paddling with his hands and feet.

That single log was presently succeeded by several logs bound together by thongs of hide or bark, making a raft on which the builder could float his family and household goods, and instead of churning the water with hands and feet the inventive navigator used a pole with which he pushed against the bank or bottom of the stream. Then a genius produced a paddle and voyages could be made farther out from shore and in deeper waters. Rafts became more elaborate; they were built up at the sides and a platform laid across so as to keep the traveler's cargo out of reach of the waves.

Somewhere a man conceived the idea of hollowing out a log with fire or with the rude stone tools he had laboriously learned to fashion. Although clumsy, awkward, and heavy, these dug-out trees possessed the ability of floating and of carrying considerable weight, and they had a certain advantage over the raft in that they could be handled more easily by a single paddler. Next came a master-builder who, studying the problem, evolved the notion of covering a light frame of wood with long strips of bark or the skins of animals. This was an immense step forward; here was a craft that could be propelled with ease, yet that was sufficiently strong to carry several voyagers.

These rafts and canoes, worked out in different ways and improved and adapted by men in widely separated parts of the world, have a great history. In America the Indian built his canoe of birch-bark and traveled far in it, daring the wildest rapids. The Canadian *voyageur* adopted it and made it his chief means of transportation in the era of discovery. To-day in New Guinea the commonest vessel is a catamaran of several logs bound together by pieces of rattan; rafts of reeds are used on the Australian coast; and the natives of Peru navigate large rafts of a very buoyant wood fitted with a wide sail and a centre-board let down between the timbers.

Neither the raft nor the canoe, however, satisfied

man's desire for navigable vessels, for he wanted a
bigger and more seaworthy craft in which to transport his goods to market; so he began to construct a
frame work of wooden ribs fastened to a wooden
keel. This new type of boat was originally held
together by cords and later by pegs. Vessels bound
by thongs are described by Herodotus as used on
the Nile and in this way the raft of Ulysses was
built according to Homer. Even to-day men construct boats in this fashion in India and the elasticity
of planks fastened together by thongs enables the
boats to ride safely through the heavy pounding surf
of the Bay of Bengal where more firmly constructed
craft would be battered to pieces.

With the step from the primitive raft to the boat
with sides and a keel went an advance in the method
of propulsion. Neither the pole nor the paddle was
sufficient, so men devised the oar and then the sail.
The ship that bore Ulysses on his long voyage back
to Ithaca after the fall of Troy is the first vessel to
be described that in structure and in means of propulsion bears an actual resemblance to the ships
we have to-day.

Egypt was the great land of traders and the Nile
its waterway. Three thousand years before the
Christian era the Egyptians were carrying on commerce in corn and cattle along the Nile and through
the Red Sea, and what manner of boats they used
may be gathered from the carvings on tombs and
temples.

Many of the boats were quite large, having a score of oars and being capable of carrying heavy cargoes. In the earliest of the pictures they are shown with a mast made in two pieces, separated at the base and joined at the top. These masts could be taken down and placed on high trestles when not needed to carry sail. The ships had straight sides with ends that rose in a high point, a beak made to represent some Egyptian god or beast or bird, and in a few cases the entire ship was modeled on the lines of a duck or swan and possessed great beauty. When a ship was intended for fighting the beak had a metal head attached to it which was used to ram enemy vessels.

The Egyptian double mast was later replaced by a single mast provided with rollers that allowed the yard to be raised or lowered according to how much sail was required, and in the pictures of warships in action the sail is usually shown rolled up like a curtain. Steering was done by paddles, sometimes by four or five, but more generally by one or two bound together and fastened to an upright post so that the paddle could be worked like a tiller. Warships had bulwarks to protect the rowers and amidships there was a raised deck to enable the soldiers to use their bows and arrows and hurl their spears over the heads of the oarsmen. At the top of the mast there was sometimes a bell-shaped platform where an expert archer or slinger was stationed, somewhat like the sharpshooters in the maintops of later ships.

The Egyptians, however, though they were great merchants, rarely sailed far from home, and were surpassed as shipbuilders and navigators by another race that dared to leave the Mediterranean, venture along the coasts of Spain and France and England and even circumnavigate the African continent. These were the Phœnicians, the first of the famous sea-rovers, traders and pirates, the remains of whose stone watch-towers on many a rocky shore attest how far they voyaged. Their ships swarmed the seas, but they made no pictorial representations of their boats and the first authentic likeness of them was found on the palace walls of their conquerors, the Assyrians, and dates back only to about 700 B. C.

From these Assyrian pictures it appears that the Phœnicians invented the bireme, a vessel with two rows of oars, one above the other, and also the trireme, which had three banks of oars similarly arranged. By this means they gained great additional oar-power and consequently speed, without increasing the length of their ships; thus they were able to make much longer voyages than earlier seafarers.

It was the Greeks who gave us the first detailed descriptions of the ships of the ancient world; those sung by Homer were biremes, not decked throughout their entire length, carrying crews of fifty to a hundred and twenty men, all of whom, except the commander, took turns at the oars. There was a great difference between the merchant ships and those intended for warfare; the former were broad and slow-moving, built to carry large cargoes, the latter were narrow and swift, constructed for speed in the chase. Homer details these characteristics of the early Grecian war-galley: it is sharp and swift, it is hollow, painted black and vermillion-cheeked, dark-prowed, curved, well-timbered, with many thwarts, and the stem and stern are high, upraised, and resemble the horns of oxen.

The trireme was the warship of Athens at her prime, though many of her galleys carried more than three rows of oars—some had four and some five banks of rowers. The men on the lowest bench used the shortest oars, the rowers sat in tiers, one man to an oar, and the benches extended from the inner side of the hull to timbers built between the decks. Some triremes had one mast, some two, each with a single sail, and the sails as well as the hulls were painted bright colors. The war galleys had a structure like a castle built on their decks, from which missiles could be thrown at the enemy; and this was the origin of the word "forecastle."

Now a new power was rising on the Mediterranean, Rome, a nation that paid little attention to ships until her increasing population felt the need of obtaining supplies from other lands. When Rome first ventured on the water she found the might of Carthage, a city of sea-traders, thwarting her at every turn,—and the result was war. The Romans must have ships, but they knew very little about building them.

Fortune wrecked a Carthaginian quinquireme, a five-banked ship, on the Italian shore. The Romans hauled her out, studied her and measured her and so learned how to construct a galley. Crews were taught to row in a framework of benches set up on dry land, and the Romans built and launched a fleet in sixty days from the felling of the first timber.

Audaciously they sailed their new ships against Carthage, and were beaten. But again they built a fleet, this time a more powerful one, and an inventive Roman constructed what was called a "corvus," a bridge that could be dropped onto an enemy vessel and that would hold its place by a heavy iron hook that penetrated the deck. By this bridge Roman soldiers could board the enemy and fight them hand-to-hand—a form of combat in which they had long been successful on shore—and by this means the new fleet defeated Carthage at Mylæ in 260 B. C. and eventually won the command of the inland sea.

The Romans improved on the warship. In addition to the boarding-bridges they built towers fore and aft and when Cæsar fought the Veneti off the coast of Gaul his ships carried great spars with curved steel heads like sickles that cut through the rigging and brought down the sails on which the enemy counted for movement. Rome became a great empire and once launched upon the sea her in-

domitable ambition would be satisfied with nothing
less than absolute mastery. When the Mediterranean was hers her galleys roved the Atlantic Ocean
and great merchant fleets sailed to Egypt and the
East. Lucian gives an account of a Roman corn
ship that left Egypt about 120 A. D. and which, after
having been buffeted by storms for seventy days,
was forced to sail through the Ægean Sea to the
Piræus, the port of Athens. This ship was one hundred and thirty feet long, with a depth of twenty-
nine feet and a width of thirty feet. Her gilded
stern was shaped like a goose-neck and her foresail
was dyed flame color. She had two masts, and the
forward one slanted at a sharp angle, thrust forward
not altogether unlike the bowsprit of later times.
Some of the Roman corn ships were much larger
than this, up to two hundred feet in length; many
carried three masts, each with a square sail, and
sometimes one of the masts had a square topsail as
well. Ships of this type were entirely propelled by
sails, and the largest of these merchantmen are
thought to have been of about one hundred and fifty
tons, the equal of a good-sized modern fishing
schooner of the Newfoundland Banks.

The oarsmen of the war galleys were rarely Romans, but were usually recruited from subject races
or were prisoners or slaves. Labor has always been
cheap along the Mediterranean and frequent wars
provided the victors with plenty of captives to pull
the sweeps. What shipbuilders the Romans became

is shown by the fact that when Cæsar prepared to invade Britain he set up a shipyard at Boulogne on the French coast and there built six hundred vessels to carry his army and supplies.

Rome loved magnificence, especially in the later days of the empire. In the fifteenth century there were found at the bottom of Lake Nemi two Roman galleys that had been built by the Emperor Caligula for pleasure ships. They were beautifully painted, the decks paved with mosaics and adorned with statues of bronze; aboard such galleys the Emperors took the cool breezes of the Mediterranean in the hot Italian summers. The Roman love of spectacles was displayed in the naval battles that were staged in immense basins wherein large fleets engaged before thousands of onlookers seated in an outdoor theatre.

It is possible that the Roman galleys that went to Britain gave the men of the North their first idea of the sail. As the power of Rome dwindled and the Hun, the Lombard and the Visigoth ravaged the southern lands the men of the Baltic and the North Sea began to emerge from their fogs and mists in their Dragon boats. Fearless and hardy sailors, the Norsemen dared all waters, and to the mixture of their race with that of the Britons is due that great love of the sea that has played so large a part in the history of England and North America.

The Viking ships were built to weather the roughest seas, low and long with curving bow and stern and great breadth of sail. One of them was dis-

covered at Gokstad in Norway in 1880; it was about
eighty feet in length, built of oak throughout, had
places for thirty-two oars, sixteen on a side, and
along the gunwales were hung a row of wooden
shields to protect the oarsmen. This was a small
Viking ship; those that were known as the Dragon
boats and the Serpents were much larger. Usually
they were constructed on one pattern whether for
commerce or warfare, carrying a single sail much
wider at the foot than at the top and decorated in
brilliant colors or embroidered in gold. At night
the crews spread a tent over the deck and slept in
leather bags. Provided with great stores of salt
meat and fish and carrying large numbers of fighting
men as well as rowers the Dragons voyaged far and
wide; the Norsemen raided the coasts of England,
overran Normandy, to which they gave their name,
pushed their prows up the Seine as far as Paris and
into the Mediterranean as far as Sicily, conquered
Iceland and Greenland and even reached across the
North Atlantic to Labrador and Newfoundland.

The Viking ship was more seaworthy than the galley of Southern Europe and came to be the pre-
dominant type of vessel for sailing the open ocean.
It was used as the model for the warships in which
the Saxons under Alfred the Great drove the Norsemen from England and for the boats in which later
William the Conqueror crossed the English Channel
and defeated the Saxons. The Serpent boat had a
raised deck fore and aft, the forerunners of the fore-

castle and quarter-deck in modern ships, and amidships was the lower main deck or waist. Here were
the oarsmen and crew who handled the sail, here also
was the mast. The merchant ships differed from
the warships only in being broader of beam.

Such were the ships of the Saxons, Edgar and
Harold, such also those of Norman William, as may
be seen from the pictures in the famous Bayeux
tapestry fashioned by William's queen, Matilda. So
well did the Vikings build from the point of seaworthiness that the American whaleboat, perhaps
the best vessel ever constructed for stormy waters,
followed the lines of the ancient Norse ship very
closely; and the Bayeux tapestry shows that the
methods of handling the Serpent boats in 1066 were
much the methods of sailors on modern fishing-ships.

The recorded history of ships begins on the Nile,
the Ægean and the Mediterranean, but it was from
the Northland that came the first great race of sea-
rovers, the direct forefathers of the English merchant adventurers and the Yankee clipper captains.

CHAPTER II
VIKING VOYAGES
TO AMERICA

II

VIKING VOYAGES TO AMERICA

VIKING means "son of the fiord," and from those narrow inlets between high cliffs in the far north of Europe sailed a daring race of sea-rovers in their long, dragon-prowed ships. Chief among them was a mighty prince known as Harold the Fair-haired, and this prince, having fought with the Jarls, or barons of his country, for more than twelve years, overcame them in a great battle of Dragon ships in the year 872 and made himself the ruler of Norway. Some of the Jarls he defeated became his retainers, but many of them were so proud that they would not own any man as overlord and therefore in their long ships they set sail with their Viking followers to adventure in distant lands. Many joined the Norsemen who were fighting King Alfred in England and Charles the Bald in France; some settled in Ireland, others in northern Scotland and the Hebrides, and some sailed as far as the Mediterranean and fought under the banner of the Byzantine Emperor against Magyar and Saracen. There were others who voyaged to Iceland and founded a new nation, that became prosperous with sheep and cattle, hay, fish, oil, but-

31

ter, wool and skins, a country where there was much
wealth and where learning was so greatly valued
that Iceland had a considerable literature in prose
and verse before there were any written works in
the modern languages of Italy or France.

This literature was in large part a chronicle of
voyages and adventures, and therein was set down
the record that in 876 one of the settlers of Iceland,
a man named Gunnbjorn, being blown out of his
course by heavy weather, had come to land somewhere on the coast of Greenland, a bleak shore, and
there, since his ship was imprisoned in the ice, the
leader and his companions had been obliged to stay
all winter. Set free in the spring, they returned to
Iceland. Word of this adventure spread, and in
983 another settler of Iceland, known as Eric the
Red, having been outlawed for killing a man in a
quarrel, decided to go in search of that land in the
northern seas that Gunnbjorn had discovered. He
manned a ship with a few companions as daring as
himself, sailed west until he reached shore and for
three years explored the coast of Greenland on each
side of the headland named Cape Farewell. In a
deep fiord, concealed by ice-bound cliffs, they came
to a clearing covered with grass, so agreeable a place
that they chose it for their home. Eric called this
place Greenland,—a name that was later given with
less appropriateness to the whole of that vast arctic
region,—and there he and his mates built houses of
blocks of sandstone, caulked up with clay and gravel.

The ruins of some of these dwellings are still to be seen.

The Vikings were not only great sailors and explorers, they desired to found colonies, and with the intention in his mind of making a settlement in Greenland Eric returned to Iceland in 986. His account of the country he had found was so enthusiastic and alluring that when he sailed again for Greenland no less than twenty-five ships went with him. This fleet met with bad weather and that peril of northern seas, the iceberg. Eleven of the ships were lost; the rest, however, at length landed four or five hundred settlers at the head of Eric's fiord. They built houses, and presently there were hamlets scattered up and down the coast, some of them as far as four hundred miles from Eric's grassy plain.

From the viewpoint of geography Greenland has long been regarded as a part of America, and therefore this settlement by Northmen led by Eric the Red in the tenth century may be considered the first colonization of the Western world by Europeans. It is true they had won only a foothold on the rim of a tract of land as large as a continent, but they were a people who held on to what they took and who were always trying to increase their holdings.

Among Eric's companions was Herjulf, and Herjulf's son Bjarni, having been away from home for some years, returned to Iceland in 986, and learning there that his father had gone to Greenland decided to seek for him. Bjarni sailed westward, but

ran into thick fogs and was forced to steer for many
days without the aid of the sun or stars. The shore
that he finally reached was not the land of fiords that
had been described to him, but a low-lying coast
covered with forests. Convinced that this was not
Greenland, Bjarni turned his Dragon ship north,
and after voyaging nine or ten days, with land frequently sighted, came to the high cliffs and fiords
that he was seeking and so to Herjulf's home.

Bjarni's adventure and discovery of the forest-
clad shore apparently caused little discussion until
he related the incidents of his voyage to certain men
in Norway, where he went about the year 994. From
these hearers the tale came to Leif, a son of Eric the
Red, who happened to be sojourning in Norway.

Roman priests had reached Norway and had converted the King, Olaf Tryggvesson, a great-grandson
of Harold the Fair-haired. Leif had also become
a Christian and when he sailed from Norway to
Greenland he took with him priests who later bap-
tised many of Eric's men. On the voyage Leif
turned over in his mind what he had heard of
Bjarni's discoveries to the south of Greenland, with
the result that he determined to explore that wooded
coast himself.

It was probably in the summer or early autumn of
the year 1000 that Leif set sail with a crew of thirty-
five men from Brattahlid, the settlement founded
by Eric at the head of Igaliko Fiord. Cruising
southward, they presently came to a barren country

where there were a great many flat stones, which led
them to give the place the name of Helluland, or
"slate-land." This is generally considered to have
been the shore opposite Greenland, either east or
west of the Strait of Belle Isle, and so probably
either Labrador or the northern part of Newfoundland.

Sailing thence still in a general southerly direction Leif's ship came to a thickly wooded land where
the voyagers went ashore and explored the territory
near the ocean. This place they called Markland,
or "wood-land"; and it is supposed to have been
some part of Cape Breton Island or Nova Scotia.
From there the adventurers stood out to sea and
sailed for several days before they again sighted
land. Skirting this coast, they discovered a bay
where a river flowed from a lake, and in this lake
they brought their ship to anchor.

Fish were plentiful and the surrounding country
was so attractive that Leif decided to winter there
and set about building huts of wood.

One day one of the crew, who had tramped inland,
returned with the news that he had found vines
loaded with grapes. Wild grapes were plentiful at
that autumn season, and because of their abundance
Leif named the country Vinland. There they remained all winter, finding the weather much milder
than in their native Iceland, and in the spring sailed
back to Greenland with a cargo of timber. On this
homeward passage the captain rescued some sailors

who had been shipwrecked near the Greenland coast
and won for himself the name of Leif the Lucky.

Leif's report of his voyage stirred other hardy
Vikings to emulate him. An expedition headed by
his brother Thorvald sailed in 1002, and reaching
Leif's huts in Vinland spent two winters there. In
the summer as they were exploring the coast they
met some savages in canoes with whom they fell to
fighting, and Thorvald was slain by an arrow. The
ship returned to Greenland in 1004 and the following year another brother of Leif, Thorstein, with
his wife Gudrid and thirty-five men sailed in the
same bark. Storms prevented their finding Vinland, Thorstein died at sea, and the leaderless expedition turned back to Brattahlid.

There now arrived in Greenland a rich and nobly
born Northman, Thorfinn Karlsefni, who fell in love
with Gudrid, the widow of Thorstein Ericsson, and
married her. Gudrid was very eager to see the
country of Vinland that Leif had visited and that
Thorstein had tried to reach, and urged her husband
to make a voyage thither. Thorfinn, a man of adventurous Viking blood, was nothing loath, and
said he would sail to Vinland and found a colony
there. With that object he set forth in the spring
of 1007 with a company of one hundred and sixty
men, a number of women, and a goodly stock of cattle
in three or four ships.

They reached Vinland without misadventure and

there a son, Snorro, was born to Thorfinn and Gudrid. A settlement was made, but after three years the colonists abandoned their home in the new country. The reason for this given in the chronicles is that, although the natives of Vinland were friendly at first and glad to barter furs for little strips of scarlet cloth, they later became quarrelsome and finally attacked the Northmen in great numbers and slew many of them. Those that were left made sail for Greenland, but on the homeward voyage one of the ships sank and her commander and half the crew were drowned.

In Thorfinn's company on this expedition had been a man named Thorvald and his wife Freydis, who was a daughter of Eric the Red. In the summer of 1010, after Thorfinn's return to Greenland, there came a ship to Brattahlid captained by two brothers, Helgi and Finnbogi. During the winter Thorvald and these brothers planned another journey to Vinland, not to establish a colony but to cut timber. The succeeding summer two ships sailed, one with Thorvald, Freydis and a crew of thirty men, the other with Helgi and Finnbogi, who had with them thirty-five men and several women.

The brothers arrived first at the huts that had been built by Leif and were carrying their supplies ashore to these shelters when the other party caught up with them and Freydis, declaring that they had no right to use her brother Leif's houses, ordered them away. Therefore Helgi and Finnbogi built new huts at a distance, and the companies from the two ships settled down in winter quarters.

Unfortunately quarrels arose between the two companies and soon there was so much ill feeling that neither party would visit the other. Then one night Freydis told her husband that the brothers had spoken evil words to her and struck her and she called on him to avenge the insult. Thorvald demurred, but Freydis became so insistent in her desire for revenge that finally she succeeded in goading him to action. He set out with his crew at night, attacked the huts of Helgi and Finnbogi, seized the men and in cold blood killed them all. The five women who were there he would have let go free, but Freydis, armed with an axe, slew them in a frenzy of hatred.

The next spring Thorvald's company sailed for Greenland in the ship of the two brothers, which was larger and more seaworthy than Thorvald's, and Freydis bribed her crew to say that the two parties had exchanged vessels and that the other company was staying in Vinland.

Crime will out, however, when knowledge of it is shared by many, and the ship had not much more than arrived at Brattahlid when word of what had happened came to the ears of Leif. He arrested three of Thorvald's men and forced a confession from them. Thus the chronicle concludes the account: " 'I have not the heart,' said Leif, 'to treat

my wicked sister as she deserves; but this I will
foretell them (Freydis and Thorvald) that their
posterity will never thrive.' So it went that nobody thought anything of them save evil from that
time.''

Therewith the chronicle known as the Saga of
Eric the Red, which furnishes most of the information concerning the adventures of the Viking sailors,
finishes its record of the voyages of the Northmen
to Vinland. From this chronicle it would appear
—and historians are generally agreed that the account is reliable—that the Northmen, sailing from
Greenland, did about the year 1000 and in succeeding years visit the coast of North America. Once
established in Iceland it was most natural that men
who were sea-rovers should make their way to
Greenland, which is nearer to Iceland than Iceland
is to Norway; and having reached Greenland it is
easy to understand that they would be curious to
discover what land lay farther to the west.

The Dragon boats of the Northmen were swifter
than the Spanish ships of the time of Columbus and
probably better constructed and more seaworthy.
They were clinker-built; that is, they had wooden
plates that overlapped, like the shingles of a house.
The keel was made of thick oak beams and the
boards of the sides were held in place by heavy iron
rivets. Some of the Viking ships had thirty oars
on each side. A boat rowed by so many sweeps,
with the head of a gilded dragon at the prow and a

high gilded tail at the stern, with a long line of painted shields hanging over the gunwales, and a sail striped with red and blue, must indeed have given the appearance of a glittering, many-legged, bright-scaled sea monster. Ships of other designs, not so large as the Dragons, were known as Serpents and Cranes.

In such ships as these the Northmen had sailed as far as Constantinople and Baffin Bay, and in such vessels it would have been easy for them to have voyaged from Greenland to North America. A ship that was blown out of her course and was sailing in a fog might readily have reached any land between Cape Race and Cape Cod as Bjarni's vessel is reported to have done in 986. Curiosity, the need of timber, the desire to found a colony were sufficient reasons for such voyages as those of Leif and Thorfinn. The accounts brought back to Greenland by these explorers regarding the climate of the country they called Vinland, the grapes, the "self-sown wheat-fields," the natives they found there, have led historians to the conclusion that Leif's and Thorfinn's settlements were situated somewhere between Cape Breton and Point Judith and possibly between Cape Ann and Cape Cod. The chronicle calls the natives Skrælings and describes them in such a way as to identify them with the copper-hued race that was later known as Indians; they were probably members of the Algonquin tribe.

The Northmen visited America, but founded no

colonies there as they had done in Greenland. Thorfinn attempted to do this, and failed, as it appears, because of the hostility of the natives, whom he could not fight as successfully as did the English later, owing largely to the fact that he had no fire-arms. This enmity of the Indians seems to have been the main reason for the abandonment of voyages to those shores by the settlers of Greenland.

The colony Eric founded in Greenland in 986 flourished for more than four hundred years and at times it numbered between five and six thousand people. It lacked the timber of Vinland and Vinland's temperate climate, but it had two great advantages over that coast, the absence of hostile savages and nearness to the mother country, Iceland.

In the twelfth century, however, some hunters of Greenland, ranging across the icefields in quest of seals and bearskins, came upon a tribe of Eskimos who were armed with stone knives and whalebone arrow-heads. In the fourteenth century war broke out between these Arctic dwellers and the settlements of the Northmen; Eskimos attacked and destroyed part of the colony in 1349, and it is supposed that they completed the destruction of the Viking occupation of Greenland sometime after 1409.

It was left to another race, that of the English, to establish permanent colonies in that new world which the Viking sea-rovers were the first of Europeans to reach.

CHAPTER III

BARBARY PIRATES

III

BARBARY PIRATES

A SHIP of Spain or Genoa or Venice, laden
with treasure from the Levant or the West
Indies, is moving in a light breeze along the
shore of the Mediterranean when suddenly from
around a headland comes a long, narrow galley, sail
spread on her two masts, the sun glittering on her
many rows of oars. The galley is a beautiful sight,
built for speed, and at a pace that cannot be matched
by the heavy merchant vessel she swings through
the water. From behind the headland comes another galley, a third and a fourth. Their prows
are pointed towards the treasure-ship and like sharp-
beaked hawks they fly at the clumsy galleon. On
the decks of the galleys the boatswains ply the lash
on the backs of the slaves at the oars, on the poop
are swarthy men in turbans, armed with scimitars,
bows and muskets. There comes a roar from the
guns of the galleys, the merchant ship retorts;
through the smoke the hawks plow on, pouring in
shot from both sides; now they are close inboard,
grappling-irons are thrown out, and over the bulwarks of the galleon scores of dark men swarm, ut-
tering strange battle-cries, and fall upon the crew
in hand-to-hand fight.

45

Savage onslaught wins the day. The galleon surrenders, her treasure goes to the strongholds of Algiers, her officers and crew to the slave-markets of the Barbary corsairs.

This was a common occurrence in the sixteenth century, and many ships of Spain, of France, of the Pope, of the proud cities of Genoa and Venice, fell captive to the turbaned men of the North African coast.

Who were the Barbary corsairs, and how did they ply their trade?

Pirates had sailed the Mediterranean ever since Jason set out in the *Argo* to steal the Golden Fleece, the Phœnicians and the Greeks had their sea-bandits, and many a Roman corn-ship, sailing from Egypt, was captured by a renegade crew and sold in a foreign market. Yet the race that was to be famous as corsairs was not by nature seafaring, as were the Phœnicians and Norsemen, and one of their rulers, the Khalif Omar, held the sea in such distrust that he forbade any of his subjects embarking on it without his permission.

The Moors of North Africa, however, in order to hold their own in warfare and trade had to have ships. So galleys were built and in them dark-skinned warriors captured the islands of Sicily, Sardinia and Corsica and landed in Spain. Thus far they were only copying the example of the Christian peoples on the opposite shore of the Mediterranean and it was not until the sixteenth century that the Moors in any numbers took to piracy.

With the fall of Granada in 1492 the last foothold of the Moorish rulers in Spain was lost and the victorious sovereigns Ferdinand and Isabella ordered the banishment of all Moslems. As a result thousands of Moorish families were driven from homes that had been theirs for seven hundred years. Many of them crossed to Africa and settled along the coast, principally at Algiers, which until then had been only a small port. As soon as they had established their families in these new quarters the Moslem men, unable to compete with the Spaniards in battle on land, decided to seek reprisal by raids at sea.

The exiles were a daring race, thoroughly familiar with the inland sea and its indented coasts, and they had a passionate belief that this was a holy warfare, waged against those who had despoiled their people and profaned their sacred places. Fierce joy there was in launching a small brigantine on the African beach and embarking for a foray into Spanish waters. The little ship needed but ten oars on a side and each oarsman was a warrior. A fair wind on the lateen sail of her single mast would carry her swiftly across the narrow stretch of water to the Balearic Islands where the brigantine would lie in hiding until a Spanish galleon hove in view. Or a squadron of brigantines could be concealed in a small river: an enemy galleon would be sighted, a

dash, and the Moorish crews were over the galleon's
sides. Back to Algiers went the Spanish prize in
part payment of the wrongs inflicted on the exiles
by the haughty Dons.

Perhaps it might be the brigantines would sail
across to the shores of that Andalusia that had been
so lately the Moors' home. Down on a Spanish village the pirates would swoop, put the soldiers to the
sword, carry off the women and the gold and silver,
rescue prisoners of their own race, and fly back to
Algiers. The African slave-markets would then be
filled with Christian men and women; and the Crescent be revenged!

Sometimes, however, the tables were turned, and
for all their speed and skill it was the Moors who
were captured, to be chained to the oars and to feel
the lash of their Christian masters.

For twenty years the pirates prospered while the
Spaniards fumed and fretted. Then Cardinal Ximenes sent Don Pedro Navarro to bring the Moors
to terms. Don Pedro took Algiers, but the pirates
fled to other strongholds on the rocky Barbary
Coast. From new harbors they made their raids,
and now they found powerful allies in the Turkish
corsairs who were waging war against all Catholic
lands.

The Mediterranean in the time of Ferdinand and
Isabella and of Columbus offered a wonderful field
for piracy. All ships bound from the outer ocean
for the ports of southern France, of Italy, and of

the Levant had to pass through either the Strait of Gibraltar or that at Malta and some had to pass through both. Riches from the newly-discovered Western world were being brought to Europe, and from the East there was an immense commerce carried on by the merchant princes of Venice and Genoa and the traders of Alexandria and Smyrna. Much of this latter commerce was bound for England and the Netherlands and, if carried by ships, had to cross the Mediterranean and so to skirt the Barbary Coast, as the northern shore of Africa, with Tunis on the eastern end, Algiers in the middle, and Tangier on the west, was commonly called. Bold men lying in wait could easily pounce upon argosies sailing near the shore.

The Barbary Coast had many natural harbors and many small streams in which the pirate-galleys, which never drew more than six feet of water, could readily hide. Back of Jerba there was a large inland sea that offered an excellent refuge, and the warships of Spain or Genoa or Venice were at a great disadvantage in the shifting shoals and tricky tides of the Gulf of the Greater Syrtes when trying to hunt pirates who knew every shoal and reef.

In addition to innumerable harbors the coast was mountainous in many places, with heights so near the water that lookouts could sight approaching treasure-ships at a great distance and give warning of enemies. Moreover, tremendous gales frequently swept the coast and sent many a storm-tossed galley into the clutches of the watchful pirates.

This Barbary Coast had had many rulers, but in the sixteenth century was divided between the Beys of Tunis, the Pashas of Algiers and the Emperors of Morocco. These rulers had not been unfriendly to Christian states and in general were no more warlike than the princes and cities on the north of the Mediterranean. They had made treaties with their Christian neighbors which prohibited piracy, but the Christians themselves were not very strict in keeping the treaties. The Genoese, the Sardinians and the Greeks were notorious sea-robbers and the increase of commerce due to the Crusades had tempted many adventurers of Europe to turn highwayman. Indeed up to the fourteenth century it was the Christians who were the chief pirates and dealers in slaves. Then with the capture of Constantinople by the Turks and the driving out of the Moors from Spain the Moslems began to take the lead in piracy and give the Barbary Coast its evil reputation throughout Christendom.

Against these men of their own race, burning with the desire for revenge on Spain and her allies, the rulers of Tunis, Algiers and Morocco were practically powerless. They had neither large fleets nor armies, their coasts were long and could not be patrolled. So though the rulers fumed and issued proclamations their anger presently subsided and they let the pirates have their own way.

To the Barbary Coast at the beginning of the sixteenth century came the Captain Uruj Barbarossa or Red Beard from the island of Lesbos, cruising with two galleots in search of treasure-ships. He looked along the shore, and the port of Tunis appealed to him as an ideal headquarters for the business he had in mind. Therefore he boldly sailed in and laid his proposition before the ruler of the country: he intended to engage in piracy and offered the Bey a fifth share of his booty in return for the use of the harbor to protect him from pursuit. The sovereign of Tunis, less scrupulous than most of the Barbary rulers, was tempted and finally agreed. The compact made, Captain Uruj sailed away.

In one of his galleots he was lying off the island of Elba when two galleys-royal flying the flag of Pope Julius II were sighted on their way to the Italian coast. The long oars were moving slowly. The galleys were some ten leagues apart, as their commanders had never encountered enemies in the waters of Elba. Uruj pointed to the ships and declared to his crew that he would take them, though the galleys were twice his size. His men remonstrated with him for such rashness; his answer was to throw most of the galleot's oars overboard to put flight out of the question.

The first towering Papal ship came on, closer and yet closer, until her lookouts saw Turkish turbans on the idle galleot. This was a strange sight in that part of the sea and the crew was called to arms.

Immediately Uruj ordered a volley of shot and bolts
and almost before the men on the galley knew what
was happening pirates climbed over the sides and
fell on them with scimitars.

A great feat it was for a galleot to capture a galley-
royal, but Uruj wanted more. He ordered his men
to put on the clothes of their captives and take their
places on the deck as if they were the Papal crew.
When the second galley, ignorant of what had happened, came up with her consort, the pirates sent
in a sudden rain of bullets and arrows and jumping
onto her bulwarks overwhelmed all opposition as
readily as before.

In triumph, with his two well-laden prizes, Uruj
the corsair returned to Tunis. He had now not only
rich spoils but plenty of Christian prisoners to pull
the oars of his ships, thus enabling him to use his
own men entirely for fighting.

Within five years Uruj had a fleet of eight pirate-
galleys and the treasure of a king, and then, finding
the port of Tunis too small for his needs, he moved
his headquarters to the island of Jerba. There in
1512 the Mohammedan King of Bujeya, who had
been expelled from his city by the Spaniards, came
to the celebrated corsair and offered him the free
use of his harbor if he would drive out the Spaniards.

The invitation attracted the corsair. He had now
twelve well-armed ships and a thousand soldiers,
and his fame had spread so widely that adventurers
were continually flocking to his standard. There-

fore in August of that year he landed before Bujeya
on the Barbary Coast, where he found the dethroned
king waiting for him with three thousand Berbers
from the mountains. Uruj immediately set siege
to the stronghold, which was held by Don Pedro
Navarro. For eight days the pirates battered the
walls and were just making a breach in them when a
shot from a Spanish gun carried off the left arm
of Uruj. With their captain unable to lead them
the corsairs preferred not to test the Spaniards'
swords, so they withdrew in their ships to Tunis,
and captured a Genoese galleot on their way thither.
At Tunis, while Uruj was recovering from his wound
in the town, his brother Kheyr-ed-din took command
of the castle of the Goletta at the entrance to the
harbor in order to protect their fleet and prizes as
they sailed into the Lake of Tunis.

Like a whirlwind on their track, however, came
twelve war-galleys commanded by Andrea Doria,
despatched by Genoa to punish the pirates for capturing the Genoese galleot. This Doria, who was
later the most famous European admiral in the Mediterranean, landed on the shore beneath the castle of
the Goletta, forced the gates, drove Kheyr-ed-din
into Tunis, pillaged the Moorish stronghold, and bore
off half of the corsair fleet to Genoa.

Uruj raged at this humiliation and as soon as his
wound had healed set to work to build a new fleet
at his island of Jerba. Then again he sailed to attack the Spaniards who had thwarted him at Bujeya.

When he reached that place, however, he found that the Spaniards had been reinforced; his Berber allies deserted him, and again he had to abandon the siege, and this time he burned some of his galleys to save them from falling into the hands of a Spanish fleet sent to take them. In his flight he came to Jijil, a town with an excellent harbor protected by steep cliffs. The people had long boasted of their independence of any ruler, but they welcomed the corsair chief as a great hero of their own race. The town suited Uruj, so he stayed there; and his raids into the Mediterranean so enriched the inhabitants that they presently chose him by acclaim the first Sultan of Jijil.

The piratical Sultan of Jijil had not been long seated on his throne when his Moorish neighbors in Algiers besought him to come to their aid and drive out a hornet's nest of Spaniards who from a fortified castle commanded the harbor of Algiers. Uruj set out with six thousand men and sixteen galleots, stopped on the road to surprise Shershel, the stronghold of Kara Hasan, a rival corsair, beheaded Hasan, and reaching Algiers sent a message to the Spanish garrison offering them safe conduct if they would surrender, an offer that they promptly declined.

Uruj planted his standard in the city, and the Algerines soon found they had imported a rescuer who was worse than the Spanish soldiers. The corsair and his followers treated the proud Moors with contempt, and then with blows; Salim, the Sheik, was murdered in his bath; and the Algerines made a secret plan for a joint uprising with the Spaniards. Uruj got wind of this and immediately quelled the revolt by cutting off the heads of the ringleaders. Then he sailed out from the harbor and audaciously met and defeated a great Spanish fleet sent against him by Cardinal Ximenes.

One Moorish town after another, Christian fleet after Christian fleet, fell to the bag of the corsair. Uruj made himself Sultan of Middle Barbary and a formidable rival of the rulers of Tunis and Fez. So many treasure-galleys had been swept from the sea by him that finally the King of Spain sent ten thousand veteran troops to make an end of him. Uruj was at Tilimsan with only fifteen hundred men when the Spaniards landed, and he fled by night towards Algiers. He had to cross a river and as he was being hotly pursued he ordered that all his gold and jewels should be scattered on the road as a bait to delay his foes. The Spaniards, however, came up with his rear-guard when only half his men were across the river and Uruj, though he himself was safe on the farther shore, recrossed the stream to rally his followers. In the battle hardly a corsair escaped the great Spanish army and the one-armed Uruj Barbarossa, fighting like a lion, perished with his men.

Uruj was destroyed, but instead of sweeping all the pirates from the Barbary Coast the Spaniards sailed home. The corsair's mantle fell on the shoulders of his brother, Kheyr-ed-din, who, though less of a firebrand than Uruj, was crafty and shrewd, and who showed his sagacity at once by sending an envoy to Constantinople to offer the Sultan the province of Algiers as part of the Ottoman realm. The Sultan was very much pleased and in return appointed the corsair chieftain Beglerbeg, or Governor-General of Algiers.

Under Kheyr-ed-din, who like his brother Uruj was called Barbarossa, because he too was red-bearded, the Barbary pirates became in reality "the Scourge of Christendom." He himself commanded eighteen galleots and his captains sailed many more. They swarmed throughout the Mediterranean, raiding the coast of Spain and the Balearic Islands, they dashed through the Strait of Gibraltar and captured fleets bringing gold from the West Indies to Cadiz. Not only merchant vessels, but great galleys-royal filled with Spanish soldiers fell into the Beglerbeg's claws.

He at length bombarded successfully the Spanish stronghold in the harbor of Algiers that had defied Uruj and set the Christian garrison to the work of building the long sea-wall that protects Algiers. Nine transports loaded with Spanish men-at-arms arrived to relieve the stronghold, but the corsair seized the whole fleet and won at a single blow more than two thousand slaves and innumerable cannon and firearms.

Thirty-six pirate galleys now ravaged the seas, seventy thousand Moors rescued from servitude in Spain joined the corsair's forces, seven thousand Christian slaves labored under his lash, and every effort made by the powerful Emperor Charles V to destroy the pirates only added to the latter's prizes in men and ships.

The Turkish Sultan Suleyman, eager to have his own people learn naval warfare from so successful a commander, summoned the corsair to Constantinople. The Barbary fleet set sail and presently the chieftain, thick-bearded, bushy-browed, and with eyes like a hawk, accompanied by his eighteen captains, appeared before the Sultan and was received with honors and gifts. He was ordered to build a new navy for the Ottoman Empire, and such was his energy that in one winter he constructed sixty-one galleys and took the sea with a fleet of eighty-four ships in the spring.

In the summer of 1534 the corsair led the new Turkish fleet out from the Golden Horn in search of prey. He surprised the Italian city of Reggio, taking many ships, captured eighteen galleys at Cetraro, burned towns and castles along the coast and carried hundreds of Christians to the Constantinople slave-markets. Emboldened by this success, he sailed across to Tunis, drove out its ruler, and added that country to the Sultan's domain. At this point, however, the Emperor Charles V intervened; much as he disliked having the pirates command the cliffs of Algiers it was far worse to have them control Tunis, since from there they could easily menace his island of Sicily. He sailed from Barcelona with six hundred ships commanded by Andrea Doria and carrying picked troops from Spain, Italy and the Rhine. This fleet fought its way into the harbor of Tunis; the corsair came out to meet it, but at sight of the imperial power his Berbers threw down their arms, the Christian slaves in the city revolted and locked the gates behind him, and Kheyr-ed-din had to fly to Bona, where with wise foresight he had stationed fifteen ships.

The army of Charles sacked Tunis, and no Barbary pirates ever showed themselves more bloodthirsty than the soldiers of this Christian Emperor. Europe hailed Charles as its deliverer from the infidel; meanwhile the corsair slipped over to Minorca, looted its chief town, took a Portuguese galleon he found there, and with six thousand prisoners and much booty retreated to Algiers. The Emperor, satisfied with holding Tunis, left Kheyr-ed-din at large.

Soon afterwards Sultan Suleyman called the corsair again to Constantinople and made him High Admiral of the Ottoman fleets. In this new capacity Kheyr-ed-din became more than ever the terror of the seas. His old opponent Andrea Doria attacked some Turkish ships and in revenge the corsair laid waste the coast of Apulia, raged through the Adriatic with seventy galleys and thirty galleots, and finally offered combat to the navy of Venice and

its allies, commanded by Doria. The corsair had
one hundred and twenty-two warships; Doria's fleet
was much larger, eighty Venetian, thirty-six Papal,
and thirty Spanish galleys, with fifty sailing galleons, but Kheyr-ed-din outmaneuvered Doria and
forced the famous Christian admiral to sail away
and leave the Mediterranean in the grasp of the
Sultan.

So strong was Suleyman now that Francis I, the
King of France, made an alliance with him against
the Emperor, and the corsair sailed a Turkish fleet
to the harbor of Toulon, where for a winter the
Moslems had their headquarters and fought beside
the French. Difficulties arose, however; the Turkish galleys were filled with Christian slaves and when
more oarsmen were needed the corsair simply sent
his press-gangs to French villages and stole as many
men as he wanted, a proceeding that not unnaturally roused the anger of his allies. Francis was
obliged to buy him off and to get rid of him set free
all the Mohammedan slaves in the French ships and
made him a present of jewels, gold and silks.
Kheyr-ed-din sailed away, stopped once more to
harry the Italian coast, and finally came to Constantinople with so much treasure that it almost
swamped his fleet.

That was the last of the exploits of this corsair
who was the greatest sea-fighter of his time. There
were in later days—for the record of the Barbary
pirates was a long one—many daring and successful

captains, but none who won such renown as Uruj
Barbarossa and his brother Kheyr-ed-din.

The ships of the Barbary pirates were usually long
and narrow, carrying a sail or two, but mainly propelled by oars. They were called galleys, galleots,
or brigantines according to their size, the galleot
being a small galley, and the brigantine about a quarter as large as the galley. The oarsmen in the days
of the great corsairs were Christian prisoners; they
were chained to the rowing benches, sometimes as
many as six pulling a single oar; frequently they
rowed for ten hours at a stretch, sometimes, in chase
or flight, for many hours more; and the power that
drove them was the lash, wielded by boatswains who
stood on long bridges above the rowers.

The plight of these galley-slaves was indescrib-
ably wretched, but the Barbary pirates dealt with
their prisoners no worse than did Christian captains with captured Moors and Turks. On neither
side was rank nor gentle breeding respected, Corsair chieftain or Spanish grandee, if he were so un-
fortunate as to be captured, had to pull his oar and
drag his chain exactly like the lowest ruffian of
Naples or Algiers. If rich he might be ransomed;
otherwise he labored at the sweeps until his galley
was captured or sunk and in the latter case he might
go down with it. Such conditions existed aboard
many European vessels almost up to the French Revolution.

In general the pirate ships were smaller and

lighter than those of Spain or France, though there were some Barbary galleys that carried castles on their prows and were as ornate and magnificent as anything Christendom could show. In most of their galleys there would be perhaps two hundred men in the crew and on the poop one hundred soldiers. Their usual mode of attack was to deceive their opponent by flying a foreign flag and when at close range to pour in sudden shot from their guns. At the order to board the fighting men jumped to the enemy's decks and finished the capture in hand-to-hand combat.

At the beginning of the seventeenth century the corsairs started to build square-rigged ships, copying European models. They were now making longer voyages, sometimes as far as to the Spanish Main. Galleys propelled by oars were impracticable for such journeys, for the oarsmen had to be fed and to do that meant the carrying of vast supplies. Sails entailed no such burden, so the galley gave way to the sailing ship and the new science of navigation. First they built galleasses, a compromise between the rowed galley and the sailed ship. Then came the Turkish caramuzel or tartan, which stood high above the water and carried eighteen or twenty guns. According to the size and the country from which the new ships hailed they were called galleon, polacca, caravel, caramuzel, and various other names. In time the galleon became the typical ship of the corsairs and in these they sailed through the

Strait of Gibraltar in 1617 and captured Madeira. Later they raided the coast of England and even ventured to Denmark and Iceland.

The Mediterranean, however, was the real home of the corsairs and there they plied their trade of piracy into the nineteenth century. They were not by nature rovers, they preferred their own shores and harbors and for centuries the merchant ships they sighted from their watch-towers were sufficient in numbers and treasure to provide them with all the booty and slaves their greed required.

CHAPTER IV
THE PORTUGUESE EXPLORERS

IV

THE PORTUGUESE EXPLORERS

PRINCE HENRY, the son of King John the Great of Portugal, having won renown in arms at the capture of the Moorish stronghold of Ceuta, established himself at Sagres, near Cape St. Vincent, in 1418, and devoted himself to promoting maritime adventure. Being possessed of great wealth, he was able to secure learned astronomers and mathematicians from all parts of Europe to assist in his councils; he built an observatory and founded a school of navigation where trained students were employed in making charts and improving the compass. In addition he engaged many daring captains and sailors and sent them out on voyages of discovery along the west coast of Africa; and such was his learning and industry that although he never went on any of these sea-adventures himself he gained the title of Prince Henry the Navigator.

There was a legend current in Europe in the fifteenth century, probably based on tales handed down from Carthaginian rovers, that it was possible to sail around Africa to India. If this were true Portugal would profit greatly by the use of such a route. At that time goods from the East had to be carried by land all the long distance to the Levant or else conveyed up the Red Sea and carried to Egypt. Venice was the point where merchandise from India was distributed throughout Europe. If a sea route could be found around Africa the expense of conveying goods would be enormously lessened and Lisbon would in great part take the place of Venice.

To sail the ocean at that time was a hazardous occupation, for the ships employed by Prince Henry were by no means the stout barks that went on voyages of discovery under Raleigh and Drake a century later. The first vessels that Prince Henry sent out were only half-decked boats with sails and crews that at the most numbered thirty-six seamen. Such ships might ride in safety the waves of the Mediterranean, but they were cockle-shell craft in the winds of the South Atlantic.

Yet the Portuguese captains and crews dared the open ocean, and their first rewards were the discovery of the island of Porto Santo by Bartholomeu Perestrello in 1419 and of Madeira by João Gonçalves Zarco and Tristão Vaz in 1420. King John and Prince Henry were delighted at these discoveries, and at once the latter set about the colonizing of the two islands and introduced into Madeira the vine and sugar-cane which are to-day the main sources of its wealth.

This was but a stepping-stone, however. Prince

Henry's object was to circumnavigate Africa, if that could be done, and the expeditions of Perestrello and of Zarco and Vaz had sailed with the purpose of attempting a southward course and doubling Cape Bojador. Perestrello, in making the attempt, had been driven out to sea and so to Porto Santo. Cape Bojador was a headland that for long defied the seamanship of the doughty Portuguese captains in their little ships.

For years Prince Henry despatched his fleets, but no ship could double that cape. They made important discoveries, however, off the northwest coast of Africa; they reached the Canary Islands and the Azores. The Canaries were claimed by Spain and King John gave them up, but the Portuguese held on to the Azores and occupied and settled them.

At length in 1434 the mariner Gil Eannes succeeded in doubling Cape Bojador, and two years later Affonso Gonçalves Baldaya reached the Rio d'Ouro. In 1441 Antão Gonçalves sailed a hundred leagues south of the Rio d'Ouro, and Nuno Tristão, the greatest of Prince Henry's captains, gained the cape on the south of the shoulder of Northwest Africa and christened it the Cabo Branco or White Cape. When he returned from this voyage Tristão brought with him several captives from this new territory, and from this resulted the trade in African slaves.

Slavery was a common practice in southern Europe at that time, and prisoners captured in war

were almost always treated as slaves and set to work
in the galleys. There were parts of Portugal that
had never been cultivated since their conquest from
the Moors because of the lack of laborers, and now
Prince Henry and other great landowners saw that
slaves from Africa would provide the needed labor.

This gave a great impetus to the voyages of the
Portuguese; exploring meant large profits when
ships returned with slaves. In 1444 a fleet of eight
vessels brought back two hundred captives who were
put to work in the fields of the Order of Christ in
the Algarves, and the following year a fleet of fourteen ships brought even more slaves.

By now the navigators were familiar with the
rounding of Cape Bojador and Cabo Branco and
were discovering that once around the stormy shoulder of Northwest Africa the coast turned abruptly
to the east. Nuno Tristão sailed to the Senegal
River in 1445 and in the same year Diniz Dias discovered Guinea, the land of the black negroes.
Guinea was a fertile country, rich in ivory and
spices and there were stories told of gold; and when
word of this reached Lisbon the merchants were
not slow in opening up trade with this promising
land.

Diniz Dias reached Cape Verde in 1446, and called
the headland by that name because of its green sur-
roundings. Then Alvaro Fernandes, sailing one
hundred leagues farther, left João Fernandes at his
own wish among the dark-hued natives of the coast.

This man stayed there seven months, studying the language and customs of the people, and when he was picked up by another ship and returned to Portugal he informed Prince Henry that, although the blacks of Africa were heathens, he had found them peace-loving and very friendly to him.

The voyages of discovery were interrupted by warfare in Portugal, and for a time the only exploits at sea were those of a Venetian, Luigi Cadamosto, who had offered his services to Prince Henry. Cadamosto's reports led to the claim being made later that he had discovered the Gambia River in 1445 and the Cape Verde Islands in 1446; but it is more generally believed that he did not reach the Gambia until a later voyage in 1455 and 1456, and that it was Diego Gomes who first found the Cape Verde Islands in 1460.

These ended the voyages of exploration that were sent out by Prince Henry the Navigator, who died in 1460. He had not achieved a sea route around Africa, but his captains had acquired sufficient information about the eastward trend of the coast to justify the expectation that a route would be found by future sailors.

It was the trade in slaves and the commerce with the rich country of Guinea that caused the King and the merchants of Portugal to maintain their interest in Africa. During the reign of John II, Diego Cão or Cam discovered the Congo, and in 1486 Bartholomeu Diaz reached Algoa Bay and rounded

the cape to the south, calling it from its stormy seas
Cabo Tormentoso, or Stormy Cape, a name which
the King, appreciating its importance to his country, changed to the more pleasing title of the Cape
of Good Hope.

King John II thought that in addition to a sea
route to India around Africa there might be a route
to Cathay or China by sailing around the continent
of Europe to the north. At his order Martim Lopez
voyaged beyond the North Cape into seas not yet
explored and found and named the island north of
Russia which he called Nova Zembla. Land routes
also interested this sovereign and he sent forth explorers who were the first Europeans to traverse
the interior of Africa, and who got as far as Tim-
buctoo. Others made their way across India, to
Arabia, to Abyssinia, and by their travels added
immensely to the knowledge of the geography of
that part of the world.

Unfortunately for the fame of John II he refused
to assist Christopher Columbus who sought his aid
on a westward voyage. He did not believe that a
route to India could be found by sailing west across
the Atlantic, and Columbus had to seek ships elsewhere than at Lisbon. The King did, however,
bring skillful shipwrights from England and Denmark and saw to it that the Portuguese builders improved their vessels.

John II had planned an expedition that should
sail to India around the Cape of Good Hope that

Diaz had discovered when he had been blown to the east by heavy gales on his voyage in 1486, but it was John II's successor Emanuel I who put that project into execution. In command of a fleet of four ships, specially built for the purpose, the King placed Vasco da Gama, who had been a soldier and an intrepid sailor. With this captain were his brother Paul da Gama and Nicolas Coelho, both experienced mariners. The fleet sailed down the Tagus River from Lisbon on July 9, 1497. After a voyage of four months the ships cast anchor in St. Helena Bay, then proceeded to round the Cape of Good Hope, and work their way up the southeastern coast of Africa. The ruler of Mozambique was unfriendly to Vasco da Gama when the latter sought a pilot to guide him across the Indian Ocean and the pilot he loaned him deserted the ships at Mombassa. The Portuguese Captain-general sailed north, however, and at Melinda, a small port to the north of Zanzibar, he secured a trustworthy pilot.

This was not the proper season of year to cross the Indian Ocean, but the fleet attempted it, and after encountering hurricanes at length succeeded in arriving at Calicut on the Malabar coast on May 20, 1498. There, following the custom of his country, Vasco da Gama set up a marble pillar as evidence of his achievement in reaching India.

The ruler of Calicut received the Portuguese in friendly fashion, but the traders of the country, fearing that a direct sea route to Europe would ruin their own commerce, incited such hostility to the newcomers that Vasco da Gama was prevented from leaving some settlers as he had planned, to start a trading establishment at Calicut. He cruised along the coast of Malabar and then sailed for home. This return voyage proved stormy and it was not until August 29, 1499 that the Captain-general arrived at Lisbon, with only fifty-five of the one hundred and forty-eight men who had started from that city with him. He was received with great honors, and the King conferred upon him the office of Admiral of the Indian Seas, with a revenue to be derived from the trade with India. For himself the King added to his other titles of sovereignty that of "Lord of the Conquest, Navigation and Commerce of Ethiopia, Arabia, Persia, and India," a remarkable claim which Pope Alexander VI approved by a Papal decree in 1502.

The Portuguese sovereign then took steps to secure proper business advantage from Vasco da Gama's voyage and sent Pedro Alvares Cabral with a fleet of thirteen ships and twelve hundred soldiers to establish depots on the Malabar coast whence valuable products of India should be shipped to Lisbon every year. On the ships went priests who were to convert the heathen.

Cabral's voyage was memorable; it turned out to be even more important to Portugal than that of Vasco da Gama had been, because, as his fleet stood out to sea after leaving the Cape Verde Islands or was blown out to sea by a storm, his sailors sighted on April 24, 1500 a country unknown to them on the west. Off the shore the surf was so heavy that Cabral could not make a landing and he had to continue some distance before he found a harbor, which he named Porto Seguro or Safe Port. There he went ashore, claiming this new country for the King of Portugal, erected a cross and called the region Santa Cruz. Exploring, he learned that the country was fertile and its inhabitants a peaceful people. He considered his discovery important and sent one of his ships with news of it back to Lisbon and with it a native to be taught Portuguese, left two men there to acquire the speech of the people and to explore, and proceeded on his voyage to India.

The name of this country that Cabral had discovered was later changed to Brazil, given it because of its richness in brazil trees.

Cabral arrived at Calicut in India and, after difficulties with the native traders there, succeeded in establishing depots for pepper and other products at Cannanore and Cochin and sailed home to Lisbon. Other navigators followed him; in 1502 Vasco da Gama reached India again with twenty ships. One of the officers he left on the coast, Vincente Sodre, became tired of the trading business and turned pirate, and was the first of those Portuguese rovers who for many years ranged the Eastern seas. In

1503 three Portuguese squadrons arrived and a fort was built at Cochin and garrisoned with nine hundred men.

The success of this military force in battle with hostile native rulers was so outstanding that the Portuguese found no difficulty in buying all the products they wanted on favorable terms and led King Emanuel to dream of conquering India; for this purpose he decided to establish a strong government on the Malabar coast.

Then began an era in which one viceroy after another sent out from Lisbon managed by force of arms and wily diplomacy to extend the hold of Portugal over great districts of India. And not in India alone did the Portuguese establish themselves, though the port of Goa on the Malabar coast became their overseas headquarters; they took and fortified Mozambique, Mombassa and Melinda on the Southeastern African coast, where their fleets rounding the Cape of Good Hope might refit and take aboard supplies; Ormuz, at the mouth of the Persian Gulf, became their headquarters for trade between Persia and Europe; and Malacca, which they settled, headquarters for the trade with Java, Sumatra and the Spice Islands.

From Malacca Portuguese adventurers explored the Moluccas and the Celebes, the coasts of Cochin China and Siam. Where the adventurers entered the traders followed; they opened up commerce with the empire of China and had their thriving depots on the island of Macao at the mouth of the Canton River, and in 1548 a Portuguese established a trading-factory near Yokohama in Japan.

East and west these daring men of the little European nation, backed by their kings, princes and great merchants, went on their voyages into strange seas and lands. After Cabral's discovery of Brazil King Emanuel sent expeditions to explore that country, two under Amerigo Vespucci, or Vespucius, in 1501 and 1503, and much of the coast down to the river La Plata was mapped by this explorer. But the reports of the country did not indicate great riches, such as Cortez had found in Mexico and Pizarro in Peru, there seemed little prospect of trade, and Portugal had plenty of profitable commerce with her new possessions to the east; therefore all attention was turned towards India, and Brazil was little regarded. It was not until 1530, when rumors spread through Portugal that gold and silver and precious stones were to be found in Brazil, that real interest was taken in that country; then colonists voyaged thither and that great section of South America was settled by Portuguese.

To Brazil went the most industrious people from the mother country and so greatly did they prosper that in the course of time, when the possessions in Asia had become a liability and a burden, it was Brazil that supplied the chief source of wealth of the Kings of Portugal.

More valuable to Portugal than the sea route

around Africa first made by Vasco da Gama, or the
depots on the Malabar coast or at Mozambique or
Malacca, was the land to which Pedro Alvares
Cabral was blown across the South Atlantic from
the Cape Verde Islands when he was sailing for the
Cape of Good Hope.

CHAPTER V
THE ARGOSIES AND
PAGEANTS OF VENICE

V

THE ARGOSIES AND PAGEANTS OF VENICE

IN the opening scene of "The Merchant of Venice" Salarino says to his friend Antonio:

"Your mind is tossing on the ocean,
There where your argosies with portly sail,
Like signiors and rich burghers on the flood,
Or, as it were, the pageants of the sea,
Do overpeer the petty traffickers,
That curtsy to them, do them reverence,
As they fly by them with their woven wings."

An argosy was a large merchant vessel, and it was because of the possession of many fleets like those of Antonio that Venice, at the height of her glory, became the envy of her sister cities of Italy and of princes, kings and popes. The Venetians were a merchant people, and their ships brought goods from the East to the marts of their city, from whence it was sent forth again to the countries on the north and west. Made rich by trade, the merchants lavished their wealth on the adornment of their city, and the beauty of Venice—a beauty more Oriental than European—was the wonder of the world.

The city owed her independence, her wealth, the proud position that was hers for many centuries, to her situation on the shores of a great lagoon that protected her from attack either from the mainland or from the Adriatic and provided her with a safe port for commerce with the East.   In the days when the rest of the Italian peninsula was being overrun by Visigoth and Lombard the Venetians on their islands successfully defied their enemies and maintained their freedom.   Fishermen for the most part at first, their interest lay wholly on the sea that washed their doorsteps, and as the settlement grew the people, by force of circumstances, became oversea merchants.

Venice early in her history boasted of fleets that brought to her markets grain and wine from Apulia, gems and drugs from Asia, wood from the Dalmatian forests, and silk, cloth and metal-work from Greece and Constantinople.   Some of these fleets sailed for Venetian traders, some were chartered to carry cargoes for cities on the mainland.   To protect the argosies from pirates a strong navy was needed and the Venetians proved themselves as stout sea-fighters as they were daring and skillful sailors.

The era of the Crusades furnished Venice with a great opportunity to add to her riches.   Kings and princes in Europe, with thousands of knights and men-at-arms, were eager to get to the Holy Land to fight the infidel.   Three Italian cities, Genoa,

Pisa and Venice, vied with each other for the profit that was to be made from conveying the crusaders. Venice had the advantage of lying farther to the east than either of her rivals, and in addition she already had fleets unequaled in variety,—swift vessels called "dromi," that were light but of large size, others known as "hippogogi," built to carry horses, galleys provided with engines for throwing bolts and stones from turrets to the walls of fortified cities,—and so it was from Venice that many crusaders embarked.

The fight for the Holy Land was waged by the knights of Christendom through many crusades with varying success, but the Venetians almost always secured profits for themselves. The republic of Venice sent a fleet of one hundred ships—great beaked vessels, larger than galleys, painted gorgeous colors, and pulled by a hundred oars—to the aid of Baldwin, King of Jerusalem, and when the city of Sidon fell the Venetians received as reward a church, a street, a market-place, and the right to use their own weights and measures, as well as jurisdiction over their own subjects in Sidon; in short, secured the establishment of a colony of Venetian merchants with special privileges. Other naval victories brought similar advantages, and so it happened that Venice came to possess free entrance for her goods wherever she traded, special concessions for her merchants, and facilities for commerce that no other state enjoyed. Pope and emperor, Turk and Christian warred with one another, and sometimes the republic fought on one side and sometimes on the other, but always the main concern of the Venetians was to gain some profit as merchants.

Salarino, in "The Merchant of Venice," referred to Antonio's argosies as "the pageants of the sea." The Venetians loved pageants, and each year on the Feast of the Ascension to symbolize the union of the republic with its encircling waters and to celebrate the conquest of Dalmatia by the Doge Orseolo they held a festival that was known as the Espousal of the Sea. On the morning of Ascension Day a great ship, called the *Bucintoro,* or *Bucentaur,* was launched from the Arsenal and rowed to the Piazzetta to receive the Doge, who was the chief magistrate of the republic, and his suite. The *Bucentaur* had two decks; on the lower one sat the one hundred and sixty-eight rowers who pulled the forty-eight oars. These men were workmen at the Arsenal and it was their privilege to row the boat on this occasion. The upper deck was hung with crimson velvet, ornamented with braid and tassels of gold, and adorned with bas-reliefs representing the arts and sciences, so that it formed a magnificent salon, typical of the Venetian love of splendor. At the stern was the chair of the Doge, set upon a dais, and above this throne was a canopy in the shape of a shell, held aloft by two cherubs, and with a gilded figure on either side, one personifying Prudence and the other Strength. Near by were carved chairs for the Patriarch of Venice, the Ambassadors, and the officers of state.

When the chief magistrate and his party had embarked at the Piazzetta the *Bucentaur* was rowed to the Church of San Nicola del Lido, where it was met by a barge, abroad which were the clergy. On this barge was a pail of water, a jar of salt, and a brush of olive-wood. The litany was recited by two canons; then the bishop repeated a prayer in Latin: "Vouchsafe, O Lord, that this sea appertain unto us. And to all those who sail over its waters give peace and quiet. We beseech Thee to hear us." Then he blessed the water and a ring.

The Doge came forward from his chair of state, and a deacon read: "Purge me, O Lord, with hyssop and I shall be clean." The bishop sprinkled the Doge and those about him and poured the remaining water into the Adriatic. The Doge took the ring and cast it through a window at the stern, crying in a loud voice: "We wed thee, O Sea, in token of true and lasting domination!"

The *Bucentaur* was then rowed back to the city, where all classes celebrated the day with feasting and merry-making.

When Philippe de Commines, the ambassador of Charles VIII of France, visited Venice in 1495 he wrote: "This is the most triumphant city that ever I saw." And the reputation for splendor increased as the great merchants built gorgeous palaces on the canals, decorated them with paintings by matchless artists, and welcomed important guests with pageantry and pomp. Wonderful was the reception the city gave to kings, such for example as the spectacle provided when Henry III of France made a visit to Venice in July, 1574.

The King was invited to stay at Murano on the evening before his entry into Venice and was entertained there at the Palazzo Cappello, which was hung with silks and cloth of gold. Forty young Venetian nobles attended him and his guard was composed of sixty halberdiers, eighteen trumpeters and twelve drummers.

In the morning a great galley was furnished to take the King to Venice by way of the Lido. On the poop-deck was a seat covered with cloth of gold for the royal visitor, on his right sat the Papal Nuncio with the Dukes of Mantua and Nevers, on his left the Doge and the foreign ambassadors. The royal galley had four hundred rowers, and behind it came fourteen other galleys with Venetian senators and nobles. To entertain the King the glass-blowers of Murano had built on rafts a furnace made to look like a great sea monster that shot flames from its mouth and nostrils, while inside the monster the workmen blew cups of the finest crystal to present to King Henry and his suite.

Then a multitude of gaily-decorated boats belonging to the different guilds of Venice appeared and maneuvered before the royal galley. Some of the boats bore priceless tapestries and works of art, others sent up fire-works, one was fashioned like a huge dolphin and on its back stood Neptune driving two winged horses and four other boatmen were costumed to represent the rivers of the Venetian republic, the Brenta, the Adige, the Po and the Piave.

The King's galley went by the Lido to the landing in front of San Nicola, where the great architect of Venice, Palladio, had built an arch of triumph, adorned with ten magnificent paintings from the brushes of Tintoretto and Paolo Veronese. At the landing the King was invited to leave the galley and board the *Bucentaur*. The story is told that the painter Tintoretto was in the crowd of on-lookers and, wishing to make a sketch of the sovereign of France, contrived to exchange his suit for the livery of one of the Doge's gentlemen and so found a place on the *Bucentaur*. There he sketched the King in pastels and showed his work to the royal treasurer, who was so much pleased with it that he induced his royal master to sit to Tintoretto for a full-length portrait, which Henry presented to the Doge as a souvenir of his visit.

Having reached the city in the *Bucentaur,* the King was entertained by exhibitions of sport between the rival clans of Niccolotti and Castellani. Two hundred men fought with sticks, as savagely as if in battle; at length the leader of the Niccolotti, the fisherman Luca, fell into the canal, and his disordered clansmen yielded the field to their opponents.

The banquet that followed was served in the hall of the Great Council. Tables were set for three thousand people, and the cooks prepared twelve hundred different dishes, modeled like ships and fishes, animals, birds, and of many other patterns. The plates were of solid silver and on the immense sideboards was a marvelous collection of masterpieces of the goldsmith's and silversmith's arts. Afterwards the royal guest witnessed the first performance of opera ever given in Italy.

Before the banquet King Henry was shown the separate pieces of wood and metal used in making a galley and when he left the Ducal Palace that night those pieces had all been put together and to his amazement he witnessed the galley launched in the canal and towed away to the Lido.

In such fashion Venice entertained sovereigns, and it is small wonder that her pageants made her renowned as the most magnificent city in Europe.

Yet this love of luxury and grandeur, although it brought fame to the republic, was also a source of weakness, because wealthy merchants, receiving titles of nobility, preferred to live in their beautiful palaces and cultivate their properties on the mainland rather than to use their talents in commerce or exploration. Venice made the mistake of allowing some of her greatest mariners to sail on voyages of discovery for other states instead of providing them with ships and money herself. Surrounded by enemies who were jealous of her riches, she permitted herself to be outdistanced by them even in trade with the East. Her armies were defeated by those of the Holy Roman Emperor, and the power of Spain on the west and of the Ottoman Empire on the east were a continual threat to the republic on the Adriatic. Instead of being able to pursue her own course single-handed Venice was obliged to bargain with one rival or another for her own preservation. In 1571 the Turks attacked Cyprus, which belonged to Venice, and although the island made a heroic resistance its defenders were forced to surrender, since the Venetian fleet arrived too late to take part in the defense.

The Turk, however, was a menace to other states as well as to Venice, and therefore the Pope and the King of Spain made an alliance with the republic to fight the common foe. A great fleet of two hundred and fifty ships was collected, with the Spanish Admiral, Don John of Austria, in supreme command, Marc Antonio Colonna in charge of the vessels of the Pope and Sebastian Venier of those of Venice. On October 7, 1571 this allied fleet came up with the Turkish ships off Lepanto in the Gulf of Corinth.

It was a clear, sunlit morning. The line of the allied ships extended for four miles and on Turkish and Christian decks the sun shone on an array of helmets, breastplates and shields that reflected the glitter like mirrors. From tall masts floated banners of many colors and designs. When the battle began the Turks attacked with the greatest vigor, and in particular assailed the flagship of the Venetians. The Venetian Admiral, Venier, although he was seventy-five years of age, was in the thick of the fighting and performed wonderful feats of valor. The tide of battle flowed this way and that. At one time the Turks on one of the ships, finding themselves out of ammunition, seized on a stock of oranges and lemons and threw them at their opponents, who with jeers fired them back. For five hours the battle of Lepanto raged, then the Ottoman fleet was destroyed. Thirty thousand Turks are reported to have perished, more than three thousand were taken prisoners and divided among the allies as slaves, ninety-four galleys were burned, one hundred and thirty were captured, and fifteen thousand Christian galley-slaves were liberated.

Of the allies eight thousand soldiers were slain, among them twenty-five nobles of Venice. One of the Spaniards who was wounded was Cervantes, the author of "Don Quixote," who lost an arm at Lepanto.

The chief glory in the engagement was won by Sebastian Venier and his Venetians. At dawn on October eighteenth a galley was sighted steering for Venice; she come up to the Lido with Turkish flags trailing from her stern and a pile of Turkish turbans stacked on her deck. Her guns boomed and shouts of "Victory" could be heard across the lagoon. Immediately the city, that had been sunk

in gloom at the loss of Cyprus, was filled with a
frenzy of joy. All shops were closed, the streets
from the Rialto bridge to the Merceria were spread
with blue cloth spangled with golden stars to represent the sky, and on the Piazza was constructed a
mammoth pyramid of Turkish trophies, surrounded
by decorations of scarlet cloth, paintings and
tapestries. The celebration of the victory lasted
four days, and as reward for his triumph Sebastian
Venier was later elected Doge and the Pope bestowed
upon him the consecrated golden rose.

The great battle at Lepanto, however, brought
little except glory to the republic. Venice wished
to follow up the victory and crush the Turks at
Constantinople, but Philip II, the King of Spain,
would not join in this plan and the Spanish Admiral
took his fleet to winter quarters. Venice could not
fight alone; and so vast were the resources of the
Turks in men and money that by the next spring
they had built and equipped a new fleet of two hundred and ten sail. Then, abandoned by her former
allies, Venice was forced to make a treaty of peace
with Constantinople and pay the Sultan 300,000
ducats. The island of Cyprus was lost and Venice
never regained it.

Her colonies fell into the hands of her rivals, and
the republic suffered greatly in trade when the
Portuguese discovered a sea-route to India around
the Cape of Good Hope. Formerly the Venetians
had enjoyed almost a monopoly in carrying mer-

chandise from the East to Europe, now the fleets of Portugal conveyed much of it direct to Lisbon. Venice was no longer a great maritime power; in the daring voyages into unknown oceans that followed the discoveries of Columbus and Vasco da Gama the Venetians took little part; they were old-fashioned sailors used to the Adriatic and the Mediterranean, and would not venture into distant seas.

With the decline of her trade the city of the lagoon lost her high rank among the states of Europe; Venice became a city mainly devoted to pleasure. Masquerades, the card table, the coffee house and the theatre absorbed the people's attention and instead of being the foremost merchant state the city was the centre of diversion in Europe. Visitors flocked to see her treasures of painting and architecture and to witness her gorgeous spectacles and ceremonies. For Venice still held to her traditions in her love of pageantry.

Through the centuries the festival of the Espousal of the Sea had been annually observed, and it was celebrated for the last time in 1796, the six-hundred-and-eighteenth time that it had been held since its first performance. The ceremony had become more and more elaborate during the centuries; there had been many *Bucentaurs* built since the Senate had ordered the first one in 1311; the last one was constructed in 1728. It was about one hundred and fifteen feet in length, with twenty-two feet beam, and was twenty-six feet deep. It stood high out of the water and was flat-bottomed, an ark suitable only for smooth water. One hundred and seventy-eight rowers propelled it, pulling forty-two oars, each of which in reality was made up of three oars, fastened together and swung as one in a single rowlock. The upper deck, fitted out like a great reception hall, was much more magnificently decorated than in the earlier *Bucentaurs*. The nine Muses, the Virtues, the Arts and such occupations as ship-building, fishing and hunting were painted on the ceiling. The figurehead of the vessel was a colossal wooden statue of Justice.

At the hour of tierce, or about eight o'clock in the morning, the bells throughout Venice broke out in jubilant peals. The Doge came from his palace with his trumpeters and standard-bearers, the Ambassadors and officers of state. All these went on board the *Bucentaur,* and as the ship moved away there followed the smaller barge of the "Doge of the Fishermen," the little "peota" of the glass-blowers of Murano, and all the gondolas of the city in gala array.

This procession swept through the lagoon to Saint Helen's Island, where the Patriarch of Venice was waiting on his flat boat. The Patriarch sent a nosegay of Damascus roses to the Doge; then the *Bucentaur,* with the Patriarch's boat in tow and also another boat in which was a choir that sang hymns specially composed for the day, was rowed towards the open sea.

As in earlier times the Patriarch, going aboard the *Bucentaur,* poured holy water on the waves and prayed for calm and quiet weather for all who voyaged in ships, after which the Doge dropped the ring into the water with the words "We espouse thee, O Sea, in token of perpetual sovereignty!"

Guns roared salutes from the fortresses, and the people in the gondolas threw flowers from boat to boat while flags were waved and cheers were given for St. Mark, the patron saint of Venice. Afterwards all went to the church of San Nicola on the Lido to hear high mass before they returned to the city.

That year of 1796 saw the last wedding of Venice and the Adriatic. Revolution flared up in the city and a few months after Ascension Day a mob grounded the gorgeous *Bucentaur* on the island of San Giorgio Maggiore and stripped it of all its gold. Four guns were placed on its decks and it was converted into a floating battery at the harbor entrance. Then came Napoleon, and on May 16, 1797 the islands of the lagoon were trodden by a conqueror for the first time in a thousand years. The one-hundred-and-twentieth Doge handed his cap of state to an attendant with the words: "Take it away; we shall not need it again."

Venice the republic was ended; but in 1866 the Queen of the Adriatic welcomed Victor Emanuel and became one of the galaxy of beautiful historic cities that make up the kingdom of united Italy.

CHAPTER VI
THE CARAVELS OF COLUMBUS

VI

THE CARAVELS OF COLUMBUS

AT the time when the Portuguese under the
leadership of Prince Henry the Navigator
were seeking a route to India and the countries beyond by sailing around Africa to the east,
there were also students of geography in Europe
who were debating whether those lands might not
be reached by a shorter route westward. If the
world were a sphere,—and it was believed to be a
sphere by most learned men,—it should be possible
to sail around it, and if one sailed far enough one
would assuredly arrive at Cathay and the Indies.
The only question was as to the distance one would
have to sail. Christopher Columbus, a native of
Genoa, who had been at one time a weaver, then a
sailor and traveler, and had studied the subject
diligently, estimated the distance across the Atlantic
Ocean—poetically called by ancient writers the Sea
of Darkness—to Cipango, or Japan, at some 2,500
miles. In this, as events afterwards proved, his
study of geography was considerably in error, for
he underestimated the distance around the globe
and overestimated the size of the continent of Asia;
but it was a fortunate error, for had the sailors
whom he later secured to make a westward voyage

with him been acquainted with the actual distance from the Canaries to what were loosely called the Indies—almost 12,000 miles—they would in all likelihood have flatly refused to attempt such a voyage.

King John II of Portugal, in whose service Columbus was employed, was chiefly interested in the plan to reach India around Africa, but this did not prevent him from listening to the arguments of the Genoese navigator in favor of a rival, and shorter, course by sailing west. He summoned a council of learned men to discuss the project, and some of them supported the views of the Genoese while others held that Columbus must be wrong in supposing that Asia extended so far to the east, and still others thought that the King had his hands sufficiently full in exploring the coast of Africa.

King John was not ordinarily unscrupulous, but in this instance he took an unfair advantage "of Columbus, for having obtained his plans the King sent out a ship with merchandise for the Cape Verde Islands and directed that the vessel, having unloaded there, should attempt a westward voyage. The sailors, however, gazing out at the wide expanse of water, refused to venture farther than the islands. Columbus learned of the deceit that had been practised upon him and in righteous indignation left the court of Lisbon and entered the service of the sovereigns of Spain, Ferdinand and Isabella, in 1486. The Spanish rulers were too much occupied with their war against the Moors to give much attention to voyages of discovery and it was not until Columbus brought his plans to the notice of the Duke of Medina Celi that he received encouragement. That nobleman entertained him at his castle at Puerto de Santa Maria and became so much interested that he decided to fit out several caravels at his own expense.

In order to do this the Duke sought the permission of Queen Isabella; but she refused her consent, declaring that she had not yet made up her mind as to whether she would send out such an expedition herself; if she did she graciously agreed to allow the Duke to share in it. This was in 1491, when the Spaniards were preparing to besiege Granada, and Columbus, seeing no immediate prospect of aid from the sovereigns, determined to try what might be done at the court of France.

In October or November of that year he left Huelva, a Spanish town northwest of Cadiz, with his son Diego, a boy of eleven or twelve. At the Franciscan monastery of La Rabida, near Palos, he stopped, according to tradition, to ask for bread and water for his son. The prior, Juan Perez, listened to the traveler's story of his great project and the many rebuffs he had received, and sent for Garcia Fernandez, a physician of Palos, and Martin Alonso Pinzon, a wealthy ship-owner and captain of that town. To these men Columbus repeated his story and so impressed them with the importance of his scheme that Pinzon declared he would like to go himself on such an expedition and the prior, who had been Queen Isabella's confessor, wrote her an earnest request to aid Columbus. On receipt of this message the Queen summoned Juan Perez to come to her at the camp outside Granada, and having talked with him sent the prior back to La Rabida with money to bring Columbus to court where Isabella promised to give him a further hearing. Leaving his son at the monastery Columbus and the prior rode mule-back to the royal camp before Granada.

When he reached the camp the arguments of the Genoese were presented to a council of scholars and were now received with much more favor than before. Some of the learned men had changed their minds in regard to his project, and the royal confessors Deza and Talavera, Mendoza, Archbishop of Toledo, Quintanilla, Treasurer of Castile, and Luis de Santangel, Treasurer of Aragon, declared themselves enthusiastically in support of Columbus. As a result Queen Isabella promised to give her attention to the matter as soon as the Moors should surrender the city of Granada.

That event occurred on January 2, 1492, and the royal flag of Spain was flung to the wind from the top of the Alhambra. Then Queen Isabella received Columbus. Long though he had waited for support for his great enterprise and difficult and discouraging as his road had been he had lost none of his faith in his plans nor abated his claim—originally made to the King of Portugal—that if he succeeded he should have great rewards. He demanded that he should be created Admiral of the Ocean and Viceroy of any countries he might discover and should receive an eighth part of all profits accruing from his voyage. To these demands Isabella objected; but Columbus, his belief in his mission fortified by an almost fanatic desire to use the proceeds from his voyage for a religious crusade against the infidel, would not recede from his position; consequently the Queen refused her support.

Again rebuffed, the white-haired Genoese mounted his mule and set out a second time for France. He had no more than started, however, when Luis de Santangel hurried to Isabella and pleaded with her not to let such an opportunity for fame and fortune slip through her grasp. His pleas were warmly seconded by Quintanilla and by the Queen's close friend Beatriz de Bobadilla, Marchioness of Moya. Isabella reconsidered and finally sent a courier after Columbus who overtook the latter as he was crossing the bridge of Pinos, six miles from Granada.

An agreement was thereupon reached, in which the Queen granted most of Columbus's demands. He and his heirs were to have the office of Admiral in all the islands and continents he might discover or acquire, he should be the Viceroy in all such places, he should have one-tenth of all gold, silver, precious stones and all other articles found there, he should be the sole judge in all disputes arising out of traffic between those lands and Spain, and he might contribute an eighth part of the cost of fitting out ships for his voyage and receive an eighth part of the profits.

Columbus at once secured from his friends the eighth share of the expense for vessels. The rest of the amount needed was raised by the treasury of Castile. The agreement was signed on April 17, 1492, and Columbus vowed to give every maravedi or gold-piece that he should receive to the work of rescuing the Holy Sepulchre from the infidel.

In May he reached Palos with the Queen's orders for ships and sailors. At that seaport Martin Pinzon and his brothers helped the royal officers in carrying out Isabella's commands. Since there were hardly any sailors who were willing to set out on such a voyage across the Sea of Darkness debtors were freed from their obligations and criminals from their prisons to make up the crews. Three ships were obtained, vessels that were commonly called caravels, a term that has been applied at different times and in different countries to ships of very varying appearance and build. It was a type of ship that was much used in the fifteenth and sixteenth centuries by the Spaniards and Portuguese for long voyages and the caravels they employed were roundish vessels, generally with a double tower at the stern and a single one in the bow, and galley rigged.

The ships that were sailed by Columbus had actually few improvements over those of the early Christian era. At his time, however, a lateen sail

was commonly carried on the mizzenmast—or third
mast from the bow—as it had been found that such
a sail had more driving power than a square sail
when a ship was heading into the wind. Of Columbus's three vessels the largest, named the *Santa
Maria* or *Capitana,* belonged to a mariner, Juan de
La Cosa. He was to command her, with an experienced sailor, Sancho Ruiz, for his pilot. This was
to be the Admiral's flagship.

The *Santa Maria* was of about one hundred tons,
and she measured from bow to stern only ninety
feet. She had three masts and a bowsprit, with
square sails on the fore and main masts and a lateen
sail on the mizzenmast. The bow was high and over-
hung the water by twelve feet; amidships the deck
was low and about one-fourth of the distance aft
it dropped down abruptly. This deck was called
the waist, and near the stern another deck rose to
about the height of the forward deck, and behind
this was reared a high sterncastle.

The Admiral's cabin was in the upper part of the
sterncastle and a door gave on to the high deck and
windows opened in the narrow stern above the water. The crew usually slept on deck, although there
were accommodations between decks for some of
them. This space which they sometimes occupied
was where the cargo and supplies were carried. The
sailors cooked their food on a box of small stones on
the main deck under the edge of the forecastle.

Martin Pinzon commanded the second caravel, the

Pinta, of fifty tons, a swifter ship than the *Santa Maria.* This vessel was owned by two men of Palos, Gomez Rascon and Cristobal Quintero, who served in the crew. The third and the smallest ship was the *Niña,* of forty tons, captained by Martin Pinzon's youngest brother, Vicente Yanez Pinzon. Neither of the two smaller vessels was decked amidships. The three caravels carried in all ninety persons.

Before dawn on Friday, August 3, 1492, these three ships sailed from Palos. The aim of Columbus was to reach the northern end of Cipango, or Japan, which, according to the map he was using, appeared to be directly on the route to the cities of Cathay that had been described by Marco Polo. His course lay to the Canaries, from whence he figured he could sail due west without shifting direction until he saw the shore of Cipango. The voyage was scarcely begun, however, when the *Pinta's* rudder was broken and unshipped, a happening which the Admiral attributed to willful mischief by Rascon and Quintero, the two owners, who did not wish their ship to take part in the expedition.

The Canaries belonged to Spain, and Columbus stopped there to repair the *Pinta.* Meantime his sailors saw an omen of evil in an eruption of Teneriffe, and reported to their captains that there were rumors of Portuguese caravels lying off the islands on purpose to capture Columbus and take him a prisoner to Lisbon.

Undeterred by such rumors, Columbus sailed from Gomera on September sixth; but the winds were so light that the three ships made only thirty miles in two days. When the breeze freshened and the shores of Ferro, the last of the Canary Islands, disappeared to the east many of the crews, filled with the thought that they might never sight land again, cried and wrung their hands.

The difficulty of controlling his sailors, who were so unwilling to proceed on such a perilous voyage, led Columbus to the expedient of keeping two reckonings, a correct one for his own use and a false one for the crews. He made only such slight alterations as he thought would not be discovered, reporting the run of 180 miles on September tenth as 144 miles, and the run of 120 miles on the following day as 108; and but for such subterfuges it might well have happened that the timorous sailors would have mutinied and turned back or even thrown the Admiral overboard.

Columbus was blessed with good weather and a friendly sea. His chief difficulty was with his men, who found causes for dismay in the slightest happenings. One of these was the action of the compass. On the night of September thirteenth the ships crossed the magnetic line of no variation and Columbus was surprised to note that the needle of the compass, instead of pointing slightly to the right of the pole star, began to swing towards the left and increased this deviation the next day. This va-

riation was also noticed by the pilots and they at
once attributed it to some freak perpetrated by the
compass in return for the audacity of attempting
such a voyage. It was only by Columbus's quick-
witted invention of an explanation and the men's
faith in his knowledge of astronomy that their ap-
prehension was allayed.

Then on September sixteenth the ships found
themselves in great masses of floating seaweed filled
with small fish and crabs. This was in reality that
great Sargasso Sea that is a wide area of tangled
vegetation. At first the caravels sailed through the
weeds easily enough, but after several days, the wind
being light, they made little headway. This gave
rise to talk among the crews concerning old legends
of strange places in the ocean inimical to mariners
where vessels were entrapped. Some thought there
might be shoals on which they would go aground, but
this fear was dispelled when they found they could
not touch bottom with their longest plummet-lines.

By September twenty-second the ships had reached
clear water; now, however, they encountered the
trade-winds and as these bore them westward the
sailors began to wonder if they would be able to
sail to the east when they wanted to return. A few
days later Columbus discovered general impatience
in the fleet at the failure to sight land. On September twenty-fifth the crews saw a mirage, which they
took to be shore, and great was their disappointment
when it disappeared the next morning. The men

became more restless, they muttered among themselves and talked of mutiny; probably it was only the sailors' confidence in the admiral's skill in navigation and their knowledge that they might need that skill on the return voyage that kept them from open insubordination.

Even so the crews became rebellious on October fourth, and Columbus had recourse to his old stratagem and told them that the day's run had been 138 miles instead of the actual figure of 189. On October seventh they had come 2,724 geographical miles from the Canaries, a longer distance than Columbus had estimated the voyage to Cipango. Thinking that he might sail to the north of that country if he kept to his present course he shifted two points to the west-southwest. Small birds were now flying over the water and he felt confident that land must be near.

The crews were becoming more outspoken and daily more mutinous, but the Admiral showed himself as determined as ever and his steadfastness was finally rewarded when signs of land were seen on October eleventh.

That night at ten o'clock Columbus from the high poop of the *Santa Maria* saw a light moving on what appeared to be shore. A little later, about two o'clock in the morning of October 12, 1492 (or, according to the "new style" of the Gregorian Calendar, October 21, 1492) a long low coast was distinctly made out five miles away. Sails were lowered and the caravels lay to. It was ten weeks since the ships had left Palos and thirty-three days since the coast of Ferro had sunk on the eastern horizon.

At dawn Columbus and many of his men went ashore in the small boats. The country where they landed was delightful to look upon and the men were wild with joy, confident that great riches awaited them; the officers embraced their leader and the sailors on their knees begged pardon for their talk of disobedience.

On the shore were naked people of cinnamon color who fled at first sight of the strange beings in the stupendous vessels that looked like great sea monsters; but they later returned and bowed and stretched out their hands to these wonderful white men, so remarkably dressed. The Spaniards approached the natives with friendly smiles and soon, making use of the knowledge acquired by earlier explorers among savage tribes, offered to exchange various trinkets, beads and bells and such things, for small ornaments of gold and bright-hued parrots. When Columbus in sign language inquired where the gold came from the natives pointed to the south, which led the Admiral to suppose that he must have reached an island north of Cipango. From the answers to his questions it appeared that the place where he had landed was called Guanahani.

According to the custom of discoverers Columbus

took possession of the island for the crown of Castile and gave it the name of San Salvador. Historians have tried to identify this island of Guanahani; no records establish its identity positively, but it was undoubtedly one of the Bahamas.

Columbus then cruised among the islands of this group for ten days, visiting four of them, and concluded that he was somewhere just east of Cathay. When asked about gold the natives always pointed south and so Columbus sailed in that direction on October twenty-fifth, thinking to visit Cipango and then proceed to Cathay, where he intended to present the Great Khan with a letter from Ferdinand and Isabella with which he had been provided.

On this course he came to Cuba, which he found extraordinarily charming, and which he took to be Cipango. He tried to talk with the natives, but such information as they gave him was of no real worth. Then he sent two messengers to seek the ruler of the country. They returned with news of having seen villages, fields of maize and cotton, and men and women smoking aromatic herbs. But they had discovered no king nor large city and had seen no gold and spices such as were reported to be found in Cipango.

Not unnaturally Columbus was confused as to these islands, which, according to his maps, should be part of Asia, yet where there seemed to be no knowledge of the Great Khan and where there was

neither gold nor spices. In his dilemma he again
questioned the natives and gained the idea from their
answers by gestures that there was a larger island,
where gold was plentiful, to the southeast.

To the southeast he therefore sailed. On November twentieth Martin Pinzon, commanding the fleet-
est of the three ships, the *Pinta,* sailed away,
deserting the others, with the intention, as some
chroniclers say, of returning to Spain before the
Admiral and claiming more credit than he was en-
titled to for the discovery of the Indies.

The *Santa Maria* and the *Niña* continued along
the coast of Cuba, exploring the shore here and there,
and Columbus found plenty of pearl oysters and
aloes and thought he discovered signs of gold in the
rivers. The cape at the end of the island he named
Alpha and Omega, since he regarded it as the far-
thest eastern point of Asia, the first land to be
reached if one journeyed across the Atlantic, the last
if one voyaged around the globe in the opposite direction. On December sixth he made a landing on
the northwestern shore of Hayti, which he christened
Hispaniola, or "Spanish land."

The natives on this island gave him information
of a land to the south called Cibao where there was
much gold, and this Columbus thought must be the
Cipango for which he was searching. Before he
could sail thither, however, misfortune wrecked his
plans. Early on the morning of Christmas Day the
Santa Maria, through the carelessness of her helms-

man, ran upon a sand-bank and was soon broken by the surf.

Columbus had now only the little *Niña,* the smallest of the three ships, and he thought that if she should be wrecked he would lose all the honor and profits of announcing his wonderful discovery in Europe. Martin Pinzon might or might not get back to Spain in the *Pinta,* but in any case Columbus wanted to report the success of his project in person to Queen Isabella. So he made his plans to return.

All the men could not sail in the *Niña* and a number of the crew, having found Hispaniola a pleasant place, where life was easy and the people friendly, were eager to remain. A blockhouse was built with the timbers of the *Santa Maria* and armed with her guns; and in this fort—called Fort Nativity—forty Spaniards were left, with supplies for a year.

January 4, 1493 the *Niña,* with the remainder of the two crews, sailed from Hispaniola on the return voyage. Two days later, as they were skirting the north shore of the island, they encountered the *Pinta,* which had tarried to allow the mariners to trade with the natives and search for gold, of which they had found some nuggets. Martin Pinzon explained that the weather had separated his ship from the other two; whether this were true or not it was a fact that the *Pinta's* foremast had been damaged and due to this Pinzon's ship was now unable to sail faster than the *Niña.*

With the trade-winds against him Columbus sailed northeast to the thirty-seventh latitude from where he could steer directly for Spain. A storm struck the two ships on February twelfth and blew so hard for four days that the caravels were nearly sunk and were driven so far apart that they lost sight of each other for the rest of the voyage.

During the storm the Admiral thought it so likely that the *Niña* would go down that he wrote out on parchment two accounts of his discovery addressed to Ferdinand and Isabella, wrapped each in a cloth and placed each in a large cake of wax which was put in a barrel. One barrel was thrown overboard, the other was kept on the quarter-deck to be flung into the sea if the *Niña* foundered.

Land was sighted on February fifteenth, but the storm was blowing so hard that the coast could not be approached, and it was not until the eighteenth that a boat reached the shore, which turned out to be the island of St. Mary, one of the Azores.

The Portuguese governor was unfriendly. He seized a party of the *Niña's* sailors and held them prisoners for five days, and only released them because Columbus threatened to such purpose that the governor thought his refusal might cause war between Portugal and Spain.

Leaving the Azores the *Niña,* heading for Cape St. Vincent, ran into another gale and was forced upon the coast of Portugal, where she took shelter in the Tagus River. Immediately word spread of what Columbus had accomplished and Lisbon was amazed and angered at the opportunity Portugal had missed. The King pretended to believe that Columbus had trespassed upon the vast territories that had been granted Portugal by Pope Eugenius IV. Again it was the thought of a possible war between Portugal and Spain that deterred the Portuguese from injuring Columbus; making the best face he could to hide his chagrin King John invited the Admiral to court and highly complimented him. On March thirteenth Columbus sailed again and reached the harbor of Palos two days later.

The people of Palos rang the church bells and flocked to the harbor to welcome the great discoverer. As they were greeting him another ship entered, the *Pinta,* and Martin Pinzon found that his plan to be first with the news in Spain was definitely thwarted. He had been driven by the gale to Bayonne and from there had sent a message to Ferdinand and Isabella setting up great claims of discovery for himself. But the news from Columbus reached the court before a reply was despatched to the claims of Martin Pinzon and when the reply was sent it forbade Pinzon to appear before the sovereigns.

Columbus was ordered to go to the rulers at Barcelona and there he was received with the greatest honors. He had brought home live parrots and stuffed birds, some pearls and bits of gold, and six natives of Hispaniola. These natives were called

Indians, since their home appeared to be in that part of the world referred to as the Indies, and it was by that name that Columbus always spoke of them. In Spain and throughout Europe it was assumed that the Admiral had discovered the eastern coast of Asia and reached Cipango and that therefore he had found a direct and comparatively short route to the land of gold mentioned by Marco Polo.

Ferdinand and Isabella were immensely elated at the thought of the untold wealth that would result to Spain, and they attributed the great achievement to the gratitude of Heaven for their expelling the Moors from Europe. They were delighted at Columbus's eagerness to make a second voyage; and for this enterprise there were plenty of volunteer sailors and a surplus of money.

So the Admiral sailed from Cadiz on September 25, 1493, with a fleet of seventeen ships and fifteen hundred men. Again he made a vow to attempt the rescue of the Holy Sepulchre with the treasures of the Indies, to raise an army of crusaders within the next seven years and another army to fight the Saracens within five years thereafter.

The ships that sailed on this second expedition comprised fourteen caravels and three larger store-ships termed carracks. Horses and mules were carried, as well as a number of European plants, for the intention was to establish a permanent colony on Hispaniola. Among the voyagers were Columbus's youngest brother Giacomo, called Diego, Juan Ponce

de Leon, who later named Florida, Francisco de Las
Casas, father of the celebrated apostle and historian
of the Indies, the pilot Juan de La Cose, in charge
of chart-making, and a goodly number of young
gentlemen of Spain, among them Alonso de Ojeda
and Pedro Margarite.

This expedition met with fair weather and land
was sighted on November third. This was an island,
which they christened Dominica. Cruising through
the Caribbean they discovered several other islands
which they named Marigalante, Guadaloupe, An-
tigua and Porto Rico. The natives here were can-
nibals, and in encounters with some of them several
Spaniards were killed with poisoned arrows. On
the night of November twenty-seventh Columbus
reached the harbor of La Navidad and fired a salute
to attract the attention of the sailors he had left
there on his first voyage.

There was no reply from shore and when the Spaniards landed the next morning they found the fortress in ruins, the chests of provisions empty, and
the graves of eleven men in the fort. The colony
of La Navidad had been completely destroyed and
none of the party of forty Spaniards was left to tell
the tale. From scraps of information that Columbus gathered from the Indians he concluded that
there had been quarrels between the Europeans and
the natives that had led to raids on both sides and
that at length a chieftain from Xaragua had wiped
out the fortress and its defenders.

A new colony was established at a place named Isabella where there was a good harbor, not far from the mountains in Cibao where gold was to be found. Twelve of the ships were sent back to Spain for supplies and more colonists, and in March, 1494 Columbus started to explore the country with a force of four hundred armed men. On his return to the seaboard he gave the command of the island to Pedro Margarite, and leaving his brother Diego in charge of the little town at Isabella he sailed with three caravels on April twenty-fourth to investigate more of the Indies.

A short voyage west brought the ships into the Windward Passage and in sight of the headland he had named Cape Alpha and Omega. Passing to the left of this, he sailed along the southern coast of Cuba. Changing his direction to the south, on May third he reached the island that still bears its native name of Jamaica.

Columbus found this island beautiful and its inhabitants more intelligent than any other natives he had met in this part of the world, but they could tell him nothing of Cathay, so he turned north and touched the coast of Cuba at a point he named Cape Cruz. He questioned the Indians and learned that they believed that Cuba was limitless, they also told him that the country to the west was called Mangon and from their description of it Columbus thought that it must be the province of Mangi, which, according to his map, lay just south of Cathay.

As they coasted along the shores of Cuba the explorers became more and more satisfied that they were on the edge of the continent of Asia. In view of this Columbus was filled with a desire to sail south and reach the Indian Ocean, round Africa and return to Spain by circumnavigating the globe. It was a great ambition and had he embarked on it he might have arrived at Central or South America; but his crews were opposed to making a longer voyage and he needed more supplies if he should attempt it, so he decided to return to Hispaniola.

Before the three ships turned back, however, all the officers and sailors declared in a formal statement their firm belief that they had reached the continent of Asia, a document Columbus wished to have to silence any critics he might meet in Spain.

On their return the caravels circumnavigated Hispaniola, a voyage that greatly surprised the Admiral, as he had supposed that Cipango was much larger than this island proved to be. He was greatly worn with fatigue and the excitement of his adventures and before his ship reached port he fell ill and had to be carried ashore and put to bed in one of the newly-built houses at Isabella.

When he recovered he found that his younger brother Bartholomew, who had been in France when the Admiral returned to Spain after his first voyage, had come out to Hispaniola in command of three ships Ferdinand and Isabella had sent with supplies. At once the Admiral appointed Bartholomew to the office of Adelantado or Governor of Hispaniola under himself, the Viceroy of the Indies.

In the Admiral's absence there had been discord and even strife in the settlement on Hispaniola. His brother Diego had proved too gentle for the task of keeping the hot-headed adventurers in order and some of the Spaniards had fought with the natives and some with each other, and finally Pedro Margarite had gathered a band of rebels and, seizing the ships that had brought Bartholomew's party, had sailed away in them to Spain.

When they reached the court of Spain Margarite and his companions belittled the value of the discoveries of Columbus, argued that both the Admiral and his brother Bartholomew were unfit to be commanders, and pointed out that the rulers of Spain were spending more money on exploring the Indies than they were ever likely to receive in return. The sovereigns apparently paid little heed to Margarite's complaints, and the latter took his criticisms of Columbus to Juan Rodriguez de Fonseca, Archdeacon of Seville, who had been placed in charge of the affairs of the Indies. Fonseca lent a willing ear to Margarite's arguments, and in this man, who was possessed of great authority, Columbus soon found that he had an enemy more difficult to cope with than any of the natives of Hispaniola.

With some of the Indians, particularly with the followers of the chieftain Caonabo, who had destroyed the fortress at La Navidad, Columbus had to fight. A party of Spaniards was caught in ambush and killed, but eventually Caonabo was captured and the Indians defeated. What with mutiny at Isabella and skirmishes inland the Admiral was very busy for a year after his return from Cuba. Then in October, 1495 four caravels with supplies arrived from Spain and aboard one was Juan Aguado, sent out by the sovereigns to learn what was going on in the colony.

His enemies, chiefly men who resented his firm hand in government, presented so many charges against Columbus to Aguado that when the latter prepared to leave Columbus thought it would be well to accompany him in order to state his side of the situation. Before he sailed some gold mines were found on the south side of Hispaniola; and this discovery, taken with what he had learned from his voyage along the coast of Cuba, resulted in a new opinion on the part of Columbus. If Hispaniola were not Cipango, possibly it might be Ophir, where King Solomon had obtained the gold for the great temple at Jerusalem. No one knew exactly where Ophir was, but it had always been supposed to be somewhere in the Indies.

The finding of gold led to the transfer of the chief settlement from Isabella to the mouth of the Ozema River at a place called San Domingo. Early in March, 1496 Columbus and Aguado sailed for Spain in two caravels. On this voyage they ran into trade-winds, which so delayed them that they had to stop

at Guadaloupe and obtain a store of cassava bread.
When they went on again they were so much impeded by head-winds that they made little progress
and were in risk of starvation. At last, however,
on June eleventh, the caravels reached Cadiz, and,
after resting there, Columbus journeyed to the court
at Burgos.

Ferdinand and Isabella welcomed him graciously
enough and nothing was said of the charges that
had been brought against him. But Fonseca nourished a grudge, and when the Admiral planned his
third voyage all sorts of difficulties were put in his
way. Yet such was the indomitable character of
Columbus that he got a fleet together and sailed with
six ships from San Lucar de Barrameda on May 30,
1498. When he reached the Isle de Ferro he sent
three of the ships directly to Hispaniola and himself
with the other three sailed to the Cape Verde Islands
and thence southwest. His object was to search for
islands near the equator and then to reach what he
considered the coast of Asia at a more southern point
than he had yet achieved, whence he might be able
to find the Indian Ocean.

This course brought the caravels into a zone just
north of the equator, where they encountered a calm
and a torrid atmosphere and could not use their sails
for eight days. But the equatorial current carried
the ships along and at length, when hardly a cask of
fresh water was left, they sighted land. Three
mountain peaks rose up from the water, forming

one large mountain on an island, which Columbus christened Trinidad.

Sailing along the coast, he came in view of land at the delta of the Orinoco River, to which he gave the name of Isla Santa. Entering the Gulf of Paria the caravels were nearly swamped by the great swells that came from several of the smaller mouths of the huge Orinoco. This water proved fresh and Columbus decided that it must have come from a gigantic stream and that such a river must be located on a vast continent. In this he was correct, for he was off the coast of South America; but this continent, of which no one had yet heard, he supposed to be closely connected with Asia, if not indeed a part of Asia.

Still searching for some strait that would take him to the Indian Ocean, he sailed through a passage which he named Dragon's Mouth, sighted Tobago and Grenada, and skirted the Pearl Coast as far as Margarita and Cubagua.

He was eager to go farther westward, but illness overtook him, and, unfitted by gout and fever for more exploring, he steered for Hispaniola and reached San Domingo on August thirtieth. There his brother Bartholomew told him of the troubles that had disrupted the colony; there had been civil warfare and Hispaniola was in a state of insurrection against its governor. For two years the work of discovery had to give place to an effort to bring about order, and meanwhile in Spain Fonseca was busily engaged in poisoning the minds of the sovereigns against Columbus.

Meanwhile also the Portuguese Vasco da Gama had rounded the Cape of Good Hope and reached the treasure-fields of India. He had brought back to his country jewels and ivory, a great collection of riches that made what Columbus had brought from Hispaniola appear very insignificant. Columbus, it seemed, had only discovered a group of islands inhabited by savages. Ferdinand and Isabella became impatient and sent Francisco de Bobadilla to look into affairs at Hispaniola; if Bobadilla found that Columbus had acted improperly he was authorized to take the government of the island from him.

This agent reached San Domingo in August, 1500. By that time the Admiral and his brother Bartholomew had put an end to the civil warfare and were achieving order, but there were some rebels in prison when Bobadilla arrived and the latter immediately demanded arrogantly that they should be handed over to him. Columbus was away from the settlement and his brother Diego, who was in charge, refused to give up the rebels; whereupon Bobadilla read aloud the royal orders, declared himself governor, released the prisoners and put Diego in chains.

All the rebellious element joined the forces of Bobadilla, and when the Admiral returned to San Domingo Bobadilla's officers at once arrested him and took him to prison loaded with chains. In the same

way they dealt with the Admiral's brother Bartholomew when he came to San Domingo.

Then Bobadilla invented a story that he had found
the three brothers guilty of rousing the Indians to
resist the sovereigns of Spain and upon this ridicu-
lous charge he put them, still in irons, aboard a ship
and ordered the captain to take them to Fonseca in
Spain.

The ship's captain wanted to remove the fetters
from the Admiral, but Columbus would not permit
it. He desired to wear the chains to court to show
how he had been dealt with. In this he judged well,
for no sooner had he arrived at Cadiz than the sight
of the great man in chains roused a fury of indignation. Great was the resentment at the hero's ill-
treatment; the sovereigns sent for him, and Queen
Isabella received him at the Alhambra in Granada
with tears and words of sympathy for the indig-
nities to which he had been subjected.

Restored to the royal favor, Columbus started out
again, intent now on finding a strait through the
continent he had discovered, so that, sailing through
it, he might reach India by voyaging west as Vasco
da Gama had reached it by an eastward passage. On
this fourth voyage his brother Bartholomew and
the Admiral's younger son Ferdinand, then fourteen, sailed with him; his fleet consisted of four small
caravels with a crew of one hundred and fifty men.
They left Cadiz May 11, 1502, and on June fifteenth
reached an island near Dominica. Columbus in-

tended to sail to Jamaica, but damage to one of the ships led to his steering to San Domingo instead. At about the same time a fleet of twenty-six or twenty-eight ships, laden with gold, was on the point of setting out for Spain, and in one of them were four thousand pieces of gold that were to be paid to Columbus as part of the reimbursement that had been promised him.

The Admiral put into San Domingo and asked permission to engage another ship to replace his disabled one; seeing signs of an approaching hurricane he also requested to be allowed to stay in the harbor and sent a message to the commander of the gold-fleet warning him of a change of weather.

His enemies, however, were still in control at San Domingo, and the Admiral was ordered to leave the harbor, and his message to the gold-fleet was unheeded. Highly indignant, he managed to find shelter for his ships and rode out the hurricane safely. But the great gold-fleet put out to sea, was caught by the gale, twenty or more of its ships were sunk, and the only one that managed to reach Spain was the vessel that carried the gold that was to be paid to Columbus.

In the calm that followed the hurricane the Admiral's ships drifted in the currents to the southern coast of Cuba. From there, in the first favoring wind, they made sail to the island of Guanaja and to Cape Honduras. Here Columbus found a higher type of civilization among the natives than any he had yet seen, and considerably more wealth; and when asked for the source of their gold and ornaments the Indians pointed to the west.

In pursuit of these lands of gold the fleet doubled the cape which marks the end of Honduras and the beginning of Nicaragua. As they sailed south towards Veragua the explorers saw lands where there were large houses and people who wore quantities of golden ornaments. At length they decided to make a settlement and seek for gold-mines in the neighborhood of Veragua.

That settlement met with misfortunes. Many of the explorers were massacred by the natives, food gave out and they found no fresh supplies. After three months they abandoned the place and headed their caravels, which were now badly leaking, towards Hispaniola. A gale almost wrecked them, and on June 23, 1503 the ships grounded on the coast of Jamaica. From there Columbus sent two men in a canoe to San Domingo to seek aid from the new governor of Hispaniola, Nicolas de Ovando.

Ovando was an enemy of Columbus, and made one excuse after another for delaying aid to the little party stranded on Jamaica. It was not until a year later, in June, 1504, that he finally sent a couple of ships to take off Columbus and his men, who were almost starved and had about given up hope of rescue.

In Hispaniola there was strife and no support from the governor for further exploring expeditions,

so Columbus sailed for Spain and after a stormy
voyage reached San Lucar de Barrameda on November 7, 1504.

A few days later Queen Isabella died, and there
was then no one to protect the Admiral from the
hostility of Fonseca. Wealth had been promised
him, but the promises were not made good. In pov-
erty, and weakened by hardship and disappointment, Columbus fell ill and died at Valladolid on
May 20, 1506.

Europe thought that Columbus had found a route
to the Indies by sailing west across the Atlantic and
that in his voyages he had discovered some islands,
none of which appeared to possess much value. No
one yet realized that between Europe and the Asia
he believed he had reached was a great new world,
two continents united by an isthmus. It was not
until many other discoverers had sailed those western seas and explored the adjacent lands that it came
to be appreciated that the voyages of Columbus had
added a vast new territory to the map of the globe.

CHAPTER VII

THE FIRST SHIP TO SAIL
AROUND THE WORLD

VII

THE FIRST SHIP TO SAIL AROUND
THE WORLD

ABOARD one of the ships of Dom Francisco de Almeida, the first Portuguese Viceroy of India, there sailed to the east as a volunteer in 1505 a young nobleman of Portugal, who had been born and bred in the wild, rugged province of Tras-os-Montes. His name in Portuguese was Fernão da Magalhães, or in English Ferdinand Magellan. By nature adventurous, he had early gone to Lisbon and at the royal court had been fired with desire to make some of those voyages to strange lands that were so largely occupying the attention of Portugal and Spain. For seven years he served in eastern lands and waters, fought with Arabs and Malays, and went on an expedition to Malacca, which was the first voyage that ships of Europe had ever made east of Ceylon.

This expedition almost met with disaster, for while the Portuguese were loading their ships with pepper and ginger the Malay ruler was planning the destruction of the visitors. The Portuguese commander, Sequeira, had no thought of treachery, and allowed Malay sailors and traders to come aboard his four ships at a time when all his boats but one had been sent ashore under charge of Francisco Serrano to bring out the cargo.

On his quarter-deck Sequeira was playing a game of chess while a ring of Malays pretended great interest in his game at the same time keeping an eye on the tall tower of the citadel on shore, from which a puff of smoke was to be the signal for them to kill Sequeira and his officers and seize their ships while other Malays massacred the boats' crews on the beach.

It was a Persian woman, in love with one of the Portuguese officers, who gave the warning that saved the Europeans. Before the signal of smoke was seen the men on several of the ships drove the Malays from the decks and Magellan, in the only small boat, rowed for Sequeira's flagship, crying out "Treason!"

The puff of smoke floated out from the tower of the citadel and the Malays on shore sprang forward to attack the white men. Serrano and some of his sailors dashed to their boats and pulled out from the beach; but most of the Portuguese were surrounded and killed. Malays in skiffs chased Serrano and he was battling against a furious horde when Magellan came up in his boat and by almost superhuman fighting managed to rescue the sailors.

As soon as the Portuguese reached their ships the Malays, in a great flotilla of skiffs, attacked the fleet; but the guns of the ships destroyed some of the skiffs and the swarm of small boats had to retire before the cannon-fire.

From that day there sprang up between Francisco Serrano and the man who had rescued him a devoted friendship.

When the Portuguese Viceroy Albuquerque succeeded in taking Malacca in 1511, he sent Serrano in command of one of the ships that made the first voyage to the Moluccas, or the Spice Islands, as they were then known.   As he was returning with a cargo of spices Serrano's vessel was driven on an island and wrecked.   This place, which at the time was deserted, was sometimes used by pirates, and soon after Serrano and his crew were cast up there a company of pirates, sighting the wreckage on the shore, landed and searched for plunder.   The Portuguese captain and his men, hiding behind the rocks above the beach, saw the marauders and at the first favorable opportunity stole down to the shore and took possession of the pirates' ship.

Their nearest refuge was the island of Amboina; and so by chance of the shipwreck Serrano came again to the Moluccas, and there he made himself the adviser and the ally of the King of Ternate.   He sent reports of affairs in the Far East to the Portuguese government, and it was his letters to Magellan that filled that ardent adventurer with the wish to follow Serrano to those marvellous, mysterious "Indies" that Europe was so much interested in since the voyages of Columbus.

In the summer of 1512 Magellan was in Lisbon, hoping to return to India; but this desire was

thwarted, because, either through some misunder-
standing with Albuquerque or some false criticism,
he found himself out of favor with King Emanuel of
Portugal. He served in the forces of Morocco and
was wounded in the knee by a Moorish lance, which
lamed him permanently. Later, in Portugal, he devoted himself to the study of nautical charts and
navigation, and from his studies came the idea of
sailing around the globe. In that new world—called
on the maps and globes the "Mundus Novus"—
reached by Columbus and explored in parts by Vespucius and Coelho and other great navigators, he
thought there must be some opening through which
he might sail westward and so arrive at the Moluccas, where Francisco Serrano was ruling with the
King of Ternate.

As a loyal subject Magellan first took his plan to
King Emanuel. Papal bulls and treaties had pre-
viously defined which part of the new regions in
process of exploration should pertain to Spain and
which to Portugal, and by these edicts of the Papacy
and the treaty of Tordesillas the Spaniards were
forbidden to sail to the Indies by way of the Cape
of Good Hope. Inasmuch as the Portuguese had a
monopoly on that route to the east King Emanuel
could see no advantage to his country in the discovery of a road to the Indies by some passage through
"Mundus Novus," a passage through which the
Spaniards might perhaps also be allowed to sail.
He therefore was not enthusiastic about Magellan's

plan. When Magellan asked permission to offer his
services to some other sovereign the King said he
might do as he pleased. Apparently the ruler of
Portugal was not very well disposed towards this
adventurous subject of his because when Magellan
took his leave King Emanuel would not offer him
his hand to kiss.

Failing to find support at Lisbon, Magellan went
to Spain, where in October, 1517 he became the guest
at Seville of a Portuguese gentleman, Diego Barbosa, who had been for some time in the service of
Spain and had great influence there. Within a few
months the guest married his host's daughter Beatriz de Barbosa, and with the help of Barbosa and
of Juan de Aranda, a high official, he succeeded in
gaining the ear of the young king, Charles V, and
also of his powerful minister, that Juan Rodriguez
de Fonseca, now Bishop of Burgos, who had been the
enemy of Columbus.

Magellan proposed to reach the Spice Islands of
the East Indies from the west, and to do that he
hoped to find a strait at the extreme south of South
America. An astronomer, Ruy Faleiro, aided him
in working out his plans, and financial assistance
was provided by Christopher de Haro, a member of
a rich Antwerp firm. On March 22, 1518 Magellan
and Faleiro signed an agreement with Charles V
by which they were to receive one-twentieth of the
profits of the voyage and to be the governors of
any lands discovered; and on August 10, 1519 a fleet

of five ships under Magellan's command left Seville
and sailed down the Guadalquivir to San Lucar de
Barrameda. Here they stayed for more than five
weeks and on September 20, 1519 put out to sea.

The flagship was the *Trinidad,* of one hundred and
ten tons; the others were the *San Antonio,* of one
hundred and twenty tons, commanded by Juan de
Cartagena; the *Concepcion,* of ninety tons, under
Gaspar Quesada; the *Victoria,* of eighty-five tons,
under Luis de Mendoza; and the *Santiago,* of
seventy-five tons, under Juan Serrano, the brother
of Magellan's friend Francisco Serrano. The crews
of the fleet numbered about two hundred and eighty,
a mixed company of Spaniards and Portuguese, Genoese and Sicilians, French and Flemings, Germans
and Greeks, one Englishman, and several negroes
and Malays. Ruy Faleiro did not sail, but an Italian gentleman, the Chevalier Antonio Pigafetta of
Vicenza, who afterwards wrote a history of the voyage, went as a volunteer in Magellan's suite, "for to
see the marvels of the ocean," as he expressed it.
Three-quarters of the expense was paid by the Spanish crown, the remainder by Christopher de Haro
and his friends.

Meanwhile King Emanuel of Portugal, much angered at the news of Magellan's expedition, had sent
rascals to Seville to try to stab the commander and
orders to his officers in the East Indies to arrest the
fleet if it ever reached those waters. Nor was Magellan without enemies in his own command, for

upon only one of his captains, Juan Serrano, could
he rely; the others, Cartagena, Quesada and Mendoza
were ready to betray him at any time.   In his crews
were many men ripe for mutiny.   The fleet had only
been at sea a few days when a small caravel overtook the flagship, bringing Magellan a message from
his father-in-law Barbosa, urging him to be on
guard, since it had come to Barbosa's knowledge that
Magellan's captains "had told their friends and relations that if they had any trouble with him they
would kill him."   Magellan sent back word that he
did not fear his captains and would do the work
he had set out on, and added messages of good cheer
to Barbosa and to his wife Beatriz and his six
months' old son Rodrigo.

The fleet left the Canaries on October third and
headed towards Sierra Leone, but ran into a calm
and could only make three leagues in three weeks.
Then came gales that buffeted the old unseaworthy
vessels,—ships that were altogether unsuited for
such a voyage,—and within a month food and water
were scarce.   Mutinous talk was heard; the captains
whispered that their Portuguese leader was not loyal
to Charles V of Spain; and Cartagena, coming
aboard the flagship one day openly insulted and
threatened Magellan.

Magellan had the insolent captain put in irons and
sent on board the *Victoria,* and gave the command of
the *San Antonio* to his own cousin, Alvaro de Mesquita.

At length they sighted South America at Cape St. Augustine, near Pernambuco on the coast of Brazil, on November twenty-ninth, and, following this shore, reached the mouth of La Plata on January 11, 1520. For three weeks they explored there, looking for a passage through the continent, but concluded that it must be the mouth of a river and not a strait.

Thence through February and March the fleet sailed south along the coast of Patagonia, meeting constant storms and cold weather, and when they found a shelter at Port St. Julian they decided to winter there.

No sooner had the ships dropped anchor than mutiny broke out. Provisions were low, the voyage had been unusually stormy, and the vessels were worn-out hulks that might easily become unusable. The fleet had sailed far to the south and since they had found no strait the crews concluded that there probably was no such passage as that for which the commander was looking. Captains and men demanded that Magellan sail no farther, but give up his wild expedition and return to Spain.

To all this Magellan turned a deaf ear. He said that he expected to find a passage to the Spice Islands and should sail on until he reached the end of the continent.

While they had been at sea Magellan had been able to control his sailors, but conditions were different now that they were in a harbor and were considering staying there through a long antarctic winter. The faithless captains poisoned the minds of their crews and arranged a mutiny. The leaders in this were Quesada, of the *Concepcion,* Mendoza, of the *Victoria,* and Juan de Cartagena, who had been superseded as captain of the *San Antonio* by Alvaro de Mesquita. On Easter Sunday night Quesada and Cartagena, with thirty men, boarded the *San Antonio* and seized Mesquita. A mutineer, Sebastian Elcano, was put in charge of the ship, men who were loyal to Magellan were disarmed, and all was done so quietly that no word of it reached the flagship.

Next morning the mutineers had three of the five ships in their control and felt that they could return to Spain whether Magellan agreed or no. They became defiant, and when a boat from the flagship approached the *San Antonio* it was ordered away with the announcement that Magellan was no longer in command. This word was brought to the Captain-general, and he sent a boat from ship to ship to discover which of the vessels were loyal to him. Only the *Santiago,* under Juan Serrano, in addition to the flagship, was faithful to him, he learned.

At this juncture Quesada sent an envoy to the flagship *Trinidad* to ask for a conference between Magellan and the rebel captains. Magellan agreed to this, but said that the meeting must take place on the *Trinidad.* The rebels would not venture to set foot on the flagship and returned word that the Captain-general must come aboard the *San Antonio.*

Then Magellan decided on a bold stroke. He thought that the crew of the *Victoria* were less disloyal to him than the men on the other two rebel ships, and therefore chose that ship for his battleground. He made ready a boat with a score of armed men he could rely on commanded by his wife's brother Barbosa, and he sent another boat, with his constable, Espinosa, and five trusty companions, to the *Victoria*. Mendoza, the captain of the *Victoria,* permitted this small party to board his ship, and once there Espinosa served an order on Mendoza to go to the flagship. Mendoza refused, and like a flash Espinosa sank his dagger in the rebel's throat. As Mendoza fell Barbosa and the men of his boat sprang over the *Victoria's* side with drawn cutlasses, caught the crew in confusion and made them surrender.

Magellan was now in possession of three of the ships, his own, Serrano's, and the *Victoria,* the command of which he gave to Barbosa. Blockading the two rebel vessels in the harbor, he opened fire from his guns on the *San Antonio* at night, and when crews from the *Trinidad* and the *Victoria* boarded that ship from both sides the mutineers yielded. The *Concepcion* immediately surrendered and the revolt came to an abrupt close.

Quesada was beheaded, Cartagena and another ring-leader were put in irons and when the fleet afterwards sailed from Port St. Julian they were set ashore, the rest of the mutineers were pardoned, and

no more talk was heard of rebellion. Later in the
winter the *Santiago* was wrecked and Serrano was
made captain of the *Concepcion*.

The little flotilla was carefully overhauled and repaired during the winter and when warmer weather
arrived the ships set forth again, on August twenty-
fourth. They encountered heavy storms which so
retarded them that they did not reach the headland
called Cape Virgins until almost two months later.
Sailing past Dungeness they came to a large bay,
which they considered might be the entrance to the
strait they had so long looked for. This was, declared Pigafetta in his account of the voyage, "the
straight now cauled the straight of Magellanus, be-
inge in sum place. C. x. leaques in length: and in
breadth sumwhere very large and in other places
lyttle more than halfe a leaque in bredth. On both
the sydes of this strayght are great and hygh moun-
taynes couered with snowe, beyonde the whiche is
the enteraunce into the sea of Sur. . . . Here one
of the shyppes stole away priuilie and returned into
Spayne."

It took more than five weeks for the ships to pass
through the many and devious turnings of the strait,
but as the water continued to be deep and salt the
navigators became convinced that this was not a
river but the real passage through the South American continent which they had set out to find. If
it were the strait, then, said some, they had made a
great discovery and had now better return to Spain,

since their larder was again almost empty. When
return was suggested to Magellan, however, he simply replied that he would continue the voyage "if he
had to eat the leather off the ship's yards."

Here the crew of the *San Antonio* rebelled, and
Magellan's chief pilot, Estevan Gomez, joined the
disaffected sailors. Mesquita, the captain of the
San Antonio, was seized and put in irons, another
captain chosen, and the mutinous crew, with Gomez
to pilot them, sailed away eastward for home. Six
months afterwards the *San Antonio* arrived in
Spain, where the rebels explained their desertion by
spreading all manner of false stories concerning Magellan.

This desertion made no alteration in that daunt-
less commander's purpose. A chronicler records
that "when the capitayne Magalianes was past the
strayght and sawe the way open to the other mayne
sea, he was so gladde therof that for ioy the teares
fell from his eyes, and named the poynt of the lande
from whense he fyrst sawe that sea *Capo Desiderato.*
Supposing that the shyp which stole away had byn
loste, they erected a crosse uppon the top of a hyghe
hyll to direct their course in the straight yf it were
theyr chaunce to coome that way."

Beyond the stormy tortuous strait opened a wide
ocean that appeared so beautiful to the discoverer's
eye that he christened it the Pacific. Intrepidly he
set out to sail across this new expanse of water, a
chartless wild that was wider than that vast At-

lantic Ocean Columbus had navigated.   For the first
time in history white men were sailing over the
greatest ocean on the globe.

For a while Magellan kept a course to the north to
escape the cold of the Antarctic, then he steered
more westerly, and on January 24, 1521 discovered
a small island which he named San Pablo. Some
idea of the distance the ships had come may be gathered from the fact that since leaving the strait that
bears Magellan's name they had already at San
Pablo sailed almost twice as far as had Columbus in
voyaging from the Canary Islands to Guanahani.

No food could be found on San Pablo nor on another desert islet they reached eleven days later,
and which they named Tiburones, on account of the
many sharks they saw in the neighboring sea. Water was as scarce as provisions; with neither food
nor drink illness came upon them. Skins and the
leather rolled around the ropes of the ships were
soaked and made to serve for sustenance. Scurvy
took toll of the crews, nineteen perished, and the
rest were so weak they could hardly handle the vessels.

It was indeed as if Magellan's sailors, coming
through the strait into the strange Pacific and voyaging westward, were like those in Coleridge's poem
"The Ancient Mariner."

"The fair breeze blew, the white foam flew,
  The furrow follow'd free;

We were the first that ever burst
Into that silent sea.

Down dropt the breeze, the sails dropt down,
'T was sad as sad could be;
And we did speak only to break
The silence of the sea!

All in a hot and copper sky,
The bloody Sun, at noon,
Right up above the mast did stand,
No bigger than the Moon.

Day after day, day after day,
We stuck, nor breath nor motion;
As idle as a painted ship
Upon a painted ocean.

Water, water, everywhere,
And all the boards did shrink;
Water, water, everywhere,
Nor any drop to drink."

The chronicle says: "In three monethes and.
XX. dayes, they sayled foure thousande leaques in
one goulfe by the sayde sea cauled Pacificum (that
is) peaceable, whiche may well bee so cauled foras-
much as in all this tyme hauyng no syght of any
lande, they had no misfortune of wynde or any other
tempest. . . . So that in fine, if god of his mercy had
not gyuen them good wether, it was necessary that

in this soo greate a sea they shuld all haue dyed for hunger. Whiche neuertheless they escaped soo hardely, that it may bee doubted whether euer the like viage may be attempted with so goode successe.''

The crews must have wondered if they would ever sight land, if this unknown waste of water had any further shore. But none now talked of rebellion, they could not turn back; with Magellan they must sail on. And on March sixth they came to a group of islands where they found people, savages of course, but savages from whom they could obtain fresh water, meat, vegetables and fruits. They need no longer starve. Yet the natives appear to have been a thieving lot, for Magellan called these islands the Islas de Ladrones, or isles of robbers.

Strengthened and emboldened, the sailors again set forth and the three ships reached on March sixteenth the islands that were later named in honor of Philip II of Spain, the Philippines. No Europeans had been there, but there were traders from China and Siam and Sumatra and from these Magellan learned that he had crossed the meridian of the Moluccas, which lay to the south, and that therefore he had actually sailed across the unknown part of the globe and by his voyage linked the continent of Europe to the eastern shores of Asia.

These islands appeared to have rich possibilities of commerce and Magellan proceeded to make a treaty of alliance with the ruler of the Island of

Sebu, by which the latter gave exclusive rights of trade to the crown of Spain. The King of Sebu was impressed by the wonderful white men and when he had made the treaty he followed it up by declaring that he and his people would like to adopt the Christian religion.

Magellan, like almost all the Spanish and Portuguese explorers, had the spirit of a crusader; he was devoutly religious and eager to convert the heathen; therefore, when he had seen the people of Sebu burn their wooden idols, he promptly set up a cross and had the natives baptized.

After he had become a Christian, the King of Sebu thought that his new religion would be an all potent power to overwhelm his enemies and at once he sent envoys to demand homage from the heathen ruler of Matan. That chieftain declined to pay homage, and when his scornful answer was related to Magellan by the newly converted King of Sebu the Christian Captain-general took upon himself the duty of humbling the pagan.

He was the crusader and the protector of his allies, and to fight in such a righteous cause was as important to Magellan as to navigate the ocean. So with his men he crossed from Sebu to the island of Matan on April 27, 1521. There the natives attacked him in tremendous force, and after a desperate fight the white men were driven back to their boats. Magellan was the last to retreat, he tried to protect his men; his helmet was knocked from his head and his right arm wounded by a spear. A blow took him unawares, bringing him to the ground, and then, in the words of his companion Pigafetta, "the Indians threw themselves upon him with iron-pointed bamboo spears and scimitars, and every weapon they had, and ran him through—our mirror, our light, our comforter, our true guide—until they killed him."

Bereft of their valiant leader, the lot of his followers was difficult in the extreme. The King of Sebu, finding that Magellan had been slain and his men repulsed by the heathen ruler of Matan, decided that the new religion was not to be relied on, and, inviting about thirty of the white men to a banquet, massacred them. Among them were the two captains who had always been faithful to Magellan, his brother-in-law Barbosa and Juan Serrano. The rest hastened to sail away from the ill-omened shores, but only one hundred and fifteen of the two hundred and eighty men who had been aboard the fleet when it left the Guadalquivir in Spain were now to be counted. The *Concepcion* proved no longer fit for navigation and was dismantled and burned.

Thus there were now two ships, the *Trinidad* and the *Victoria*. Espinosa was chosen commander of the *Victoria* and the pilot Carvalho was appointed Captain-general in place of Magellan. Later Carvalho proved incompetent and was succeeded by Sebastian Elcano, one of the men who had mutinied at Port St. Julian. The two vessels stopped at Bor-

neo, and then reached the Moluccas, where they
learned that the King of Tidor had had Francisco
Serrano murdered.

In the Moluccas the two ships stopped to trade.
When they set out again, on December eighteenth,
the *Trinidad* sprang a leak; and in consequence it
was decided that in order not to lose the favoring
east monsoon the *Victoria* should head for the Cape
of Good Hope, while the *Trinidad,* after having been
repaired, should, when the monsoon was reversed,
sail for Panama. In this figuring that the easterly
breeze which had sent them across the Pacific was
a monsoon and changeable like the Indian winds the
navigators were in error, as they afterwards discovered. The two ships parted company; on the
Trinidad, which was now captained by Espinosa,
were fifty-four men; on the *Victoria,* commanded by
Elcano, there were forty-seven; a total of one hundred and one left of the original company.

The *Trinidad,* having been repaired, sailed on
April 6, 1522, with the westerly monsoon to aid her,
but when she arrived in the North Pacific she ran
into the northeast trade-wind and in trying to get
away from it went up to the fortieth parallel and
beyond it. Famine and illness were aboard and her
crew headed about and made again for the Moluccas.
The ship reached land without her mainmast and
with only nineteen of her crew of fifty-four. These
were captured by hostile Portuguese, and ultimately

only the commander Espinosa and three sailors got back to Spain.

The other ship, the *Victoria,* continuing westward, as had been agreed on, rounded the Cape of Good Hope on May 16, 1522, with her crew depleted by hunger and scurvy, her foretopmast gone and fore-yard badly sprung. On June eighth she crossed the equator. Need of food compelled her crew to stop at the Cape Verde Islands, where the sailors obtained supplies by deceiving the Portuguese with the story that they were only returning from a voyage in the Atlantic. Their secret, however, leaked out; a Spanish sailor who was one of a crew of thirteen sent ashore for rice, having drunk too much for caution, told of Magellan and the Spice Islands. Immediately the thirteen sailors were seized and a boat was sent out to order the *Victoria* to surrender. Instead of obeying, the little ship spread her canvas and sped away from the Cape Verde Islands on July thirteenth. September 6, 1522 the *Victoria* sailed into the Guadalquivir with her Captain Sebastian Elcano, the Chevalier Antonio Pigafetta, and sixteen others, the first ship that had ever made the voyage around the world.

Wonderful was the achievement of Columbus; he made the greatest voyage in history, since it brought the New World to the knowledge of the Old; but as a feat of navigation that voyage was surpassed by the achievement of Magellan, who, with ships that

were hardly seaworthy, with mutinous captains and
sailors, through countless perils and trials, sailed
through the strait that bears his name at the southern
end of South America, first emerged into the Pacific
and crossed it to the islands that lie close to Asia.
Greatest of navigators was this Portuguese gentleman and the record of his career is one of steadfast
loyalty and courage, that of a very prince of adventurers in that great age of daring sailors.

The *Victoria,* with Elcano and seventeen men returned to Spain, and Espinosa and three of the crew
of the *Trinidad* did likewise. Magellan had fallen
in April, 1521; in September of that same year his
little son Rodrigo died, and by March, 1522 Magellan's wife Beatriz had learned from the Portuguese
Indies of the fate of her husband on the island of
Matan and of her brother Barbosa on the island of
Sebu. In that month the sorrow-stricken wife of
Magellan died.

On Sebastian Elcano, a man who had mutinied on
the coast of South America, but whom fortune had
sent home as Captain-general, the sovereign of Spain
conferred the crest of a terrestrial globe encircled
by the words *Primus circumdedisti me* (Thou first
encompassed me) and also a pension of five hundred
ducats. Espinosa likewise received a crest of nobility and a pension.

The name and fame of Magellan are inscribed on
the map of the world.

CHAPTER VIII

DISCOVERERS IN THE NEW WORLD

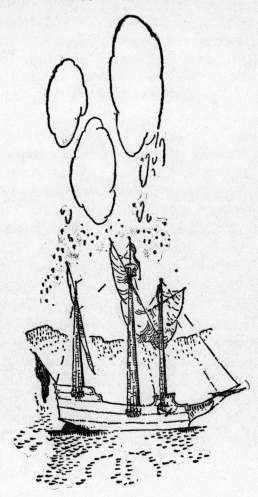

VIII

DISCOVERERS IN THE NEW WORLD

ADVENTUROUS mariners in ships that were absurdly small, according to modern standards, followed in the wake of Columbus and bit by bit added islands, coasts and rivers to the map of "Mundus Novus" that the geographers of Europe were making. There was John Cabot, a native of Genoa, who moved to Venice and later to Bristol in England and who made a voyage in 1497, under letters patent from King Henry VII of England authorizing him and his three sons "to sail to the east, west, or north, with five ships carrying the English flag, to seek and discover all the islands, countries, regions, or provinces of pagans in whatever part of the world."

This was rather a large order, and showed that the ruler of England was not a whit less eager than his brother sovereigns of Spain, Portugal and France to lay claim to all the as yet unexplored places of the world. John Cabot sailed from Bristol in May, 1497, apparently with a single ship named the *Matthew,* or *Matthews,* probably accompanied by his son Sebastian, and a crew of eighteen men. On this expedition they discovered what was thought to be the coast of China. On a second voyage, made in 1498,

with five or six ships, John Cabot is said to have
explored a part of the shore of North America; and
later Sebastian Cabot went on several western voyages. The records, however, do not establish exactly what parts of North America the Cabots
reached; but they themselves appear always to have
considered that their discoveries were on the coast
of China.

A mariner who added a good deal to the map of
the New World was a Florentine, Amerigo Vespucci
or Vespucius, who made four important voyages,
two in the service of Spain and two for Portugal.
He charted the coast of Brazil, and his accounts of
his explorations ultimately gained for him the honor
of having his name of Amerigo given to the whole
western hemisphere.

The sixteenth century is filled with the romantic
adventures of many intrepid sailors. One such mariner was Juan Ponce de Leon, who had accompanied
Columbus on his second voyage, and who sailed from
Porto Rico with three caravels in March, 1513, with
the object of finding the fabled Fountain of Youth,
which was said to be situated on the island of Bim-
ini, north of Hispaniola. On Easter Sunday, which
is called in Spanish Pascua Florida, he sighted the
coast which he christened Florida.

After the *Victoria* returned to Spain in 1522 with
word of what Magellan had accomplished the government of Spain sent Garcia de Loaysa to the strait
known by Magellan's name. One of Loaysa's ships

encountered a storm in the South Atlantic and was driven past the entrance to the strait and as far south as Cape Horn. The first navigator to sail around this point was the Dutchman, Schouten van Horn, in 1616, for whom the cape was named.

The Spaniards were trying to find a passage to the Indies through the southern part of the New World and the French were sending their explorers to the north. The English were also voyaging in the western seas. Sir Francis Drake, setting out in 1577, passed through the Strait of Magellan and went as far north as northern California or southern Oregon, claiming the coast for England and christening it New Albion. Thence he crossed the Pacific and made the second circumnavigation of the world.

Both the English and the Dutch merchants, eager to secure the immense profits they thought would result from commerce with Asia, were sponsoring expeditions to find a northern passage from Europe, either to the east or the west. For the Muscovy Company of London Henry Hudson, an Englishman, sailed in 1607, skirted the shores of Greenland, reached a point nearer the North Pole than any earlier navigator had attained, but, finding great masses of ice in his way, was obliged to return. The following year he made another voyage to see if there might be a route to China through the waters between Spitzbergen and Nova Zembla. When he failed to find a passage there the

Muscovy Company decided to send out no more expeditions and the mariner went to the Netherlands, where he offered his services to the Dutch East India Company.

This company agreed to employ him, and on April 4, 1609 Hudson sailed, with a crew made up of Netherlanders and Englishmen, one of whom was Hudson's son, to try to reach China by a route to the northeast. His ship was a small merchant vessel of about eighty tons named the *Half Moon*. This ship had three masts and was built with a steep sheer fore and aft and with a narrow high stern transom decorated with a crescent moon. She had a short and rather high forecastle, a main deck that was of almost equal dimensions in length and breadth, and a low half-deck, above which was the hood of the steerage where the helmsman took his station, and on top of that a diminutive poop cabin.

The *Half Moon* reached the North Cape of Norway early in May, but when Hudson approached Nova Zembla he found the ice too thick for him to force his way through, and so he altered his course to the west, with the intention of looking for a passage through North America.

Early in July the *Half Moon,* with her foremast gone and her sails badly tattered, came upon some French fishermen on the Banks of Newfoundland. On the eighteenth she reached a good harbor on the coast of Maine, where Hudson refitted his ship with a new foremast and repaired the sails. On August fourth he sighted Cape Cod and two weeks later anchored off Chesapeake Bay. Instead of entering here, however, Hudson turned, spent a day exploring the bay that was afterwards called the Delaware, and then sailing north approached on September third land where there appeared to be three separate rivers. On that day he came to an anchorage off Sandy Hook.

The next day the *Half Moon* found a very good harbor near the New Jersey shore, and natives were allowed on board the ship to barter for knives and beads. On September fifth Hudson landed and was given an enthusiastic welcome by the Indians, who greatly admired the strange dress of the captain and his crew. On their part Hudson's men liked the roasted Indian corn which furnished the natives' chief food, and learned something of the red men's habits. The Indians, it seemed, always carried maize and tobacco with them, they had pipes made of red copper, with earthen bowls, and they wore ornaments of copper around their necks. Their boats were made of hollowed-out trees. Their weapons were bows and arrows with stones for points. They were friendly, but were inclined to help themselves to the white men's goods without asking permission and were exceedingly crafty in hiding what they had purloined.

On the sixth of September John Colman and four others rowed from the *Half Moon* in a small boat, made soundings of the Narrows, and passed through

Kill van Kull to Newark Bay. The neighboring
shores appeared to them very pleasing country, well
wooded and bright with flowers. As they turned
back to the ship, however, two Indian canoes attacked the boat and Colman was slain by an arrow.

Three days afterwards Hudson sailed from the
lower bay into the Narrows, and on the eleventh he
came into the large river of the north and rode all
night in a harbor that was sheltered from every wind.
In the morning Indians, paddling out to the *Half
Moon* in twenty-eight canoes, brought beans and
oysters. The weather was fine, and as Hudson
looked about him from his deck, admiring the Narrows that opened to the ocean and the wide river that
flowed above Weehawken with a broad, deep channel
between palisades crowned with forests and the
verdant shore of the island of Manhattan, he recorded that the country "was as fair a land as can
be trodden by the foot of man."

That evening the ship anchored above Manhattan-
ville, and on the next day reached the vicinity of
Yonkers. On the fourteenth a strong southeast wind
carried the *Half Moon* into the Highlands. At
dawn on the following morning mists hid the land-
scape but as they were dispersed before the sun the
mariners saw the beautiful country around West
Point. With a good south wind the *Half Moon*
sailed on up the river, passing the bend at Hyde
Park, and anchored a short distance below Red
Hook, within view of the range of the Catskill Moun-

tains. Here the captain again traded with the
Indians and took on board fresh water, and by evening of the seventeenth reached a place just above
the location of the modern town of Hudson.

The commander went ashore in a native canoe
with the chief of a tribe known as the River Indians
and was conducted to a house built of oak bark,
circular in shape and with an arched roof, where
were stored the maize and beans of the last harvest.
Outside the house enough maize and beans were drying to load three ships. Food was served the guests
in red wooden bowls, hunters brought in pigeons,
and preparations were made for a feast. When
Hudson refused to wait, the Indians, thinking that
he feared they might use their weapons, broke their
arrows and threw them into the fire. The Captain
liked the country of the River Indians and wrote,
"Of all lands on which I ever set my foot, this is the
best for tillage."

Up the river the *Half Moon* went and on the nineteenth came to the landing of Kinderhook, where
the Indians brought aboard beaver and otter skins.
Hudson sailed his ship no higher; but a small boat
went on up a short distance above Albany to where
the river was only seven feet in depth and the soundings uncertain.

On September twenty-third Hudson turned the
Half Moon and sailed down to the ocean. On the
way his men explored; they found the country on
the west possessed of excellent soil with a quantity

of large oaks, walnuts and chestnuts, and they saw many places that they thought would make admirable sites for settlements. On October first the ship passed south of the mountains and on the fourth Hudson sailed out of the mouth of the great river that bears his name.

After a pleasant voyage the *Half Moon* reached Dartmouth in England. There the ship was held by English officers who claimed the services of the captain and the English sailors. Hudson sent an account of his discoveries to the Dutch East India Company, and from his report the attention of Dutch merchants was called to the value of the fur trade along the Hudson River and this led to the Dutch settlement of New Netherland.

The Dutch refused to search further for a northwest passage, but the English formed a new company and sent out Hudson again in the ship *Discovery*. He had hunted in the region between Maine and Chesapeake Bay for a passage through the continent; now he turned farther north, and sailing past Iceland, Greenland and Frobisher's Strait he reached on August 2, 1610 the far northern strait that is known by his name. Sailing through this he came into the great inland sea of Hudson's Bay and thought he had found a passage through to the west.

He found no outlet that autumn, however, and at length resolved to winter there and search again in the spring. His crew murmured at staying in such arctic quarters for which they had made no provision. Spring came, but the food was exhausted and the sailors mutinous. So, when he was on the brink, as he believed, of discovering the long-sought northwest passage, Hudson had to turn back and steer for Europe. For two days the ship was surrounded by ice-fields, and the crew's resentment against their captain increased. Then, in a wild rage, the sailors seized Hudson, and he, with his only son and seven others, four of whom were sick, was thrown into an open boat. Philip Staffe, the ship's carpenter, demanded and was given permission to go with Hudson; the small boat was cut adrift and the ship sailed away through the lanes of ice. The boat's occupants were never heard of again, and the captain and his companions perished in the waters or on the shores of Hudson's Bay.

Henry Hudson had left his name on the great river that flows through the state of New York and on a strait and an immense stretch of water in the northern part of Canada, but he had not found a passage through the continent. Such voyages as he and others had made, however, seemed to limit the search to the route that had been partly explored by John Davis in 1585–1587. Davis had discovered the strait named for him; and in 1615 William Baffin pursued Davis's route farther and discovered Jones and Lancaster Sounds and the sound christened in honor of Sir Thomas Smith, the first governor of the East India Company.

Frobisher, Davis, Hudson, and Baffin had tried to find a way by water across North America from the Atlantic to the Pacific. The Russians were making overland journeys from Europe to the rich markets of China. They crossed Siberia and in 1706 added the peninsula of Kamtchatka to their possessions. Then Peter the Great wished to determine the question as to whether Asia and America were joined together at the north or separated by a strait, and in 1724 appointed the Danish navigator Vitus Bering to the command of an exploring expedition.

Bering and his men crossed the wilderness of Siberia and launched the small ship *Gabriel* in the early summer of 1728 from a place near Cape Kamtchatka. From there they sailed north, keeping in sight of the coast, and on August eleventh reached an island which Bering named St. Lawrence. On the fourteenth he left East Cape astern and sailed into what appeared to be an open sea; after voyaging there for a day he turned back and passed through the strait without sighting the opposite coast. In 1741 Bering sailed again with two ships, the *St. Peter* and the *St. Paul,* and arrived at the coast of Alaska, and by this voyage he established the location of the strait that bears his name and completed in a rough outline the map of North America.

So the discovery made by Columbus in 1492 was

followed up by men of many nations until the contour of "Mundus Novus" was revealed to the geographers and merchants of Europe who had been for so long a time intent on finding a westward passage to the riches of Cathay and the Indies.

CHAPTER IX
THE *GREAT HARRY*

IX

THE *GREAT HARRY*

THE good people of the English seaport of Dover saw a magnificent sight on May 31, 1520, when their sovereign, King Henry VIII, set sail from their harbor aboard his splendid ship, the *Henri Grâce à Dieu* or *Great Harry*. She was not large for her epoch, being probably of about one thousand tons, but she was as ornate and gorgeous a vessel as ever swam the waves.

King Henry loved magnificence, and on this occasion he was embarking to meet the King of France, Francis I, at the Field of the Cloth of Gold. The French sovereign was famed for his splendor and therefore it was fitting that the ruler of England should arrive at the French coast in a ship that might represent the pomp and wealth of England.

The *Great Harry* was built for warfare as well as for visits of state. She had four masts and a long bowsprit, square sails, top castles, top sails, top gallant sails, and a very high stem and stern. The yards were provided with iron hooks to catch or cut the rigging of an enemy ship. The top masts were not lowered. Altogether she was a very high and heavy, and probably very unseaworthy, ship.

It was usual for all war vessels of that time to carry along their rails rows of shields called a "pavese." On the *Great Harry* these shields or targets were displayed even around the tops. They were placed in groups of four, ornamented respectively with the following devices: the cross of St. George on a silver ground, a golden fleur-de-lys on a blue ground, the Tudor rose on a green and white ground, and a golden portcullis on a red ground.

When she carried King Henry to France the sails of the *Great Harry,* specially made for the occasion, were of cloth-of-gold, damasked. Long forked pennants, on most of which were the cross of St. George, flew from the mast-heads, the yardarms and other parts of the vessel. At the corners of the poop were banners bearing the Tudor dragons on a green and white ground, and at the corners of the forecastle the royal arms of England flew from gold-tipped lances.

The high sides of the ship were filled with gothic windows, that were beautifully painted and gilded. The stern rose in curving tiers and the after part of the poop was studded with ornamental windows and many large guns. Every gift of the shipwright and ship-artist had been lavished on the *Great Harry,* and she must have been a wonderful sight as she sailed out from Dover, her great golden sails filling with the wind, her banners and pennants flying, and the royal trumpeters playing martial music.

Yet, fine as she was, it is questionable how well

she could breast the seas. She landed King Henry, but after he had met Francis I, and feasted and jousted with him at the Field of the Cloth of Gold he did not return to England aboard the *Great Harry*. Perhaps the ship had tumbled him about too much, or perhaps his overthrow in a friendly wrestling match with the jovial Francis had something to do with his decision. He chose another ship.

Almost all the large ships that were built in that era to satisfy the pride of the King or the nation were so cranky or badly balanced that they were extremely unsafe except in a fair light wind. Generally they were incapable of working to windward. Moreover their lower port-holes were so close to the water that, except in a calm sea, they were apt to founder. The *Mary Rose,* one of Henry VIII's great ships, went down for this reason with all her crew. Their heavy after overhangs also made them pitch badly, and the beak on the bow split the waves and broke the seas before the waist of the ship was washed down. Unsuitable for long voyages, they were only fitted to display their pride close to the shores of England.

CHAPTER X
ENGLISH ADVENTURERS

X

ENGLISH ADVENTURERS

THE mantle of the Viking fell on the shoulders of the English sailor of Devon. In the island that is Britain, and where the blood of Celt, Saxon, Norman and Dane had united in one strain, there sprang up a race of men who made the era of Queen Elizabeth famous for its great sea-captains.

Columbus, Vasco da Gama, Vespucius, Magellan, Ponce de Leon, and almost all the mariners who played principal rôles in the first act of that wonderful drama known as the Discovery of the New World were men of Southern Europe, and to Spain and Portugal went the glory and rewards of their marvellous exploits. Englishmen kept at home, and then suddenly, when the Spanish Dons appeared to have the Western World tight in their grasp, sailors of the island in the northwest corner of Europe, launched their ships and sailed forth to defy the might of Spain.

Spain in the middle of the sixteenth century was the most powerful nation in the world. Her statesmen, her soldiers, her sailors, had great reputations; with the annexation of Portugal in 1581 the wealth of that country and its colonies was added to Spain's

169

and Philip II boasted that all America, all Africa, rich territories in Asia, and the finest Atlantic ports of Europe belonged to his crown.

The settlements of Spain in the West Indies and along the Spanish Main, which was the name for the Spanish possessions in South America north of the Orinoco River and in Central America, were well guarded and to them came trains of pack mules bringing gold and precious stones, the ocean was covered with Spanish ships carrying the treasure home; and then uprose the English merchant adventurers, and, sometimes as peaceful traders, sometimes as pirates, they fought for a share in the riches of the New World.

Such an adventurer was Sir John Hawkins, merchant and buccaneer, who brought many a full cargo to England, some honestly come by, some taken by force. On September 16, 1568 he anchored his fleet in the harbor of San Juan de Ulloa on the coast of Mexico, and the next day a Spanish fleet, commanded by Don Francisco de Lujan, appeared outside. The Spaniards sailed in, and friendly messages were exchanged by the two commanders; but when Lujan had perfected his plans he ordered an attack on the English and the guns of his fleet, which was vastly superior to that of Hawkins, overwhelmed his adversaries. One English ship was sunk; three, including Hawkins' flagship, the *Jesus,* were captured. Hawkins, with some hundred of his men, escaped to a small vessel, the *Minion,* and got away, followed by his kinsman, Francis Drake, in a pinnace, the *Judith*. In the hands of the Spaniards he left a part of his fleet, the profits of the voyage he had been making, fifty-seven negro slaves and much merchandise, which totaled a very large sum. Drake got back to England without difficulty in the *Judith;* Hawkins, finding the *Minion* overcrowded and lacking provisions, had to land about a hundred of his men, and the ship's company almost perished of starvation and sickness before they reached Devon.

This treachery of the Spaniards to Hawkins inflamed England, and particularly it inflamed Francis Drake, who was filled with a lust for revenge. He determined on a private war with Spain, and so set out from Plymouth in 1572 with two ships, the *Pascha* of seventy tons and the *Swan* of twenty-five. He sailed to the Spanish Main and made a bold attack on Nombre de Dios; failing there, he lay hid for fifteen days, watching for Spanish vessels to come out from the harbor; then he captured a string of mule trains loaded with treasure on their way across the Isthmus. With the plunder of a number of raids, he returned to Plymouth, to be greeted as a hero by his native Devon.

With the wealth he had won he fitted out three frigates and sailed with them to Ireland, where he fought for England as a volunteer. Crowned with new laurels, he was presented to Queen Elizabeth, and through her patronage was enabled to make his next voyage. This was to be nothing less than a passage through the Strait of Magellan, through which no Englishman had yet sailed. Embarking on December 13, 1577, with five small ships and a crew of one hundred and sixty-six men, he reached Brazil and on August 21, 1578 entered the Strait of Magellan. Thence he coasted past Chile and Peru, seizing Spanish vessels and attacking Spanish settlements ashore and acquiring much booty, reached the west coast of North America, crossed the Pacific, and in September, 1580 entered the harbor of Plymouth. In honor of his circling the globe Queen Elizabeth visited his ship and conferred on him the honor of knighthood and also directed that his vessel, the *Golden Hind,* should be preserved as a monument of England's glory.

Philip II, jealous of English trade, laid an embargo on all English ships in Spanish ports. England retorted by placing a corresponding embargo on Spanish vessels, by interfering actively in the war Spain was waging in the Low Countries, and by the Queen's commissioning Drake to proceed on a war of reprisals against the Spanish settlements in the West Indies and elsewhere.

The next expedition of Sir Francis was, like most of those of the English merchant adventurers of that era, a business as well as a privateering voyage. Queen Elizabeth furnished two ships of war, but the bulk of the fleet was made up of nineteen mer-

chant ships from London and the west of England;
in addition there were some eight or ten pinnaces
and private vessels that sailed on their own account.
Drake was the commander-in-chief, Martin Frobisher was Admiral of the London forces, and
Richard Hawkins, son of Sir John, Francis Knollys
the younger, a kinsman of the Queen, and many
others of note were in the party.   About thirty ships
sailed from Plymouth on September 14, 1585.
Everything that was Spanish they attacked.   They
sacked and burnt Santiago and Porto Praya in the
Cape Verde Islands, gutted San Domingo, seized
Cartagena on the Spanish Main and held it to ran-
som.   For a month they cruised off Cape St.
Antonio and considered attacking Havana, but decided that its fortifications were too strong; then,
sailing up the coast of Florida, they plundered and
burnt St. Augustine, which was a settlement of
some two hundred and fifty houses.   At Roanoke
Island in Albemarle Sound Drake took on board his
ships the colonists who had been sent out the year
before by Sir Walter Raleigh, and returned to
Portsmouth in July, 1586.   He brought home booty
valued at from sixty to sixty-five thousand pounds,
and the damage he had done in capturing Spanish
ships and attacking Spanish settlements was tremendous.   Philip II hated the English more than
he had before, and began preparations to conquer
their country.

The King of Spain was gathering ships and men

and supplies for this purpose when on April 2, 1587 Sir Francis Drake sailed out from Plymouth with thirty ships. On April nineteenth he arrived off the port of Cadiz and had no difficulty in defeating the seven galleys that tried to oppose his entrance. The harbor was full of shipping and Drake and his lads from Devon promptly fell upon it. He sent this message to England: "We sank a Biscayan of 1200 tons, burnt a ship of 1500 tons, belonging to the Marquis of Santa Cruz, and 31 ships more of from 1000 to 200 tons the piece, carried away with us four laden with provisions, and departed thence at our pleasure, with as much honor as we could wish."

This exploit, typical of the audacity and daring of this famous sea-rover, Drake referred to as "singeing the King of Spain's beard."

After this raid on Cadiz he lay in wait for Spanish coasting vessels on their way to Lisbon, took many of them and burnt their cargoes, and completed his expedition by capturing a richly-laden homeward-bound Spanish East Indiaman off the Azores.

While Drake was harrying the Dons on land and sea other venturesome Englishmen were sailing to explore the New World and attempting to make settlements there. Four ships, commanded by Sir Humphrey Gilbert, set forth in June, 1583, with the object of establishing a colony in Newfoundland. When the settlers reached their goal, however, they found neither the climate nor the land to their liking

and asked to be sent back to England. Some were
sent off in one of the vessels; another of the ships
was wrecked. With the other two Gilbert sailed
south along the coast, he himself aboard the little
ship *Squirrel* of only ten tons. Presently the crews
of the two ships, worn out with hunger and in great
want of clothes, persuaded Sir Humphrey to turn
towards England. They sailed east across the
Atlantic, but when they were to the south of the
Azores on September ninth a great storm, with "ter-
rible seas, breaking short and pyramid-wise," struck
the two ships. Sir Humphrey was heard to call out
from his deck, "Be of good cheer, my friends; we
are as near heaven by sea as by land." Then the
little ship *Squirrel* sank, with the commander and
his men.

From the sea-girdled land of Devon came Sir
Walter Raleigh, whom his contemporaries called the
"Shepherd of the Ocean." He was a half-brother
of Sir Humphrey Gilbert, and sailed with him on
an expedition against the Spaniards. He won the
favor of Queen Elizabeth, and, nothing daunted by
the mischance that had befallen Sir Humphrey's
attempt at colonization, he determined to explore
and settle America.

Raleigh's first expedition, sent out in 1584 in two
ships under command of Philip Amydas and Arthur
Barlowe, reached Florida and followed the coast
north as far as the inlet between Albemarle and
Pimlico Sounds, in what was then the Indian King-

dom of Axacan, now North Carolina. The time of
arrival was midsummer and the country was beautiful. Above the underbrush rose tall red cedars,
the vines were full of wild grapes, deer, turkeys and
snow-white cranes were in amazing abundance.
The Indians welcomed the white men with friendly
greetings and gifts. The English explored and
found the region "most plentiful, sweet, wholesome
and fruitful of all other." When the two ships returned to England in the autumn of 1584 the
captains gave such a glowing account of what they
had seen that the Queen christened the country
Virginia, as the Virgin land.

Virginia was the name given for a long time afterwards to a great region of North America, a territory so vaguely outlined that a writer of that era
says of it: "The bounds thereof on the East side
are the ocean, on the South lieth Florida, on the
North Nova Francia, as for the West thereof the
limits are unknown."

Enthusiastic over the report of his captains,
Raleigh proceeded to obtain from Queen Elizabeth
a patent which gave to him and his heirs the pro-
prietary right over all territory in Virginia that
they should occupy, subject to the payment of one-
fifth of the produce of all mines of precious metals
to the English crown. With the object of securing
land he then embarked a company of settlers in 1585,
under the command of Sir Richard Grenville, another son of Devon. Grenville founded his colony

on Roanoke Island in Albemarle Sound; but the commander was more interested in capturing Spanish prizes than in the colony, the settlers quarreled with the Indians, many of them became homesick, and when Sir Francis Drake with his fleet arrived there after his great privateering expedition the colonists sailed back to England on his ships.

Grenville was not a colonizer; he was a sea-fighter, and his fame rests on the great battle he made with his little ship *Revenge* against the ships of Spain. He attempted a second time to found a colony in Virginia, and this met with a mysterious fate. White, the Governor, went to England in 1587 to obtain supplies for his settlers and left at Roanoke eighty-nine men, seventeen women, and eleven children, among whom were his daughter Ellinor and his granddaughter Virginia Dare, the first English child born in America. When Governor White returned he found the settlement deserted. Before he had sailed to England he had directed that if the people moved from Roanoke Island they should carve the name of the place to which they intended going on some conspicuous object, with a cross if they went away in distress. The Governor found the name "Croatan" cut in a post, but without a cross. Croatan was the name of an Indian town on the coast; but the white settlers were not there. The Indians knew, or pretended to know, nothing concerning the exodus of the colonists from Roanoke, and no explanation was ever given of the disappearance of that band of more than one hundred English people.

After these failures Sir Walter Raleigh abandoned his attempts to settle Virginia and resigned his rights in North America to a company of merchants, preserving a rent to himself and one-fifth of whatever gold might be discovered. Ill fortune came upon him, and at length, when he was a prisoner in the Tower of London, he secured his freedom by offering King James I to find a gold mine on the coast of Guiana without trenching on any Spanish possessions. For this purpose he sailed on March 17, 1617 and reached the mouth of the Orinoco River on December thirty-first. Raleigh himself was ill with fever and remained at Trinidad while he sent five small ships up the Orinoco under his trusted captain Lawrence Keymis, with whom went Raleigh's son Walter and a nephew.

These ships, on their way to the place where the gold mine was thought to be, came upon a Spanish settlement, and a fight ensued, in which Raleigh's son was killed. Keymis continued his search for the mine, but found none and returned to report to his commander. Quarrels and a mutiny followed, and the fleet sailed back to England. King James had said that if Sir Walter should attack any Spanish colony on his expedition his life should be forfeit, and on this charge Raleigh was arrested, and this man of many talents, soldier, colonizer, historian and poet, was executed on October 29, 1618.

Hawkins, Drake, Raleigh, Grenville, all were men of Devon, all were adventurers by sea, to whom the waters of the Atlantic and the Caribbean offered a glorious field on which to fight the Dons and the lands of the New World a no less glorious field to search for gold. Their names stand high in the roll of England's great sons, for they were intrepid sailors and soldiers, knights of the open sea.

CHAPTER XI
THE SPANISH ARMADA

XI

THE SPANISH ARMADA

THE largest fleet of fighting ships that was ever assembled, and the most magnificent to look upon, was gathered in the harbor of Lisbon in the spring of 1588. There were six squadrons in the fleet and in each squadron were vessels of every size and style. There were sixty-five great galleons, huge towering castles, with main timbers four and five feet thick, the smallest of them of seven hundred tons, and the largest, *La Regazona,* an Italian, of thirteen hundred tons. Appropriate to the religious crusade on which they were to embark many of the galleons had been given names from the Church, one had been christened in honor of St. Philip, others for St. John, St. James, St. Martin, St. Matthew, the Lady of the Rosary, and all bore the crusader's emblem of the cross on their sails.

Next in size to the galleons were four galleasses, each mounting fifty guns, and carrying four hundred and fifty sailors and soldiers and three hundred slaves to pull the oars. Besides these there were four large galleys, fifty-six armed merchant ships, and twenty caravels and pinnaces. Excluding the

183

caravels and pinnaces, there was a total of one
hundred and twenty-nine fighting ships in the fleet.

Of cannon there were two thousand, four hundred
and thirty, the finest that Spain could produce. Of
provisions there were enough to feed forty thousand
men for six months. There were about eight thousand sailors, nineteen thousand soldiers, a thousand
gentlemen volunteers, six hundred priests, servants,
and officers of various capacities, and two thousand
galley-slaves, these being for the most part Turks,
Moors, and heretics from the Low Countries.

The fleet was commanded by a great nobleman,
the Duke of Medina Sidonia, and under him were
celebrated admirals in charge of the six squadrons,
among them Martinez de Recalde, one of Spain's
best seamen, Pedro de Valdez, who had commanded
a fleet off the Netherlands, and Miguel de Oquendo,
a gallant young officer of high renown. The land
forces were headed by Don Alonzo da Leyva, a man
so popular and accomplished that hundreds of high-
born Castilian adventurers had sought the privilege
of service with him.

This was the great Armada, long a dream of Philip
II, King of Spain. With this fleet he planned to
conquer England, on whose throne sat the heretic
Queen Elizabeth. Already master of vast possessions in Europe and America, conqueror of Portugal
and tyrant in the Low Countries, Philip was moved
by his greed for power as well as by his bigotry in
religion to stamp out what he considered the viper's

brood of the Protestant English. For three years
he had expended all the treasure that had come to
Spain from his colonies in the New World on the
ships, the equipment and supplies that were needed
for this crusade.

At Dunkirk Philip's general, the Prince of
Parma, had collected an army and a flotilla of flat-
bottomed boats, and as soon as the Armada should
have cleared the English Channel of Elizabeth's
navy this army was to cross and, protected by the
great fleet, land on the coast of England.

For months the port of Lisbon had been filled with
men of many nations, summoned there by the King
of Spain; there were Spaniards, Portuguese, Ital-
ians, Irishmen, Scotchmen, Englishmen who hated
the Protestant Queen; the faithful from all lands
had flocked to this great enterprise against heretic
England; but though they were to make common
cause they quarreled continually among themselves.
Spain itself was scarcely united; Andalusians, Cas-
tilians, Catalans, speaking tongues hardly understood by each other, had their private ancestral
feuds. Cavaliers from Burgos or Leon might be
enthusiastic, but not so ardent were Castilian and
Portuguese peasants, impressed into service from
their farms and kept under guard lest they should
escape. The Spaniards and Portuguese fought in
the streets of the town, and carried their quarrels
even to the ships' decks.

On May 19, 1588 (old style) this great fleet, that

had been so busily preparing, sailed down the Tagus
River from Lisbon.

Against this great Armada, this fleet that was the
largest ever gathered together, setting forth to conquer England, what could that nation muster?   England had a small navy, a few tall fighting-ships, and
had recently built four new vessels on a model
designed by Sir John Hawkins, who had been a sea-
robber and slave-hunter, but was now at the head of
Queen Elizabeth's naval administration.   In these
four new ships the high forecastles and sterns that
distinguished the galleons of that time had been
lowered, the keels had been lengthened and the lines
made finer and sharper, innovations at which most
of the old sailors grumbled, since they thought such
changes would make the ships unfit for any but the
smoothest waters.

England was a country of traders and merchant
adventurers, and the merchants in every port were
called on to arm and contribute as many private
ships as they could. London provided thirty,
Southampton, Plymouth, Bristol and others gave
each its share. Sir John Hawkins had four or five
ships, Lord Howard of Effingham two, Sir Francis
Drake a squadron, composed of privateers, that answered England's call.

When the English fleet took the sea under command of Lord Howard it numbered about one hundred vessels and there were some forty more ships
watching the coast at Dunkirk. In comparison

with the Spanish galleons the largest of the English fleet—which were known as the Queen's ships— looked small; but they were more heavily armed with guns than the Armada and less cumbered with foot-soldiers. Instead of christening their ships for patron saints, as was the Spanish custom, the English had given their vessels such names as the *Victory,* the *Dreadnought,* the *Revenge,* the *Lion,* and the *Bull.*

The Armada left Lisbon in a strong northerly breeze. The tall galleons, with their great sides standing high above the water and their masts carrying little canvas in proportion to the ship's size, did not work well to windward, and it took three weeks to reach Finisterre. There a gale was encountered, and the ships were scattered, some standing out to sea and others into the Bay of Biscay. Their orders had been that, in case of such an event, they were to make for the Bay of Ferrol; but as the wind shifted to the west some of the scattered fleet were unable to do this and instead were driven into Santander. Then the weather moderated and by the sixth of July the whole Armada collected in the Bay of Ferrol, with no more damage done than a few masts sprung and a number of yards and bow- sprits lost overboard.

Several days were spent in repairs and on July twelfth the Armada swept out from Ferrol and took its farewell of Spain. Beautiful must have been the sight to the watchers on the shore: the many ma-

jestic galleons, with countless banners flying and the
red crosses on their sails, the decks crowded with
the flower of the fighting men of King Philip. In
the lead was the commander, Medina Sidonia, in the
San Martin, and throughout the fleet there was
dignity and order, for now petty jealousies had disappeared before the common interest in their great
crusade.

That first evening out from Ferrol the wind
dropped and the sails flapped idle, but next morning
a breeze sprang up from the southwest and the fleet
ran before it; in two more days the ships were off
Ushant, and the fastest of the pinnaces was sent to
the Prince of Parma at Dunkirk to inform him that
the Armada might be expected shortly in the English Channel.

The fleet, however, had now come into the latitude
where storms had raged all the past winter and
spring, for it had been an unusually boisterous season on the coast of England. As the Armada lay
off Ushant a gale overtook it; the vessels did not
dare to run farther; four galleys were driven in
upon the French shore and wrecked, and a galleon,
the *Santa Aña,* sank with ninety sailors, three hundred soldiers and fifty thousand ducats in gold.

The storm blew itself out in two days, and with
the skies clear the fleet, forming again in order, proceeded north. By the nineteenth of July it had
reached the English Channel and at dawn the next
day an English fishing-boat, its crew counting the

number of the Armada's ships, was sighted by the fleet. The fishing-boat was chased, but got away. Soon afterwards on that same morning, however, a small boat was captured, and the Spaniards learned that the English fleet was in Plymouth Harbor. Medina Sidonia called a council to consider whether they should sail in and attack the English ships at anchor. But he was not a daring commander, and, since the orders of King Philip had been to make straight for Margate Roads and assist the Prince of Parma, Sidonia decided not to turn aside at Plymouth.

Had the Spanish commander determined to attack, however, he would not have caught the English napping or unprepared, for long before the Armada had sighted the Lizard the ships of the Spaniards had themselves been seen, and on the night of July nineteenth beacons had flared from headland to headland to tell all England that the enemy had come.

The news of the Armada's arrival was indeed salvation for the English fleet. The Admiral, Lord Howard, Drake and Hawkins and the other captains had been handicapped in their preparations in innumerable ways; Queen Elizabeth had changed her mind a dozen times regarding her naval policy; the Royal Treasury had doled out funds in the most niggardly fashion for building, arming and provisioning ships; the fleet had only been kept together by the greatest thrift and good management on the part of the captains and by the aid of private money; and when the Armada appeared the vessels that were to defend England had but one week's supplies on board and powder and shot sufficient for only one day's fighting, according to English figures. Now that the enemy was off the coast the English captains and crews rejoiced that they could engage him before lack of ammunition and food rendered their ships useless.

Bonfires along the shore and swift messengers on horseback carried the tidings to cottage and village and city, and men armed and hastened to their posts. If England were to be invaded the enemy should pay dear for every foot of land he won. The Earl of Leicester, who commanded the land forces, had 16,000 men at Tilbury on the Thames, with 30,000 more hurrying to form behind him to protect London in case the Spanish fleet should enable the Prince of Parma's army to arrive on English soil.

On that same night of July nineteenth when the beacons were set blazing Plymouth Harbor was a scene of great activity. The large ships, the Queen's ships, and some of the privateers were warped out behind the protecting shore of Mount Edgecombe. Vessel after vessel was placed so that she could readily clear away to sea, and when the Spaniards were first sighting the Lizard forty English ships were lying ready for action behind the headland.

Next day lookouts reported to Lord Howard, the

English Admiral, that one hundred and fifty Spanish vessels had been seen off Cornwall. Some of these were only tenders bound for Flanders, but they were sailing under the escort of the Armada, and their presence served to convince the English that the strength of the enemy had not been exaggerated.

Immediately the English weighed anchor, but did not yet show themselves. At dusk the Spaniards had their first glimpse of Plymouth, and then Sidonia saw that, whether he turned aside here to fight or sailed on to Margate Roads, Lord Howard was ready for him.

It was too dark for the Spaniards to estimate their enemy's strength with accuracy, but feeling confident that his fleet greatly outnumbered Lord Howard's Sidonia signaled his squadrons to lie to for the night and prepare for battle at daybreak.

In the moonlight the Spanish lookouts saw sixty or seventy English ships slip out from Plymouth Sound and take positions to the Armada's rear, just beyond cannon-shot.

On the following morning the sea was calm, but by eight o'clock the wind had sprung up from the west and the Armada made sail with the intention of closing with the foe. Then, to the Spaniards' vast surprise, they found that the English could approach or withdraw as they pleased; the high-walled, broad-bowed galleons of the Armada went lumbering clumsily in the wake of the low-sided, sharp-prowed English ships that could sail two feet to the Spaniards' one, dash in, fire a round, and speed away as suited them.

The action began with the *Ark,* which flew Lord Howard's flag, and three other English ships sailing along the entire rear line of the Spaniards, firing into each galleon, and then coming round and repeating the fire on the return. The *San Matteo* luffed, in the hope that the English would try to board her, but they sailed on, content to pour in broadsides.

Not only the speed of the English ships, but the accuracy and rapidity of their fire astonished the Spaniards, who tried to close in on the enemy, but found themselves each time evaded.

The rest of the English fleet copied the tactics of the *Ark,* and this continued all the morning; the vessels of the Armada kept on firing, but as they were to leeward and leaning over to the wind their shots flew high and rarely touched the enemy.

The flagship *San Juan* had her mizzenmast shot through, many spars cut away, her captain wounded and fifteen men killed, and other Spanish ships were so much damaged that Sidonia, seeing that his vessels could not injure the English but would be shattered themselves, gave the signal to make sail up the Channel and ordered the squadron commanded by Martinez de Recalde to protect the rear.

By now the wind had risen and promised a stormy night. As the Armada sailed away Lord Howard kept close to Recalde and fired occasional shots. The Spanish squadrons, fearing to be cut off if they separated, crowded together. A rough sea came up from the west and at dusk the 1200-ton galleon *Capitana*, the flagship of Pedro de Valdez, fouled the *Santa Catalina* and broke her bowsprit. The foremast went over the side and the galleon fell behind. Valdez fired a distress gun, and two galleasses attempted to take his ship in tow, but the waves were so high that the cables broke. Valdez was the only commander who knew the English Channel and the Duke of Medina Sidonia sent boats to take him and his crew from their battered vessel. Valdez, however, would not leave his ship. In the darkness Lord Howard, pursuing, saw the galleon, but thought her abandoned, and so sailed by. A privateer from London came up and kept firing at the wrecked ship until midnight, and in the morning Sir Francis Drake, who had been chasing some smaller ships, sighted the galleon and called on her to surrender.

Valdez struck his flag, and Drake took his prize to Torbay. There casks of reals were found in her hold and some tons of gunpowder, most useful to the English. The powder was put aboard the *Roebuck*, a swift trawler, which at once sailed to join Lord Howard's fleet.

Meantime another Spanish galleon had met with disaster. This one was commanded by Miguel de Oquendo, who, however, was not on board that night.

Officers and men, angered by the success of the English during the day, were quarreling among themselves and the ship's captain struck the master gunner with a stick. The master gunner, a German, was so enraged that he went below-decks and, having stuck a burning linstock into a barrel of powder, leaped through a porthole into the water. The explosion that followed blew off the deck from bow to stern and sent two hundred sailors and soldiers flying up with it. The galleon, which was one of the largest of the Armada, was so strongly built that her masts stood and she remained afloat. Sidonia at once ordered boats to the ship. A few of the crew who were unhurt were taken off the galleon; the wounded could not be moved and were left aboard the wreck, which was captured and towed to port by the English in the morning. There were gold-pieces in the hull and some barrels of gunpowder unharmed by the explosion; so again the English found their need partly supplied by the Spaniards.

The night had been stormy, but the following morning was fine and the sea quiet. The Armada was now off Portland and the English three or four miles to the east. Lord Howard was to leeward and so had lost the advantage he had held on the previous day. If the Spanish commander had forced another engagement immediately he would have had better chances of success, but he preferred to rest his crews and allow them to regain their confidence, which had been badly shaken. Meantime he despatched a letter to the Prince of Parma at Dunkirk, describing the first day's fighting and asking the Prince to send him pilots who knew the Channel, for he admitted that he should not know how to navigate those waters if he were overtaken by a storm.

Next day Sidonia, being to windward of the enemy and with his crews somewhat refreshed, bore down upon Lord Howard to offer battle. As the English headed out to sea he supposed they were flying from him, and attempted to give chase. The Spanish galleons varied considerably in speed, and the *San Marcos,* outstripping the others, was soon far in advance of her mates. Thus it happened that, when the breeze changed, as it customarily did in the Channel in summer, and as the English anticipated, Lord Howard was to windward of the *San Marcos,* which was several miles away from her fleet.

The plan of the English, outnumbered as they were in vessels and very short of ammunition, was to avoid a general engagement and instead to pick off and destroy separate Spanish ships. Therefore they now attacked the *San Marcos;* the galleon fought gamely and single-handed against several for an hour and a half; then Oquendo came to her rescue, and Lord Howard, who had about run out of powder, was obliged to draw off and await fresh supplies from shore.

By this time word that the Armada was in the Channel had spread throughout England and from every harbor came sloops and fishing-smacks bringing recruits to the fleet. That night the Spaniards counted a hundred enemy sail and every hour saw the number steadily increasing.

The following morning the sea was again calm. Lord Howard had received no supplies of shot or powder, though he had sent messengers to the ports, and his fleet lay six miles away from the Armada, waiting until their magazines could be restocked. The Duke of Medina Sidonia, thinking that the English were afraid to fight, ordered his galleasses to attack them. Howard contrived to stand off the galleasses, and that night of July twenty-fourth sufficient ammunition reached him to allow of one more day's fighting. The night was dark and quiet; at dawn the Spaniards saw two of their provision-vessels being towed away by some English small boats, and as the breeze rose Alonzo de Leyva in the *Rata,* accompanied by two galleasses, started to pursue them. Simultaneously Lord Howard decided to attempt for the first time a close engagement.

The English admiral, aboard the *Lion,* sailed straight into the main body of the Armada, steering for the *San Martin,* from which flew Sidonia's flag, and firing broadsides at every galleon he passed. As the *Ark* came up the Spaniard Oquendo brought his ship athwart her course and the two vessels col-

the night when he had anchored in Calais Roads his Flemish pilots had stolen away in the cockboats and escaped to Flushing, and he was now entirely dependent on his Spanish shipmasters who knew almost nothing of these waters.

As it happened,—although Sidonia did not know it,—the English also were in bad case. Their spirit was as determined as ever, Lord Henry Seymour had joined Lord Howard with the squadron of the Straits and forty privateers were reported ready for service in the Thames, but Seymour's crews were provided with only one day's food and Howard and Drake could supply their men with only five meagre dinners and one breakfast more; in addition they had only enough powder for a single day's fighting and none seemed to be forthcoming from London. Within a week at the most starvation would drive every English ship from the water and leave the Channel in the Spaniards' possession.

In this extremity Lord Howard called a council of war in his cabin and it was decided to try to drive the Armada out from Calais Roads by fire-ships. Eight vessels unfit for active service were selected, and their hulls filled with inflammable material and their rigging smeared with pitch. The night was cloudy with promise of a gale, the moon would not rise until morning, and the tide was setting towards the place where the Spanish ships were crowded together.

At midnight the lookouts on the Armada spied

dim objects drifting near their galleons and then
suddenly saw flames leap up and spread from sail
to sail.

At the sight panic struck the Spaniards. Sidonia,
instead of ordering out boats to tow the fire-ships
from his fleet, fired a gun from the *San Martin* as
signal to his vessels to slip their cables and make
out to sea. This the captains did, and the Armada,
scurrying out from the Roads, lay to six miles from
shore, intending to return in the morning to the anchorage off Calais.

But the English were not idle. Drake, with part
of the ships, hung close to the enemy, Howard with
the others stayed near Calais to try to drive the
slowest of the Spanish fleet up on the coast. At
dawn the largest of the Spanish galleasses went
aground on Calais Bar. Howard sent out boats to
capture her. The galleass had seven hundred men,
sailors, soldiers and galley-slaves, aboard; but her
guns in the slanting position she had taken on the
bar were useless for defense, her commander was
killed by a musket-shot, the galley-slaves sprang
overboard, many of the sailors and soldiers followed
them, and the English boarders took possession of
the ship.

Sidonia had every intention of returning to his
anchorage at Calais, but Sir Francis Drake had determined that the Spaniards should be driven out
into the North Sea. The wind was rising and threatened a gale. During the night the Spanish ships

had drifted some distance, and as Sidonia signaled them to make back to Calais Drake with his own squadron and Seymour with his came on the scattered enemy with the advantage of wind, speed and seamanship on the English side.

All morning Seymour's squadron, wasting none of their powder by firing at long range, poured into a group of Spanish galleons a rain of shot at such short distance that the enemy were utterly confused. Drake fell on Sidonia and Oquendo, and, aided by the wind and the unwieldiness of the Spanish ships, drove galleon close to galleon and forced the huddled mass of clumsy vessels towards the shoals that lie off the coast of Flanders.

Howard joined the others at noon. The Spaniards worked their guns awkwardly; the cannon, on rolling platforms, fired by gunners unused to rough seas, sent their shot harmlessly up into the air or down into the water. Every shot of the English told. From eight in the morning to sunset on that twenty-ninth of July the English fired steadily, until almost their last cartridge was spent. Three large Spanish galleons sank. Three others went drifting in wreckage towards Ostend. By night the bulk of the Armada, shattered, demoralized, crippled, was driving shorewards, and the English, exhausted by the day's work, hauled off to rest and wait for supplies.

Sidonia attempted to bring order in his battered fleet and signaled to make sail for the North Sea, which now appeared his only refuge from his pursuers. The *Santa Maria,* a wreck, went down with all her crew. When the roll of the Spanish ships was called it was found that four thousand men had been killed in the day's fighting or had been drowned. The galleons were leaking, their masts were splintered, their rigging and sails ripped to shreds; they could not return to Calais, for the English were now between them and the Roads; to stay where they were would be to court complete destruction; so they made what speed they could north through a northwest wind and a mountainous sea.

The English, although they were out of ammunition, seeing the Spaniards flying, made bold to follow them, and at dawn next day Sidonia discovered the ships of Howard and Drake close on his weather beam. Now on one side of him were his enemies, on the other side the long shoals that fringe the coast of Holland. Without pilots Sidonia was helpless. But in this desperate plight the wind shifted and to the Spaniards' immense satisfaction their ships were lifted away from the banks towards open water.

Howard and Drake had to fall back and the Armada escaped the English sailors' clutches.

The Spaniards now had a wind that would permit them to return to Calais and try to join forces with the Prince of Parma, but to attempt that would be to risk another encounter with the English. To decide on his next step Sidonia called a council of war and asked his officers whether it seemed better to them to return to the Channel and make for Calais or to go back to Spain by sailing around the Orkneys and Ireland.

The pride of the Spaniards had been broken by the gun-fire of the English on the preceding day and most of the captains preferred to take the latter course, which they supposed would be far safer than again challenging the English cannon. And though some of the commanders expressed themselves as willing to dare another engagement it was evident that the crews of the Armada had lost all taste for fighting.

Calderon, an experienced ship-master, said that the west coast of Ireland was dangerous; not so dangerous, argued others, as again meeting Howard and Drake. So it was decided; and the Armada sailed on into the North Sea that day and the next.

Lord Howard had also called his officers into council, and as the Channel was now unguarded they decided that Lord Henry Seymour must return there with his squadron, since the Prince of Parma might attempt to cross from Dunkirk. Seymour and his men greatly wanted to share in the fight that was expected with the Armada, but, obeying the council's orders, thirty ships of the squadron turned round that night and made their way back to the Channel.

Drake and Howard, with ninety vessels and provisions for five days, stuck to the Armada's rear, as confident of success as the Spaniards were disheartened. Drake sent a message to Sir Francis

Walsingham in England: "We have the army of
Spain before us, and mean, by the grace of God, to
wrestle a fall with it. There was never anything
pleased me better than seeing the enemy flying with
a southerly wind to the northwards. God grant ye
have a good eye to the Duke of Parma, for with the
grace of God, if we live, I doubt not ere it be long
so to handle the matter with the Duke of Sidonia
as he shall wish himself at St. Mary Port among his
orange trees."

When he saw the English fleet reduced by the departure of Seymour's squadron Sidonia again considered the possibility of turning back to Calais, but
the storm, which rose in might, and his lack of pilots decided him to stick to his course and sail for
the Orkneys.

The southwest gale struck the Armada with all its
power, and as the sea grew rougher some of the
ships, their spars broken or their hulls leaking,
dropped astern. In these unfamiliar waters and in
the teeth of the tempest the one desire of the captains and crews of those galleons that were still seaworthy was to press on and they made no effort to
help the battered laggards but left them to founder.

The English, pursuing through the North Sea,
thought that the Spaniards might be making for the
Forth, with the aim of landing in Scotland. But
the Armada did not stop there. The gale had now
become a hurricane; and as the English had only
supplies for three days aboard it seemed foolhardy

to follow north. Drake concluded that the Spaniards were probably heading for Denmark, and sent two pinnaces to watch their course. The rest of the English fleet, disappointed, but facing starvation, steered for Margate in search of food.

The Armada still counted a hundred and twenty ships of the hundred and fifty that had sailed from Spain. For five days the tempest blew and through fog and rain and seas that grew wilder and wilder as they left the shelter of the Scotch coast the ships, built for southern latitudes and manned by crews weakened by lack of nourishment and illness, fought their way. For almost a week they were out of touch, out of sight, of one another. On August ninth the sky cleared and it was seen that many of the galleons had lost their masts and yards and that the wind had split the sails of many others. That night the gale rose again and with it came fog.

By the thirteenth of August the fleet was scattered far and wide, and Sidonia had only a remnant of his vessels within sight. He called a council on his flagship. By now the crews were suffering from hunger, thirst and cold; those who had been wounded were dying by hundreds; their situation was desperate. The council determined, however, that at all costs they must keep off the coast of Ireland. So again on they went, through eleven more days of storm, while galleon after galleon dropped away from the flagship. On the fourth of September Sidonia, with fifty-two ships, all of which leaked at every seam, got past the Blaskets and was in safety. The commander and his officers and men were utterly spent with their battle with furious waters and perilous reefs.

Thirty ships of the Armada had been sunk or captured in the English Channel. Sidonia had fifty-two. The rest, nearly seventy in number, had been driven far and wide through the seas of the north, had gone down in the ocean or been wrecked on coasts where their crews were taken prisoner or killed in fight. Many a galleon had met her end on the cliffs of Ireland; the galleass that carried Don Alonzo da Leyva and the young lords of Castile had struck a rock off Dunluce and two hundred and sixty bodies were washed ashore. In that month of September more than eight thousand Spaniards perished between the Giant's Causeway and Blasket Sound. It seemed as if a curse had hounded the great fleet of Spain.

Fifty-four vessels ultimately got back to Spanish ports with between nine and ten thousand men. The ships were battered hulks, the crews were worn and ill. Spain was in despair. Sidonia had returned, but all the other great captains, Pedro de Valdez, Alonzo da Leyva, Recalde, Oquendo, Moncada, were lost. All but a third of the greatest fleet that had ever sailed lay beneath the waves or on the shores of the northern isles and Ireland, and Philip the Second's dream of conquering England was ended with the Armada.

CHAPTER XII
THE *MAYFLOWER*

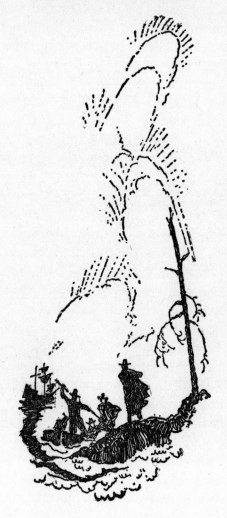

XII

THE *MAYFLOWER*

THERE sailed down the Thames from London on July 15, 1620 (old style) a ship that is famous in American history. This vessel was of about one hundred and eighty tons burden, one of the larger ships of the merchant service of England; beyond that there is no exact description of her, and a picture of the *Mayflower* must be drawn from accounts of other ships of her size and class. From these records she appears to have been of heavy build, though not ungraceful, with a high poop and forecastle; broad of beam, short in the waist, low between decks, and of square rig with a lateen sail upon her mizzenmast. She probably had three masts. Her high stem and stern made her what is known as "a wet ship." She had considerable cabin space, and for this particular voyage was doubtless fitted out with extra cabins to accomodate the large number of passengers.

Like all merchant ships of the time the *Mayflower* carried several guns, the heavier ones mounted on the spar-deck amidships, the lighter astern and on the rail, with a gun of longer range and larger calibre upon the forecastle. Probably her guns numbered eight or ten in all. The flag under which she sailed was what became known as the Union Jack, which had been ordered by King James of England in 1606 to replace the earlier English ensign, the red cross of St. George on a white field. The Union Jack represented the uniting of the Kingdoms of England and Scotland, and its design was formed by superimposing the red cross of St. George upon the white cross of St. Andrew on a dark blue field.

This ship had been chartered in London about the middle of June, 1620, on behalf of certain merchant adventurers of England and of the English congregation of "Separatists" (later known as "Pilgrims") who were at Leyden in Holland, and who jointly proposed to found a colony in North America. The captain or master engaged for the ship was Thomas Jones, a seaman of a very remarkable history; one who had sailed the Eastern seas in the corsair *Lion,* been a prisoner in London for misconduct, master of the cattle-ship *Falcon* on a voyage to Virginia, and who, after serving the Pilgrims on the *Mayflower,* was to become buccaneer again, commanding the little ship *Discovery* off the coasts of New England and Virginia, and to sail his prize, a Spanish frigate, captured in the West Indies, into the port of Jamestown, ending his career as he began, a pirate.

The journal of the *Mayflower* records that she was to sail "towards 'Hudson's River' in Virginia." Pursuing her way down the Thames to the Channel, she came on July nineteenth to Southampton, where she stayed some days, making ready for sea and awaiting her consort, the pinnace *Speedwell,* of sixty tons, that arrived on July twenty-sixth with some seventy passengers from Delfshaven in Holland.

The *Speedwell* was leaky and required repairs, but on August fifth the two vessels sailed from Southampton, the *Speedwell* with thirty passengers and the *Mayflower* with ninety.

Who were the Pilgrims that were setting out in the *Mayflower* and the *Speedwell?* They were English men and women who wanted to worship God in liberty of conscience and who, finding no such freedom as they desired in England, where they had often been persecuted for their opinions, had determined to find a home outside of that country where they might make a new England, linked to the mother country but free from her established church. Some of them had gone to Holland, where they had heard there was freedom of religion for all men, and had located at Leyden, but as news came of the great virgin continent across the Atlantic Ocean their desire for a home of their own, and for farmlands, led them to plan to go to America. Moreover they wished to have a share in the great struggle for religious liberty that was taking place, and were moved, as one of their leaders said, by "a hope and inward zeal of advancing the gospel of the kingdom of Christ in the remote parts of the New World; yea, though they should be but as stepping-stones unto others for performing so great a work."

The northern part of Virginia attracted them;— Virginia was the name given to a large section of America, and its boundaries were so loosely defined that it was considered by some to cover almost all the more fertile land on the North Atlantic coast;— therefore they had sent John Carver and Robert Cushman from Leyden to London to obtain the consent of the Council for Virginia to settle on that part of the seaboard. Many obstacles were put in their way, and it was finally only by the aid of some London merchants who were interested in American fisheries that the Pilgrims were able to secure the two ships for their expedition.

The Pilgrims who were at Leyden sailed from Delfshaven in the *Speedwell,* and those who were in England embarked on the *Mayflower*.

The *Speedwell* had been repaired at Southampton, but the two ships were still in the Channel when the smaller vessel was again found to be leaking badly. Therefore both vessels put into Dartmouth, where the *Speedwell* was unloaded and overhauled. That done, they sailed again, but three days later the *Speedwell* found herself in trouble and the two ships made for Plymouth where it was decided to send the *Speedwell* to London with eighteen or twenty of her passengers and transfer the remainder with part of her cargo to the more seaworthy *Mayflower*.

So the *Mayflower* sailed alone from Plymouth on September 6, 1620, with one hundred and two aboard.

Fine warm weather in the first part of the voyage was succeeded, to quote from the ship's log, by "a sharp change. Equinoctial weather, followed by strong westerly gales; encountered cross winds and fierce storms. Ship shrewdly shaken and her upper works made very leaky. One of the main beams in the midships was bowed and cracked. Some fear that the ship could not be able to perform the voyage."

The vessel pushed on, however, and milder weather came with late October. A son was born to Stephen and Elizabeth Hopkins and christened Oceanus Hopkins in honor of the sea. On November eighth land was sighted and the next day the *Mayflower* approached the bluffs at Truro on the tip of Cape Cod.

Their plan had been to settle in Virginia, and they had set out from London with the intention of locating somewhere in the country along the Hudson River, where report said there was excellent farmland; what actually happened was that the Pilgrims came to one of the least fertile sections of the Atlantic coast. Cape Cod in November may have looked like a precious haven to men and women who had been for two months at sea, but its long lines of sand dunes and wind-swept forests could hardly have appeared to them a land blessed with plenty.

After a conference between the master of the ship and the leaders of the Pilgrims the *Mayflower* tacked about and stood for the southward, but as she presently encountered shoals and breakers she put round again for the Bay of Cape Cod. Some of the Pilgrims were dissatisfied at the abandonment of the plan to locate on the shore of Virginia, but most of them felt as did Edward Winslow, who said: "Winter was come; the seas were dangerous; the season was cold; the winds were high, and the region being well furnished for a plantation, we entered upon discovery."

Tossed for sixty-seven days at sea, with food and fuel mostly spent, cold, homesick, and some of them ill, it is not to be wondered at that most of the ship's passengers preferred to land on the shores off which they had come to anchor rather than to seek another coast which could only be reached by further voyaging in winter weather.

On November eleventh the Pilgrims held a meeting in the main cabin of the ship and drew up a Compact which was signed by all the men, forty-one in number, on behalf of themselves and their families. This compact established a government for the colony they intended to found based on equal laws enacted for the general welfare. They then chose John Carver to be their governor.

Of that same day the *Mayflower's* log records: "Got out the long-boat and set ashore an armed party of fifteen or sixteen in armor, and some to fetch wood, having none left, landing them on the long point or neck, toward the sea. Those going ashore were forced to wade a bow-shot or two in going aland. The party set ashore returned at night having seen no person or habitation, having laded the boat with juniper-wood.''

The Pilgrims had reached America, but it was a bleak, inhospitable shore. Behind them was the ocean, in front the wilderness with its savage denizens. The nearest French colony was at Port Royal; five hundred miles lay between their anchorage and the English plantation of Virginia.

They had brought a shallop with them, but when it was unshipped it was found to need repairs and sixteen or seventeen days elapsed before it could be used. Meantime Captain Miles Standish, William Bradford and others went ashore to explore and returned two days later to report that they had seen Indians and had followed them for ten miles without coming up with them; in addition they had discovered a buried store of corn and had seen deer.

The weather now became very stormy, and the ship's master told his passengers they must find a permanent location as he wished to return to England. On November twenty-seventh the log records that a ''strong exploring party'' landed. ''Wind so strong that setting out from the ship the shallop and long-boat were obliged to row to the nearest shore and the men to wade above the knees to land. The wind proved so strong that the shallop was obliged to harbor where she landed. . . . Blowed and snowed all day and at night, and froze withal. Mistress White delivered of a son which is called 'Peregrine.' The second child born on the voyage, the first in this harbor.'' The men who had gone ashore ''were tired with marching up and down the steep hills and deep valleys, which lay half a foot thick with snow.'' They discovered a quantity of maize, but no place that seemed suitable for a settlement.

Day by day the leaders explored the coast and camped at night on the frozen meadows. One morning at dawn a war-whoop and a shower of arrows told of attacking Indians. The redmen withdrew, however, without an encounter. The ship's log says of that afternoon that the exploring party in their small boat ran into ''a severe gale . . . in which their rudder-hinges broke, their mast was split in three pieces, their sail fell overboard in a heavy sea, and they were like to have been cast away in making a harbor which Master Coppin'' (a pilot, who had been in these regions before) ''thought he knew, but was deceived about. They landed on an island at the mouth of the harbor.''

It was on the ninth of December that the party, made up of Carver, Standish, Bradford, Winslow, and some others, looked across from this small island to the encircling shore. That day they rested and repaired their boat. The next day was the Sabbath and they kept it with due observance. On Monday, the eleventh of December, the exploring party landed on the mainland at Plymouth. Having studied the harbor, the shore and the neighboring country, they agreed that this was the place for their settlement.

Four days later the *Mayflower* was moored off this shore. The journal says on December fourteenth: "The colonists have determined to make settlement at the harbor they visited, and which is apparently, by Captain John Smith's chart of 1616, no other than the place he calls 'Plimoth' thereon." This name of Plymouth, appropriate because it was the name of the last port in England from which they had sailed, they adopted for their chosen site, and there they began the building of their new home, which was to be the first colony established in New England.

Exposure to cold and wet had weakened many of the Pilgrims and it was no easy task for them to make a habitation in a winter season of frequent storms of sleet and snow. Every man, it was agreed, should build his own house. In addition there was other work to do, the construction of a common-house and the protection of the settlement from Indians. Frequently men who went to explore the near-by country lost themselves in the wilds and parties had to be sent out to search for them. The Pilgrims' journal reports that on January twelfth some of the settlers were missing and fears were entertained that they might have been captured by Indians. On January fourteenth the journal states: "At anchor in harbor. About six o'clock in the morning, the wind being very great, the watch on deck spied the great new rendezvous on shore on fire and feared it fired by Indians, but the tide being out, men could not get ashore for three quarters of an hour, when they went armed. At the landing they heard that the lost men were returned, some frost-bitten, and that the thatch of the common-house only was burnt by a spark, but no harm done the roof. The most lost was Governor Carver's and Master Bradford's, both of whom lay sick in bed, and narrowly missed being blown up with powder. The meeting was to have been kept ashore to-day, the greater number of the people now being there, but the fire, etc. prevented. Some of those sick in the common-house were fain to return aboard for shelter. Fifth Sunday in this harbor."

In February a band of Indians was found lurking near the settlement and the colony organized for defense, with Miles Standish as captain. But the Indians did no harm, and in March Samoset, an envoy from the Sachem Massassoit, came to Plymouth and a treaty of amity was made between the Pilgrims and the natives.

Early in March the weather moderated; but illness had taken heavy toll of the settlers and the survivors were still in want and great privation. The *Mayflower* made ready to return in April. "In the sixteen weeks the ship has lain here," says the journal, "half of her crew (but none of her officers) have died, and a few are still weak. . . . A bad voyage for the owner, Adventurers, ship, and crew."

On April fourth the journal records: "Sails loosened and all ready for departure except Governor's letters. Last visits of shore people to ship. Sail with morning tide, if wind serves. One hundred and ten days in this harbor.'' And on the next day: "Got anchors, and with fair wind got under way at full tide. Many to bid adieu. Set colors and gave Planters a parting salute with the ensign and ordnance. Cleared the harbor without hindrance, and laid general course E.S.E. for England with a fine wind. Took departure from Cape Cod early in the day, shook off the land and got ship to rights before night. All sails set and the ship logging her best.''

Thirty-one days later the *Mayflower* arrived safely in England.

In spite of illness and hunger, of loneliness and homesickness, and the lack of almost everything they were used to in the way of comforts, not one of the Pilgrims returned in the *Mayflower*. They were men and women of indomitable faith and resolution, and what they had set their hand to that would they do. On that wintry, wind-swept shore they held to their determination to found a home that should be a haven for all who sought liberty of conscience. "Out of small beginnings," said Bradford, "great things have been produced; and, as one small candle may light a thousand, so the light here kindled hath shone to many, yea, in some sort to our whole nation.''

The *Mayflower* and her band of Pilgrims have had their reward in the pages of history. Of that vessel wrote Thomas Carlyle: "Hail to thee, poor

little ship *May-Flower*—of Delft Haven—poor,
common-looking ship, hired by common charter-
party for coined dollars,—caulked with mere oakum
and tar,—provisioned with vulgarest biscuit and ba-
con,—yet what ship Argo or miraculous epic ship,
built by the sea gods, was other than a foolish bum-
barge in comparison!"

Liberty, courage and faith: these were the guid-
ing stars of the simple, heroic little band that crossed
the ocean in the *Mayflower* and founded New England.

CHAPTER XIII
DUTCH SHIPS

XIII

DUTCH SHIPS

THERE is a saying that the city of Amsterdam was built upon herrings, and it is recorded that Dutch shipping owes much to the fact that in the fifteenth century the herring began to spawn in the North Sea instead of in the Baltic, thereby making the "haring-vliet" or mouth of the Maas and the "Schotsman" shoal, off the island of Walcheren, two of the most valuable fishing grounds of Europe. In the days when the Dutch were becoming the rivals of the Spaniards, French and English in the fields of commerce the fishing boat of the Netherlands was as important a vessel as the more pretentious merchantman.

The position of the Low Countries and their fisheries made the Dutch a sea-faring people, they fished their own waters and sought fish as far away as the seas around the Orkneys, the Shetlands and the coast of Ireland. They learned how to cure and barrel the fish and by their industry enjoyed a monopoly in supplying the markets of northern and central Europe. In 1560 the value of the year's fishing trade to Friesland, Holland, Zeeland and Flanders amounted to the very large sum of £300,000. In the latter part of the seventeenth century the Dutch were

employing 8000 ships and 200,000 hands, and were
earning £5,000,000 a year from their fisheries.   Herring were to be found in plenty off Great Yarmouth
on the east coast of England and sometimes there
would be as many as one thousand Dutch fishing
vessels off that town and ten thousand Dutch sailors ashore, drying their nets and buying provisions.

The two principal types of fishing craft used by
the Dutch in the North Sea were the buss and the
dogger. A picture of an early "haring buys," as
it was called, shows a large open boat, about thirty
feet in length, with two masts, each carrying a square
sail. The Dutch buss of the middle of the seventeenth century was usually a ship of from sixty to
two hundred tons, having three masts, the after one
short and fitted with a sail employed generally for
riding with the ship's head to the wind. The fore
and main masts were so constructed that they could
be lowered in order to offer less resistance to the
wind when the boat was riding to its nets. Frequently a single square sail was carried on each of
the two larger masts, although sometimes the buss
had a square main topsail. Sometimes a type of
studding sail was used and occasionally also a jib
on a temporary bowsprit.

The jib first appeared in use on ships of the Netherlands. A triangular sail had long been employed
and the lateen sail was very popular in early days.
The chief difference between the lateen sail and the

jib consists in the fact that the former utilizes a
spar for its support while the support of the jib
is a rope which also serves as a support for the
mast. Some Dutch sailor of the early sixteenth century rigged up a sail on the fore stay of his boat,
with the thought that, as a lateen sail worked well
astern, another sail of similar shape might be made
to work at the bow, and this contrivance of his took
its place as a regular form of rigging. This triangular sail, however, although it was common on small
boats in the sixteenth century, did not come into use
on large ships until the latter part of the seventeenth
century and the beginning of the eighteenth.

The buss belonged to the same family of ships as
the Schevennigen "pink," which is used in modern
times off the coast of Holland. The dogger was not
unlike the buss. It had two masts with square sails,
and was what was known as a line-fisher, since it did
not use nets, being employed chiefly for catching cod
and ling.

When the buss or the dogger had made their hauls
the fresh fish were carried into harbor in boats of a
fast-sailing type called "vent-jagers."

The finest Dutch ships were those of the Dutch
East India Company and in the seventeenth century
these were stately vessels with three masts and a
bowsprit and carried topgallant sails on the fore and
main masts. They had lofty sterns and two decks
of guns. They were, however, somewhat smaller
than the merchant ships of England or France, and

had flatter floors and drew less water, which was an important factor in clearing the shoals that abound near the coast of the Netherlands. They were excellent vessels for the northern seas, and Dutch shipwrights became so skilled in constructing them that Peter the Great worked in the shipyards of the Netherlands in order to reproduce their handiwork in Russia.

With these merchantmen the Dutch prospered and when Cromwell was Lord Protector of England the Dutch were doing the bulk of the world's carrying trade and owned four-fifths of all the merchant ships on the seas.

Then England became jealous of the Dutch power and prohibited fishing off the coasts of England, Scotland and Ireland. In 1651 there was issued the English Navigation Act which prohibited the importation of goods into England except in English ships or in the vessels of the country that produced the goods. This was aimed at the Dutch merchantmen and in the next year there broke out the first of the wars between the Low Countries and England.

Spain and England had fought for commercial rivalry, so now the Dutch, who had succeeded to much of the Spaniards' trade, found themselves in conflict with the English. The Low Countries, or the United Provinces, as they were called, had grown exceedingly prosperous from their fisheries, manufactures and carrying trade, and it was said that the profit they had made from the export of cured fish was greater than the value of all the treasure brought from the New World by the galleons of Spain. The geographical position of the United Provinces, between France and the Baltic and at the mouth of the great rivers of Germany, helped largely to win for their people the title of the "wagoners of all seas." But the situation of England gave her a splendid strategic position in opposing the Dutch, for ships of the United Provinces sailing to the Mediterranean had to pass through the English Channel at its narrowest point.

When war broke out between the two countries in 1652 the navies of both nations won laurels on the seas and the Dutch Admirals Tromp and Ruyter proved themselves the equals of the English commanders Blake and Monck. The Dutch, however, lost so much of their trade in two years of warfare that they negotiated for peace with Oliver Cromwell.

Then in 1664 the English seized the Dutch colony of New Netherland in North America and war broke out again the following year. Dutch ships under Ruyter and Cornelius de Witt sailed up the Medway as far as Chatham and burned an English fleet as it lay at anchor. Peace was made two years later and England exchanged her colony of Suriname in South America for the Dutch New Netherland.

Once more in 1672 the two countries came into

conflict on the water and again the Dutch proved a
match for the English, for "the wagoners of all
seas" showed themselves as capable of handling
warships as of sailing their favorite busses and
doggers.

CHAPTER XIV
TALL EAST INDIAMEN

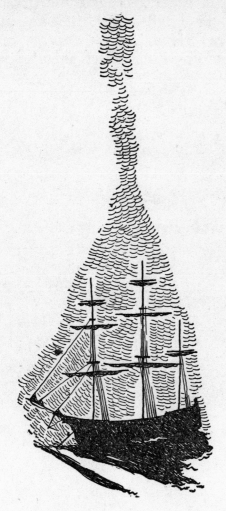

XIV

TALL EAST INDIAMEN

"THE United Company of Merchant Venturers of England Trading to the East Indies," more generally known as the East India Company, was a privileged child of the English government for more than two centuries, and carried on an exclusive and exceedingly lucrative trade between England and the Far East. For the long voyages around the Cape of Good Hope the company built splendid ships that bore the name of East Indiamen, vessels that were very much like ships of war, with carefully drilled crews, equal to those in the Royal Navy, since the East Indiamen in voyaging to Bombay, Calcutta or other ports had to navigate waters that were much frequented by pirates and in addition England during the seventeenth and eighteenth centuries was often at war.

These tall ships were constructed for seaworthiness rather than for speed and money was lavished on their building; one of 1325 tons is reported to have cost £53,000, an extraordinary sum for those days. With its monopoly of trade, however, the company could well afford such prices, for sometimes a ship earned three hundred per cent on her entire cost of construction in a single round trip

from England to India or China. Fortunes were
easily made and not uncommonly the ship's master
shared in these, for on many voyages he was allowed
to trade on his own account in a space of the ship's
hold set aside for his uses; masters of East Indiamen were known to have made as much as £10,000
for themselves on a single voyage.

When the Portuguese explorers found a sea route
to India they opened up an avenue of trade that
quickly relegated the Mediterranean to a sub-
ordinate position and spurred the mariners of other
nations to compete with them. The Portuguese, the
Spaniards, the Dutch, the French, sought commerce
with the East and found it vastly profitable; and by
the beginning of the seventeenth century England,
through the East India Company, was taking a hand
in the competition for this valuable trade.

At the village of Blackwall on the Thames River
the ships for the East India trade were built, a wonderful succession of them; from the year 1582
hundreds of East Indiamen were launched at Blackwall, and when the English people objected to the
monopoly of trade so long held by the East India
Company and Parliament in 1833 withdrew the
charter and threw open the Far Eastern trade to
all British merchants, Blackwall still went on building merchant vessels, the famous Blackwall frigates,
the clippers and the ships of the Peninsular and
Oriental Navigation Company.

In April, 1582 the first of these ships, the *Edward*

Bonaventure, sailed from Blackwall, and, joining the *Leicester* at Southampton, headed west for India, but finding a Spanish fleet in the neighborhood of the Strait of Magellan was forced to return to England.

In 1599 a number of merchants in London presented a petition to Queen Elizabeth asking for a monopoly to trade with the East Indies, and this petition was granted for a term of fifteen years on the last day of 1600, which marks the commencement of the East India Company.

In 1601 a small fleet of vessels sailed from the Thames with a cargo of iron, lead, tin, and gifts for the rulers of India, rounded the Cape of Good Hope and reached Sumatra in June, 1602. In September, 1603 the fleet returned to England with a large cargo of pepper, and this voyage was regarded as so successful by the English government that the original grant of a monopoly for fifteen years was indefinitely extended in favor of the East India Company and their ships became the great carriers between England and the Orient.

With the firm establishment of this trade the company set to work to build vessels suitable for such long voyages. Early in the seventeenth century the largest merchant vessel that had been built up to that time in England was constructed for the Indian service, the *Trades Increase,* of about eleven hundred tons; this ship was too big for the builders' knowledge of naval construction, and, although she reached the East safely, she fell over on one side while she was being careened in order to have her sheathing examined, and made no more voyages.

Shipbuilding had now become a profitable business and in 1612 the Shipwrights Company was incorporated. The East India Company leased a yard at Deptford in 1607 and soon was employing five hundred carpenters, caulkers, ship fitters, joiners, riggers, painters and other workmen. By 1612 the yard at Blackwall was well established and that part of the Thames had become a hive of industry in the building of a merchant marine.

How profitable was the trade is shown by the fact that the profit from the first twelve voyages averaged not less that 138 per cent. By 1681 the company owned thirty-five ships of from 100 to 775 tons, and in 1683 a £100 share in the business was worth £500.

The shipyard at Blackwall became one of the great sights of England. Samuel Pepys, the author of the famous diary, says that he went there in 1661 to see the new wet dock and the "brave new merchantman *Royal Oake,*" which was about to be launched. That other celebrated keeper of a diary, John Evelyn, relates that in 1662 he went to Blackwall with the Duke of York and boarded an East Indiaman where they drank punch and "canary that had been carried to and brought from the Indies, which was indeed incomparably good."

By the end of the seventeenth century the Eng-

lish merchant ships had become the chief traders of
the world and had greatly outdistanced their rivals,
the Spaniards and Dutch. English explorers had
opened up new countries and the English fighting
fleets had partially cleared the seas for the nation's
commerce. Always a great trading people the
English were shrewd enough to see that the ocean
was the road for them to follow in pursuit of wealth
and the government did everything it could to
foster the interests of its merchants overseas. Its
favorite child was the energetic and daring East
India Company.

The Blackwall yards had by the middle of the
seventeenth century a wet dock, three dry docks, and
a number of slips, and here the splendid tall ships
were built; celebrated vessels such as the *Falmouth,*
a three-master of 668 tons, carrying topsails and
top-gallant sails and with elaborate bow and stern
and ornate figurehead; the 642-ton *Osterley;* the
Valentine and *Ajax,* each of 655 tons; and the huge
Bombay Castle, of 1612 tons, armed with seventy-
four guns, which the company presented to King
George III.

In 1789 the Brunswick Basin was begun at the
Blackwall yards and here the bowsprit and all the
masts of the *Lord Macartney* were raised and fixed
in the record time of three hours and forty minutes.
A few years later was launched the *Warren Hastings,* which became one of the most famous of the
company's fleet.

These ships were frigate-built, but, although they were larger, they were not much speedier nor better constructed than the merchant vessels of a century before. Towards the close of the eighteenth century, however, two families of ship-builders, the Wigrams and the Greens, began to come into notice, and it was they who eventually revolutionized English merchant marine architecture.

Many adventures befell the East Indiamen. On January 31, 1804 sixteen of the fleet, ranging in size from twelve hundred to fifteen hundred tons, under command of Captain Nathaniel Dance in the *Earl Camden,* set out from Canton for England with a cargo worth many thousands of pounds. With the sixteen ships went a convoy of forty other vessels, which were to accompany the fleet as far as their courses would allow.

For two weeks the voyage was uneventful; then at daybreak one of the ships, the *Royal George,* signaled that she had sighted four strange sails to the southwest. Dance thereupon ordered the *Royal George, Alfred, Bombay Castle,* and *Hope* to take a nearer look at the strangers. On the flagship was an officer of the Royal Navy, Lieutenant Robert Fowler, who had been in command of a vessel that had been wrecked. He offered to go in the brig *Ganges,* which was one of the convoy, and so the *Ganges* joined the other scouts. Soon these signaled that the strangers were a French squadron, composed of a line-of-battle ship, three frigates and a brig.

England and France were at war, and the East Indiamen would be a rich prize for the enemy squadron. Dance formed his fleet in line of battle in close order. Admiral Linois of the French ships put about as soon as he could reach the wake of the East Indiamen, but preferred to delay his attack until daylight next morning; and so the two fleets lay to, the men at their quarters. At dawn they were three miles apart, the French to windward.

The French admiral had been on the lookout for the great China fleet. He ran up his colors and the merchant ships ran up theirs. At nine in the morning, as the enemy had not opened fire, Dance formed the order for sailing and proceeded on his course. Linois edged in closer, and when the English commander saw that his opponent was attempting to cut off the rear of his fleet he signaled his ships to bear down in line and engage when they came abreast of the enemy.

Early in the afternoon the French opened fire and the China fleet returned the bombardment and kept it up so hotly that after three-quarters of an hour the French 74-gun flagship *Marengo* and her consorts stopped their firing and stood away under full sail to the east.

The merchantmen had beaten the warships. Dance gave the signal for a general chase, which lasted for two hours, when he halted his fleet, lest they should sail too far from the mouth of the Strait of Malacca, for which he was making. For this exploit great credit was given the East Indiamen, which, in spite of their heavy cargoes, had by skillful maneuvering and bold action put to flight ships that were waiting to capture them. The East Indiamen were fighters and many were as battle-scarred as the heavy English ships-of-the-line.

The early nineteenth century was the great era of the East India Company, when to serve on one of its merchant ships was equivalent to serving in the Royal Navy. The ships were smart, and the wealth of the company and its long and honorable record gave the captains and officers a social standing equal to that held by officers in His Britannic Majesty's regular sea-forces. The position of commander was eagerly sought, it carried great prestige and many a captain, profiting by the privilege of doing a certain amount of trading for himself, was able to retire from the service after several voyages and purchase a ship for himself.

On board an East Indiaman of twelve hundred tons there would be in addition to the captain six mates, a surgeon, purser, master-at-arms, midshipmen and a score of other petty officers and a crew of one hundred and thirty. The captains were chosen from those who had sailed to India or China as chief or second mate. The company was liberal with pensions to men who had served it faithfully and provided well for those who were wounded and for the families of men killed in the company's business.

In those days there was always likelihood of an East Indiaman being engaged in battle with the French. When the *Warren Hastings* sailed she carried twenty-six guns on her main or lower deck, fourteen on her upper deck, and four on her poop. With this armament she left England in February, 1805, arrived at China, and set out for home; on the return voyage, however, four of her main deck ports were caulked up to make space for an extra store-room and those four guns placed in the hold, and four of her upper deck guns were also stored below.

On June twenty-first in the morning the *Warren Hastings* sighted a stranger, which turned out to be the French 40-gun frigate *Piémontaise*. The East Indiaman was of 1356 tonnage against the Frenchman's 1093; but the latter had a crew of 385 against the former's 138, and could fire a broadside of twenty-three guns against the *Warren Hastings'* eighteen. Except in tonnage, the *Piémontaise* was much the more powerful vessel and moreover was built for fighting.

The French frigate shook the reefs from her topsails and made for the Indiaman, which kept to her course. A little later the Frenchman hoisted the British flag, and, although the merchantman was confident the other ship was French, she ran up her colors and her private signal. The frigate did not answer the signal, but continued to approach, and presently the *Warren Hastings,* perceiving that the other ship's intentions were hostile, shortened sail and cleared for action.

At noon the *Piémontaise* hoisted her French ensign in place of the British; then opened fire and destroyed part of the merchantman's rigging. The frigate continued to pour in broadsides, which killed and wounded a number of the English crew, splintered the foremast and carried away all the fore-shrouds on the port side and the merchantman's ensign. This flag, however, was soon hoisted again at the *Warren Hastings'* maintopgallant mast-head.

The French ship kept up her cannonades. The *Warren Hastings,* with her foremast crippled, in a heavy wind and high sea, answered the enemy's fire. In the exchange of broadsides the merchant ship now lost more men and her mainmast was badly damaged as well as much of her rigging. Soon she had only her maintopsail set; broadsides knocked her spanker boom to pieces and carried away the mizzenmast which fell in such a direction as to prevent the use of every gun on her upper deck. Her lower deck was ablaze and her rudder was out of service.

For over four hours the East Indiaman stood up to the French frigate, and then was forced to lower her ensign. She had surrendered, but unfortunately in the heavy sea and with her rudder disabled she became unmanageable and crashed against the Frenchman. The enemy took this to be an attempt to ram their vessel, and some of the French crew, leaping aboard, attacked and wounded the captain and several other officers before their rage was appeased. Then the frigate took the merchantman in tow, a very valuable prize with her China cargo.

The East India Company, in its pursuit of trade, practically ruled India and built up an organization that took over much of the government of the natives. It became a great power, of enormous use to England; but it held a monopoly of trade and after two hundred years of privilege people began to question its right to keep all the Far Eastern commerce to itself.

Parliament commenced to inquire into the company's rule in India and as a result the company lost its Indian monopoly in 1814 and the trade was thrown open to all merchants who would provide ships of more than three hundred and fifty tons. The trade with China was still reserved to the company, and this commerce, especially the tea trade, was very profitable.

With the Indian ports, however, free to all English merchants there were soon so many ships trading there that the demand increased for the right to trade with China also. At length, therefore, in 1833 the last of the company's exclusive rights was withdrawn and the famous "United Company of Merchant Venturers" ceased to be an important factor in English commerce.

Yet in large part Great Britain owes her supremacy in India to the company that for two centuries sent from the Thames to Bombay, Calcutta and the China ports that great fleet of East Indiamen that fought their way through the seas with such persistence and valor.

CHAPTER XV

SHIPS OF THE AMERICAN
COLONIES AND REPUBLIC

XV

SHIPS OF THE AMERICAN COLONIES
AND REPUBLIC

THE settlements along the Atlantic coast of North America differed greatly in soil and situation, as well as in the character of the colonists. The men who came to Plymouth in the *Mayflower* found a bleak shore with little profit to be made from agriculture, the Dutchmen who followed Hudson to the vicinity of his river arrived at a country well watered and fertile and affording splendid opportunities for trade in furs, while to the south the rich fields of Maryland and Virginia appeared a land of golden promise to those who sought plantations. The sea was more important to the New Englander than to the Southerner and the former looked to the ocean for his livelihood as the latter looked to the land.

Many a European indeed, landing on the northern shore, immediately lost his taste for settlement, preferring to retrace his steps across the water rather than to battle with such a rocky soil. So a little party that had come to the mouth of the Kennebec, having spent a winter there, built what they termed a "faire pinnace of thirty tons," named her the *Virginia,* and sailed back in her to England.

Other settlers proved more hardy, however, and it was not long before New Englanders, seeing little prospect of developing farming, turned their attention to fishing and to shipping. Fish were plentiful off their shores, and these, with lumber, provided opportunities for trade with other colonies and even with the West Indies.

In 1631 shipbuilding commenced in Massachusetts with the launching of the 60-ton sloop *Blessing of the Bay* on the Mystic River, and as early as 1640 the *Desire* of Salem was trading to the West Indies for cotton, tobacco and negro slaves. The *Desire* made a voyage to England in the very creditable space of twenty-three days. In 1643 the *Trial* left Boston, and went to Malaga, from where she brought back wine, fruit, oil, linen and wool. A ship of four hundred tons, the *Seafort,* was built at Boston in 1648, but was wrecked on the coast of Spain. Many shipwrights had come with the early Puritan settlers and by 1660 the building of vessels had become a leading industry in Salem and Boston, Newbury, Ipswich and Gloucester.

According to the records ships of many types entered and sailed from Boston in 1661 and 1662; there is mention of a shallop, a pinnace, a barque, a pincke, a buss, a ketch and a snow. Some of these represent types of vessels that were experiments of the builders and were soon abandoned. The shallop was a two masted boat with a lug sail on each mast, —the lug sail being a quadrilateral stretch of

canvas bent upon a yard that hangs obliquely to the
mast at about one-third of its length,—and was
square sterned and of light draught, so that it was
especially fitted for bay and inland waters. The
pinnace, easy to build and very serviceable, was
popular for fishing and the coast trade. She was
usually an open boat, sharp at both ends, and ordinarily had two masts with square sails. Pinnaces, half-decked for shelter, sometimes made
voyages to the West Indies and even to England, as
did the little *Virginia* that was built near the Kennebec. The snow, which was much larger than
either the shallop or the pinnace, had square sails
on her two masts and was the predecessor of the
brig that later became so popular.

In general the colonial ships of New England,
however, were small single-decked sloops, the most
suitable type for the coasting trade, and lateen-
rigged ketches, which were the favorite boats of the
fishermen. North of Cape Ann as well as south of
it shipbuilding flourished; the first vessel regularly
built for a transatlantic packet was constructed at
Richmond's Island in Maine in 1631; and from 1674
to 1714 the New Englanders launched 1332 ships.
Said Lord Bellomont, the Royal Governor: "I believe there are more good vessels belonging to the
town of Boston than to all Scotland and Ireland."

Due to this attention to the shipwright's trade it
was natural that New England should have provided
many of the ships that were needed for commerce

by the other colonies, where the settlers were more interested in farming or the fur trade than in building ships. Soon vessels owned in New England were carrying the bulk of the commerce from Chesapeake Bay to England and the southern ports of Europe. Edward Randolph wrote of the ship owners of Massachusetts in 1676: "It is the great care of the merchants to keep their ships in constant employ, which makes them trye all ports to force a trade, whereby they abound with all sorts of commodities, and Boston may be esteemed the mart town of the West Indies."

There is a story that a builder of Gloucester, Massachusetts, in 1713 constructed a vessel with two masts and rigged them with fore-and-aft sails. For a head sail he used a triangular stretch of canvas; and his boat was the first to carry this particular arrangement of sails. When she was launched and took to the water a spectator exclaimed, "Look! See how she scoons!"

To this the builder answered, "Very well. A scooner let her be."

So from that word to "scoon"—which meant to skip like a flat stone over the water—came the name of the schooner, a type of ship that was soon seen everywhere on the Atlantic. She largely displaced some of the earlier vessels, such as the ketch, which was a two masted ship with square sails on both masts, and the pink or pinkie, which was sharp at both ends, somewhat like the Viking boats, and rigged with two fore-and-aft sails.

With the schooner came the era of codfishing, and commerce on a larger scale. Massachusetts traded with the mainland of South America, carried log-wood and mahogany from Honduras to London, exchanged fish and wood for the products of the Dutch East Indies, and brought back from the French West Indies quantities of molasses to feed her distilleries. Presently New England rum was taking the place of beer and cider as the favorite American beverage.

While the early settlers of New England were busy fashioning oak timbers and pine spars for their ships the colonists of New Netherland on Manhattan Island and along the Hudson River were carrying on a thriving trade for the Dutch West India Company. Soon after Henry Hudson made a report of his voyage up the river Dutch mariners crossed in the wake of the *Half Moon.* One of these was Adriaen Block, who arrived in 1613 in the ship *Tiger.* On a November night this vessel was burned off the southern point of Manhattan Island. Block wintered there and built a new ship which he named the *Restless.* In this he explored the Housatonic and Connecticut Rivers, Narragansett Bay and two small islands, to one of which he gave his own name.

In 1631 two Belgian shipbuilders visited the

settlement on Manhattan Island and were so much impressed with the excellent timber there that they persuaded Governor Peter Minuit to construct a vessel of eight hundred tons, which was christened the *New Netherland*. This ship, which was probably one of the largest merchant vessels in the world at that time, sailed to Holland, but the West India Company was displeased at the cost of its building and no other ships of such large proportions were built in the colony for nearly two hundred years.

For their journeys into the interior of the country after furs the Dutch colonists made much use of canoes; they were not greatly interested in fishing and many of the vessels employed in their commerce were European-built. But as New Amsterdam on Manhattan Island became more and more important as a seaport the settlers took to shipbuilding and even for a time rivaled the shipyards of New England in supplying vessels for other colonies until the English Navigation Act of 1651, restraining colonial commerce to English and colonial ships, gave the builders of Massachusetts a great advantage over the Dutch.

When the Dutch colony of New Netherland became the English colony of New York the shipping from Manhattan Island greatly increased, and the city at the mouth of the Hudson River assumed the foremost place among the seaports of the North Atlantic Coast. Schooners and merchant vessels of all kinds, packet ships and later clipper ships were built in New York's many yards.

Up the Delaware River at William Penn's city of Philadelphia there was also much shipping, and there were many wealthy merchants, one of the best-known of whom was Stephen Girard, who made a great fortune in commerce with India and China in his four celebrated ships, the *Helvetia, Montesquieu, Rousseau,* and *Voltaire.*

As to the Virginians, they were not great ship-builders; they were far more interested in agriculture than in fishing or in constructing vessels for overseas trade. At first most of the ships they used in commerce were English-built. Their seaports were few compared to those of New England. There were some 'longshoremen who made their living by their nets, and in the tidal rivers and the bays a primitive boat was to be found which was called the bugeye. This vessel had double ends; the bottom was made of several logs bolted together; timbers were fastened to this bottom and side planks spiked to the timbers. Usually these boats had two masts with a jib, and, although they were very heavy, the bugeyes could make good speed.

Nor were the colonies south of Virginia as much interested in ships as in plantations. Charleston in South Carolina had its merchant fleets, but whereas the ambitious young fellow of Maine or Massachusetts followed the calling of the sea his brother in the Carolinas or Georgia preferred to seek his fortune in cultivating crops of rice, indigo and cotton.

The New England merchants were essentially shrewd and far-sighted, and soon after the Revolution they reached out for the Far Eastern trade. The *Harriet,* of Hingham, a sloop of fifty-five tons, sailed in December, 1783, from Boston with a cargo of ginseng for China. She stopped at the Cape of Good Hope, where she encountered several English East Indiamen, and the captains of these ships, to avoid American competition, purchased the sloop's cargo for double its weight in Hyson tea. The *Harriet* returned home, without completing her voyage to China. A New York ship, the *Empress of China,* of three hundred and sixty tons, reached Canton Roads in August, 1784, and is said to have been the first American-built vessel to sail to China. The next year a Baltimore ship carried the flag of the new republic to the Canton River, and in 1787 the *Grand Turk* of Salem made the round trip voyage to China and was the first Massachusetts vessel to reach those waters.

The United States wanted the tea and silks and china of the Far East, but had few wares to offer the Chinese in return. Rumors came, however, that the Russians were trading in furs with the mandarins, and this suggested a new project to the Yankee merchants. Six of them, representing Boston, Salem and New York, organized a company to export furs from the northwestern coast of America, and sent out the ship *Columbia,* of 212 tons, from Boston on September 20, 1787, with the 90-ton sloop *Lady Washington* as tender.

These two small vessels sailed south and after an unusually long voyage, due to stiff westerly gales in the South Atlantic, rounded Cape Horn, the first North American-built ships to achieve that passage. They reached the coast of Oregon about a year after they had left Boston and stopped at Nootka Sound, which was the fur-trading centre of Vancouver Island. It was too late in the season to obtain a full cargo, and on that almost unknown shore the crews spent the winter, the ships anchored in a cove, the sailors sheltered in log huts. By the next summer, before they had obtained as many furs as they wanted, their supplies ran low, and Captain Kendrick, who commanded the expedition, sent Captain Gray off for China in the *Columbia,* and the *Lady Washington* remained on the coast.

The *Columbia* reached Canton, and, exchanging her furs for tea, continued on around the world to the home port of Boston. When she arrived there on August 9, 1790, after a three-year voyage that had covered 41,899 miles, the guns of the city roared a welcome to the little ship that had been the first to carry the United States flag around the globe and Governor Hancock gave a dinner in honor of the officers. That voyage of the *Columbia* inaugurated the fur trade of the Northwest.

In this fur trade the ship-merchants of New York and Philadelphia were soon outdistanced by those of Boston, and in 1801 fourteen out of the sixteen vessels on the northwest coast hailed from the latter port. In this trade small ships were used. One vessel, the *Massachusetts,* of almost eight hundred tons, the largest ship built up to that time in an American shipyard, sailed from Boston in 1790, but had a most unprofitable voyage and was sold in Canton to the Danish East India Company, and after that the merchants preferred ships of lesser tonnage. The usual vessels were brigs and ships of one hundred to two hundred tons, with copper bottoms to keep clear of weeds in the seas of the tropics. They carried large crews to fight hostile Indians and these crews were skilled in repairing the damage sustained by the ships on the reefs and ledges of rocky shores that were practically unmapped.

These ships, although small, were very sturdy; they did not try for speed, but were content to carry their heavy cargoes in safety. Usually after leaving their home port on the North Atlantic they would stop at the West Indies and again at the Falklands. In the Pacific they might go ashore at the Galápagos Islands and then head for Hawaii, which was a favorite resort of traders of all nations, fishermen from China and the Malay waters, Russian hunters of the sea otter, and British and Yankee sailors.

When they reached the Northwest there was the

business of barter with the Indians for furs, and the Indians had to be handled diplomatically or they might go on the warpath. Frequently a ship spent a winter securing a full cargo of furs to carry across the Pacific to the markets of China.

A great deal of money was made in the China trade and many a Yankee sailor, who had shipped first at seventeen and risen to be mate and captain, was able to retire to a home ashore with a snug fortune by the time he was thirty. The seamen were an able lot, in general superior to the crews of the navy; they were not impressed into service, but followed the ocean because of their liking for it.

It was thought a good joke in Boston when Frederic Tudor in 1805 proposed to ship ice to the West Indies from his father's pond in Saugus. People said the ice would melt and swamp any ship that was filled with such a cargo. Tudor made experiments and hit on packing the ice in white pine sawdust. Then he sent one hundred and thirty tons of ice to Martinique in a brig.

The cargo reached port, but there was no demand for it, and Tudor had to set to work to educate the people of the tropics to the use of ice. He kept at it, built ice-houses in several ports, borrowed from time to time as much as $280,000 to carry on his plans, and at length, after the War of 1812, secured from the English government a monopoly of the ice trade with Jamaica. Next he obtained exclusive rights in Cuba, and other American merchants began to take note of Tudor's ice commerce. Between 1817 and 1820 he extended his profitable business to Charleston, Savannah and New Orleans.

Then some merchants of Calcutta asked for a consignment of ice, and Tudor sent them a cargo of one hundred and eighty tons in the ship *Tuscany*. He wrote to his ship's captain: "As soon as you have arrived in latitude 12° north you will have carried ice as far south as it has ever been carried before, and your Ship becomes a discovery ship and as such I feel confident you will do everything for the eventual success of the undertaking; as being in charge of the first ship that has ever carried ice to the East Indies."

The *Tuscany* landed the cargo safely, and soon the Anglo-Indian residents of Calcutta were enjoying iced beverages and calling for more shipments of this product of New England.

In fourteen years Tudor had paid off his debts and was making a fortune from a trade which later circled the world.

In his diary this pioneer American merchant says of his early ventures: "I found myself without money and without friends, and with only a cargo of ice in the torrid zone to depend on for the supply of both." When he had succeeded he made this entry: "Thus is the winter of my discontent made glorious summer. . . . Drink, Spaniard, and be cool, that I who have suffered so much in the cause may be able to go home and keep myself warm."

CHAPTER XVI
BUCCANEERS OF THE
ATLANTIC COAST

XVI

BUCCANEERS OF THE ATLANTIC COAST

THE buccaneers were heroes or villains, according to the point of view of the nation they helped or injured. The Spaniards looked on Sir John Hawkins and Sir Francis Drake as piratical rascals, and well they might; to the English, however, they were magnificent adventurers, and with equally good reason. If sailors plundered the enemy their lawlessness was praiseworthy; if they robbed one's own people they were villains.

The wealth of the Spanish West Indies and the Spanish Main attracted the buccaneers as the rich ships of the Mediterranean attracted the Barbary corsairs. The English colonies in North America were for some time after their settlement too poor to be worth plundering, so the pirates confined their attention to the Spanish ports. King Charles II of England, who had at one time "heard of the harbouring of pyrates and ordered such persons brought to justice," later conferred knighthood on Morgan, the chief of the buccaneers, and made him Governor of Jamaica; and in the streets of the English colonial towns many a pirate swaggered, welcomed by the citizens because he had doubloons to squander that had come from Spanish galleons. The goods the buccaneers brought in they sold at low prices to colonial merchants, and many a fortune was based on articles smuggled in under the eyes of officers who took a share of the loot.

More than that, many reputable merchants actually took a hand in buccaneering ventures. A company of twenty-two merchants of New York fitted out a ship for John Hoar, an Irish buccaneer. Governor Fletcher granted him a commission as a privateersman, and Hoar sailed in 1695. The next year the company sent out the ship *Fortune* to Madagascar with "goods suitable for pirates," and this vessel supplied Hoar with provisions in exchange for the booty he had seized on the sea.

A privateer was a private armed ship, not attached to the navy, but licensed to prey on the enemy, and "letters of marque" were permits issued to trading vessels which authorized them to capture enemy ships they met on their voyages. The step from being a privateersman to being a pirate was a short one and "letters of marque" covered many a crime committed on the ocean. In the waters of New England a buccaneer named Dixey Bull plundered fishermen and traders as early as 1623, and in the first years of the eighteenth century it was estimated that there were fifteen hundred pirates on the Atlantic coast.

In general the buccaneers plied their trade between Cape Fear in North Carolina and the island of New Providence in the Bahamas. The little island of Tortuga off the northwest coast of Hispaniola in early days was their favorite resort and at one time there were no less than twenty pirate ships at anchor there. Later St. Kitts and Jamaica were added to Tortuga as bases, whence buccaneers sailed out to lie in wait for any ship, now English as well as Spanish, that promised suitable plunder.

The buccaneers preferred fast and seaworthy vessels, but they made use of all kinds that came to their hands. Sometimes they sailed a large ship with three masts, sometimes a two-masted sloop, or it might be they ventured forth in a bark with a single mast or in a piragua, which was a small open boat with one lateen sail. Usually their vessels had many cannon. Morgan's ship on his voyage to Panama carried twenty-two large guns and six small ones of brass. De Lussan sailed in a pirate fleet that had for its flagship a frigate of thirty-six guns.

They called themselves Brethren of the Coast. Frequently they flew the flag of their nation, but some buccaneers had their own flags. Cook flew a red flag with yellow stripes and a hand and sword, and Sharp a red flag with a cluster of green and white ribbons. In the eighteenth century the pirate ships were generally low rakish-looking schooners that carried at their mast-head the flag called the Jolly Roger.

Among the buccaneers Captain Kidd was one of the most celebrated, and he is often described as the very pattern of a pirate, although he was probably not as black as he was painted and was scarcely more unscrupulous than the hypocritical merchants and royal officers who profited by his unlawful deeds. He seems to have been at first a successful privateersman, and had many backers and friends among the gentry of New York, one of whom, Colonel Robert Livingston, recommended him to the English government "as a bold and honest man to suppress the prevailing piracies in the American seas." In August, 1691, he brought in a prize ship to New York, and paid the King his tenth share of the prize and the Governor his fifteenth, which shows that he was regarded as an honorable servant of the crown. Through the influence of Colonel Livingston he secured command of the English ship *Adventure* in 1695 and cruised in her to Madeira, Madagascar and the Red Sea. This was a piratical voyage and he captured a number of ships, one of which, the *Quedah Merchant,* of four hundred tons, he brought to the West Indies. His seizure of lawful trading vessels, however, raised a great outcry in England and the colonies, and when he returned to his headquarters at Gardiner's Island near New York he found himself denounced as an outlaw. Lord Bellomont, the royal Governor, who had been glad to share in some of Kidd's prize-money, offered him a safe-conduct to come ashore; but once in the Governor's grasp Kidd was arrested and sent to England for trial as a pirate and there executed.

Kidd was supposed to have hidden treasure at various places along the Atlantic coast; whether he did this or not he certainly slipped valuable loot into the pockets of men in high places who befriended him as long as it was to their advantage to do so and who did not hesitate to betray him when that served their interest.

For a picture of a thorough-going pirate one should turn to Edward Teach, who was known as Blackbeard. He was a native of Bristol, England, and began his career on the sea as a privateersman against the French in the West Indies. The first ship he sailed as a pirate was the *Queen Anne's Revenge,* of forty guns. In this, and in many other vessels, he plundered the shipping of all countries and raided the Atlantic coast.

Teach took his name from his long black beard, which he wore plaited in two braids. He dressed in silk and velvet and great silver-buckled shoes. He carried a dirk and cutlass and a brace of pistols in his belt and in a sling about his neck and chest were thrust six extra pistols. Often a flaming slow-match hung over each of his ears, and when he was thus accoutered and bristling with arms he must have made an extraordinary appearance.

One day in 1718 Blackbeard's ship, flying his black flag, arrived off Charles Town in South Carolina. A long-boat pulled ashore and a message from the pirate captain was presented to Governor Johnson. Blackbeard stated that his crew was in need of medicines and declared that unless the drugs he listed were immediately sent out in his boat he would present to the city the heads of Samuel Wragg, a prominent merchant, and of several other citizens whom he had recently captured in a ship sailing for England.

The Governor was furious at the pirate's audacity, but the friends and families of the prisoners insisted that the medicines should be sent. When the drugs reached Blackbeard he robbed his captives of their possessions and set them ashore. Chuckling over his exploit, the pirate sailed away. But Johnson and the people of Charles Town were now thoroughly aroused, and in a few days Colonel Rhett, with the sloops *Henry* and *Sea Nymph,* fitted with eight guns and carrying about seventy men each, set out to catch the buccaneer.

Colonel Rhett heard that the pirate was near Cape Fear and sailed in that direction. Reaching there, the crews of the sloops saw the pirate ship lying up the Cape Fear River, well shielded from attack. Early the next morning the buccaneer's big vessel, the *Royal James,* came speeding down the river, her guns cleared for action, evidently intending to fight her way past the sloops to the open sea.

Rhett brought his ships in close and drove his opponent out of the channel so that she became grounded on a sand shoal. The sloops also ran aground, the *Henry* close to the *Royal James* and the *Sea Nymph* farther downstream.

It was ebb-tide and none of the ships could expect to change position for some hours; the hull of the pirate ship was turned towards the *Henry*, and the latter's deck was fully exposed to the enemy's fire.

Colonel Rhett undauntedly opened fire and the pirate answered with a broadside, which swept the *Henry's* deck. The buccaneers had all the advantage, and seeing the deadly effect of their cannonade they called to the South Carolinians to surrender. The latter refused and kept up the fight for five hours, when the tide turned and the *Henry* floated off from the shoal. Bringing his ship about, Rhett made ready to grapple with the *Royal James* and board her. The pirate crew, however, seeing that the *Sea Nymph* had also now floated free and was coming to the aid of her consort, mutinied against their captain, who would have fought to the last, made him a prisoner, and surrendered their ship.

Then, to his great surprise, Colonel Rhett discovered that he had not captured Blackbeard, but another pirate captain, Steve Bonnet. With this buccaneer and his crew in irons and with the *Royal James* Rhett returned to Charles Town in triumph.

From the town Steve Bonnet contrived to escape in woman's dress with one of his men in a small boat. It was supposed that he planned to join the ships of another pirate, believed to be Moody, who had been seen off the harbor with a large ship of fifty guns and two others captured by him on their way south from New England. To capture these

vessels four ships were made ready in Charles
Town, one of which was the *Royal James,* and three
hundred men volunteered for service. Then word
came that Bonnet had not reached Moody but was
hiding on Sullivan's Island. A search party was
sent out and brought Steve Bonnet back to Charles
Town.

The pirate ships had been seen at anchor inside
the bar of the harbor, and Governor Johnson sailed
his fleet at night to a fort near them. Early in the
morning the Charles Town vessels sailed across the
bar, with their guns concealed. The pirate, supposing that the ships were peaceful merchantmen,
let them sail by, then, closing in behind them, ran
up the Jolly Roger and called on them to surrender.
Johnson, who had now succeeded in getting the
buccaneers between his fleet and the town, hoisted
the royal ensign, threw open his ports, and fired a
broadside. The pirate at once headed for the open
sea and managed to reach it. Johnson, following
the rover chieftain, signaled the *Royal James* and
the *Sea Nymph* to attack the second enemy ship.

These two came up with the enemy and the ships
fought yard-arm to yard-arm. The pirates were
driven from their guns and the South Carolinians
boarded the enemy vessel and captured it in hand-
to-hand fighting. Meantime Johnson was pursuing
the first ship; a stern chase is a long one, but the
Governor's vessel was faster than the pirates', and
though the crew of the latter threw overboard boats

and cannon to lighten their ship, the buccaneers' vessel was overhauled and taken.

When the hatches of the pirate ship were lifted thirty-six women were found in the hold. The ship was the *Eagle,* which had been carrying indentured servants from England to Virginia. The buccaneers had seized her and kept her, passengers and all. Again a mistake had been made in the identity of the pirate commander; he was not Moody but Richard Worley, and he had been killed in the fighting aboard the smaller of the two ships.

Blackbeard escaped the men of South Carolina, but soon after he had sailed from Charles Town with the medicines for his crew he was caught up with by two small ships from Virginia under command of Lieutenant Maynard. Maynard's men boarded the pirate's vessel and the Lieutenant fought and killed Blackbeard, not, however, until the buccaneer had received twenty sword-cuts and as many pistol wounds.

The day of the pirates' reckoning shortly arrived; an English fleet scoured the seas for them, seized their headquarters at New Providence and swept them from the West Indies.

CHAPTER XVII

THE *VICTORY:* A SHIP-OF-THE-LINE

XVII

THE *VICTORY*: A SHIP-OF-THE-LINE

THE *Victory*, famous as the flagship of Lord Nelson at the Battle of Trafalgar, was typical of the warship that had succeeded the galley, a vessel designed to carry as many cannon as possible and by dispensing with rowers to use all the deckroom for mounting guns. She was what was known as a line-of-battle ship or a ship-of-the-line; with three masts, spreading square sails, and with high sides that gave her a bulging, clumsy appearance. The lofty forecastle and sterncastle that had given a majestic, although somewhat top-heavy, appearance to war-galleys of the earlier era were absent from this type of ship; the term "forecastle" was used only for a part of the bow, and the sterncastle had become a raised deck at the stern of the ship and was called the quarter-deck. The stern was the most elaborately ornamented part of the vessel, and was something like a house with many windows, overlaid with scrollwork.

Such a ship had about seven hundred men in her crew, who slept in hammocks lashed to hooks between decks. The *Victory* carried one hundred guns on her three gun-decks, muzzle loaders, mounted on wooden carriages set on wheels. These cannon were tightly secured in their places,—for if one should break loose in a pitching sea it might do great damage,—and each had its muzzle protruding through an open port. Ammunition was piled beside it and each cannon had its own gun-crew.

In battle, fleets of such ships approached each other slowly, strung out in single file, crews on the gun-decks, officers on the quarter-deck, sharpshooters with muskets in the mast-tops ready to take aim at men on the enemy's decks. As though engaged in a stately processional the lines of ships would advance towards each other until the flagship gave the signal to fire. Then the guns would roar their opening broadsides and shots go crashing into the opponent's bulwarks. Still closer they would draw through the clouds of smoke; each ship would come alongside one of the enemy, grappling-irons would be thrown out, and the fleets would be fighting duels in pairs, the rigging of the ships entangled and their spars caught. Then the crews would engage each other with pistol and cutlass on their own or their opponent's decks.

Napoleon, Emperor of the French, was planning to invade England, and had prepared a strong French fleet, which was augmented by many Spanish vessels. England, depending on her sea-power for her safety, had a splendid navy which blocked the attempt of the French Admiral Villeneuve to enter the English Channel in the summer of 1805. Baffled there, the French fleet steered for Cadiz and anchored in that port. Outside the harbor of Cadiz there were English ships-of-the-line under Admiral Collingwood on watch for the vessels of the allied fleets of France and Spain, and these English ships were shortly reinforced by many more.

On September 14, 1805 Napoleon sent orders that the allied ships at Cadiz should put to sea at the first favorable opportunity, join seven Spanish ships at Cartagena, go to Naples, and land the soldiers they had on board to reinforce his troops there. If they met an English fleet of inferior numbers they were to fight a decisive action. On its part the English government was determined to confine the allied fleets at Cadiz or defeat them if they came out, and for that purpose sent Horatio Nelson, Viscount Nelson of England and Duke of Bronté of Naples, the victor of the Battle of the Nile, to take command.

Nelson arrived off Cadiz on September twenty-eighth, bringing with him three ships-of-the-line. In all he had twenty-seven vessels of this type at his disposal. On the fifth of October the French Admiral Villeneuve held a council of his French and Spanish officers, and they agreed that, although the condition of their ships did not justify them in expecting a victory over the English, Napoleon's orders were too peremptory to be disobeyed and they must make a sortie.

Easterly winds were needed to get the allied fleets out of Cadiz, and until October fourteenth the wind blew steadily from the west. Then, on the eight-

eenth, Villeneuve learned that Napoleon, impatient
at his admiral's lack of vigorous action, had replaced him in command by Admiral Rosily and that
Rosily was at Madrid on his way to Cadiz. Stung
by the thought of being disgraced before the men of
his fleet, Villeneuve determined to put out to sea
before his successor could arrive.

That day Nelson wrote in his diary: "Fine
weather, wind easterly; the combined fleets cannot
have finer weather to put out to sea." The next
morning, October nineteenth, at half-past nine the
signal sent from the frigates near shore and relayed
from ship to ship until it reached Nelson fifty miles
from land announced the tidings for which every
English captain and sailor was eagerly waiting—
the word that "The enemy are coming out of port."

The allied fleets were composed of thirty-three
ships-of-the-line, eighteen of which were French and
fifteen Spanish, accompanied by five French frigates
and two French brigs. The two fleets were under
one command, that of Admiral Villeneuve, from
whom the Spanish Admiral Gravina took his orders
either for cruising or battle. Of the allied ships
four were three-decked vessels, of from one hundred
to one hundred and thirty guns, all four of them being Spanish, and one, the *Santísima Trinidad*, the
largest ship then afloat. Of Nelson's twenty-seven
ships seven were three-deckers of ninety-eight to one
hundred guns, and he had one eighty-gun ship against
six of that size with the allies.

A fleet of thirty-three ships-of-the-line could not be easily handled, particularly when leaving port, and although the movement out from Cadiz began soon after daylight on the nineteenth it was not finished that day. Only twelve ships stood clear of the bay when the wind lessened and they were becalmed outside. Next day the rest set sail and by early afternoon the allied fleets were united and heading to the northward and westward, planning to gain room to windward for entering the Strait of Gibraltar.

Nelson's intention was to cut the enemy off from the Mediterranean, through which they wished to sail to Naples, in accord with Napoleon's orders. Therefore, as soon as he learned that Villeneuve was leaving Cadiz, the English Admiral hoisted signal for a general pursuit to the southeast, towards Cape Spartel.

The twentieth of October was ushered in by heavy winds from the southwest. At dawn the British fleet was between Cape Trafalgar and Cape Spartel, near the mouth of the Strait of Gibraltar. The thick weather made it impossible to see any distance, but the English were confident that the allies could not yet have reached that position. At seven in the morning the frigate *Phoebe* signaled Nelson that the enemy were bearing to the north, so the British ships wore and took that course, parallel to the allies, and sent out lookouts. Shortly after noon the weather cleared and Sir Henry Blackwood, in command of the British frigates, saw the allied fleets close to his ship. Giving the command to a junior captain, Blackwood sailed his own ship to speak to the Admiral, and sent Nelson the message, "The enemy appears determined to push to the westward."

Nelson wrote in his diary: "That they shall *not* do, if in the power of Nelson and Bronté to prevent them." He signaled to Blackwood, "I rely upon your keeping sight of the enemy."

The English Admiral was much of the time that day on his flagship's poop, and, on one occasion, coming to a group of midshipmen, he said, "This day or to-morrow will be a fortunate one for you, young gentlemen." At dinner he remarked to some of his officers, "To-morrow I will do that which will give you younger gentlemen something to talk and think about for the rest of your lives, but I shall not live to know about it myself." He added that he expected to capture a score of the enemy's fleet.

The main bodies of the opposing forces did not come in view of each other on October twentieth. The allies were now heading in a favoring wind to the southward, making for the mouth of the Strait of Gibraltar. At midnight the two fleets were ten miles apart.

At daybreak on the twenty-first the British ships were pointed to the northward, the allies still to the south. Far out on the eastern sea-line rose the height of Cape Gibraltar. Shortly before seven in the morning Nelson gave his signals: "To form the order for sailing"; then "To prepare for battle."

The *Victory* altered her course, heading for the enemy. Admiral Collingwood, in charge of the second division of the British fleet, did likewise, and the other ships fell into line behind their leaders. Twelve ships were in the column in the wake of the *Victory* and fourteen followed the *Royal Sovereign,* Collingwood's flagship; the two columns kept about a mile apart.

Villeneuve now saw that the English meant to engage him, and wishing to keep Cadiz, some twenty miles to the northeast, under his lee, he signaled the allied ships to wear together. The allied fleets now headed north and the Spanish Admiral Gravina, who had been leading the column, became commander of the rear-guard.

The French Admiral had recognized the fact that the British fleet, incomparably more expert than his own, would not be satisfied to attack in the old-fashioned manner by coming down in a parallel line and engaging from van to rear; he knew they would try to concentrate their fire on a part of his flotilla. His own officers and men, however, were too inexperienced to make it possible to counter the enemy's movements; therefore he ordered his ships to form the line and left the individual captains free to act as each thought best when the battle began.

A very light breeze was then blowing, and though Villeneuve gave his orders at six in the morning the rearrangement of his squadrons was not executed until about ten o'clock. Then no accurate line was formed; the allied fleets took their position in a curve some five miles in length, the ships not following one another, but in many groups of two and some of three abreast.

Meanwhile aboard the *Victory* all was ready for battle. Nelson had come on deck, and was watching his fleet move forward. His main concern was to keep the enemy from reaching Cadiz and therefore he wasted no time in forming regular columns. Each ship had all sails set and the place of each was determined by her speed or by the position she had taken when the movement began. The aim was to get the heads of the columns into action as quickly as possible so as to break up the enemy's order.

Collingwood's ship, the *Royal Sovereign,* easily held the lead in one division, followed by the *Belleisle;* and the *Victory* in the other division. Captain Blackwood, who had come aboard the flagship and who recognized the exposed position of the leader, urged Nelson to allow one or two other ships to precede the *Victory.* "Let them go," was the Admiral's answer, but he gave no orders to slacken speed to permit them to pass him. And later, when the *Téméraire,* an English three-decker, in attempting to get ahead of the *Victory* pushed her bows to the flagship's quarter, Nelson called out to her commander, "I'll thank you, Captain Harvey, to keep in your proper station, which is astern of the *Victory.*"

Presently the Admiral turned to Blackwood, who

was standing with him on the poop, and said, "I will now amuse the fleet with a signal." He asked if Blackwood did not think a signal was wanting, to which the latter replied that he thought the whole fleet understood very clearly what they were to do.

Nelson considered a few minutes, as if searching for the right message; then said, "Suppose we signal 'Nelson confides that every man will do his duty.'" The officer to whom he was speaking suggested that he replace "Nelson" with "England." The Admiral was delighted with the change and called to the signal officer, "Mr. Pasco, I wish to say to the fleet 'England confides that every man will do his duty.'" Then he added, "You must be quick, for I have one more to make, which is for close action."

Pasco answered, "If your Lordship will permit me to substitute 'expects' for 'confides,' it will be sooner completed, because 'expects' is in the vocabulary, and 'confides' must be spelt."

"That will do, Pasco; make it directly," ordered Nelson.

So the famous line "England expects that every man will do his duty!" was signaled to the fleet.

The two English squadrons were heading to the north of east, Collingwood to the right and leeward, Nelson to the north and windward. Collingwood's ship, the *Royal Sovereign,* was steering for the *Santa Ana,* when, just at noon, the French ship *Fougueux,* the second astern of the *Santa Ana,* fired the first gun of the battle. Immediately all the ships hoisted their colors and the admirals their flags. As the *Royal Sovereign* sailed on, not yet answering the enemy's fire, Nelson exclaimed to his officers, "See how that noble fellow Collingwood carries his ship into action!" And Collingwood said to his flag-captain, "Rotherham, what would Nelson give to be here!"

Nelson, turning to Blackwood, remarked, "Now I can do no more. We must trust to the great Disposer of all events, and to the justice of our cause. I thank God for this great opportunity of doing my duty." He then gave the order for close action.

The *Victory* was two miles away from the *Royal Sovereign* when the latter broke through the enemy's line and had to sail a mile and a half to reach the allied fleets. Then Villeneuve's flagship, the *Bucentaure,* fired a shot at her, to try the range; it fell short, but soon other shots passed over the *Victory.* Now that she was in reach seven or eight ships near the *Bucentaure* opened fire on Nelson's flagship, for Villeneuve wished to prevent her gaining a position from which she could use her broadsides. For forty minutes, while she sailed on, the *Victory* was an unresisting target for her enemies, her sails were riddled with shot and a number of her officers and men fell. Still she kept her headway, making for the enemy's flagship while the allied vessels crowded around her. The mizzen-topmast was shot away, and a shot reached the quarter-deck where Nelson and Captain Hardy were standing. "This is too

warm work, Hardy, to last long," said the Admiral.
He gave high praise to his crew, and they deserved it,
for twenty men had been killed and thirty wounded,
and not a single shot as yet had been fired from the
Victory's guns.

Nelson's objective was still Villeneuve's flagship,
but to engage the *Bucentaure* effectively the *Victory*
required room to turn under her opponent's stern
and come up alongside her. As the *Victory* drew
near the *Bucentaure* Captain Hardy, seeing three
ships crowded behind the allied flagship, reported
to Nelson that he could sail close under her stern
but could not round-to nor pass through the line without running on board one of these three ships. Nelson said, "I cannot help it, it does not signify which
we run on board of. Go on board which you please:
take your choice."

The *Victory's* bows soon crossed the wake of the
Bucentaure and the English ship passed within thirty
feet of her enemy's stern, her long yardarms strik-
ing the French rigging. Then as each gun came
to bear the English crews fired; shots tore through
the *Bucentaure's* woodwork and the thick smoke,
driving back, filled the *Victory's* own decks.

The cannonade swept Villeneuve's flagship from
bow to stern; that first fire wrecked twenty French
guns and killed or wounded four hundred of the
Bucentaure's crew. Then, leaving the following
ships of the division to deal with the flagship, the
Victory ran on board the *Redoubtable,* a French

seventy-four, whose cannon had been blazing at her.

These two ships, drifting before the wind, engaged in a mighty duel. The *Victory* had many more guns, but the *Redoubtable* had a great advantage in small-arm fire on the upper deck and in her mast-tops, where many musketeers were placed.

Nelson did not favor the use of men in the tops because of the danger of fire, but in that fight the French sharpshooters aloft did tremendous damage. It was now the work of the two crews to use their weapons at short range; meantime the English Admiral and Captain Hardy paced the quarter-deck on the side away from the *Redoubtable*. Above them was the enemy's mizzen-top, filled with musketeers. Nelson, in his Admiral's uniform, with the stars of four decorations sewn on his breast, furnished a conspicuous target. A bullet struck him, and he fell to the deck, exclaiming to Hardy, "They have done for me at last."

All around him men were falling from the fire in the French tops. There were so few on the *Victory's* upper deck that the enemy tried to board, but were speedily driven back. Nelson was carried below. Meantime the ships that had followed the two English leaders had broken into the allied order and were obeying the directions Nelson had given in advance of the battle.

On the ships at the heads of the columns had fallen the brunt of the fighting, for they had dashed impetuously on the swarm of enemy vessels that blocked

the way. On the *Victory* and the *Téméraire* in one
division and the *Royal Sovereign* and the *Belleisle*
in the other was sustained one-third of the whole loss
in the English fleet. They won through, however,
broke the enemy line and opened the way for their
followers, who attacked a disordered foe, that was
now tardily reinforced by the van of their fleet which
had so far been out of action.

Before the onslaught of the English columns the
allied ships fled or surrendered. Villeneuve's flagship was captured and the Spanish Admiral Gravina assumed command of the allied fleets. Of the
five allied ships that came up late one was cut off
and taken by the English *Minotaur* and *Spartiate*,
the other four sailed southwest to sea. Gravina, seeing the field lost, shortly before five o'clock in the
afternoon retreated towards Cadiz, signaling all his
ships that still flew their flags to follow him. Eleven
ships-of-the-line, six Spanish and five French, got
safely into port at Cadiz.

To quote an English officer who was on the *Belleisle:* "Before sunset all firing had ceased. The
view of the fleet at this period was highly interesting, and would have formed a beautiful subject for
a painter. Just under the setting rays were five
or six dismantled prizes; on one hand lay the *Victory* with part of our fleet and prizes, and on the left
hand the *Royal Sovereign* and a similar cluster of
ships. To the northward, the remnant of the combined fleets was making for Cadiz. The *Achille*,

with the tricolored ensign still displayed, had burnt
to the water's edge about a mile from us, and our
tenders and boats were using every effort to save
the brave fellows who had so gloriously defended
her; but only two hundred and fifty were rescued,
and she blew up with a tremendous explosion.''

Eighteen of the French and Spanish ships were
taken, and that sea-fight of October 21, 1805,—known
as the Battle of Trafalgar, from the cape near Gibraltar,—established beyond question England's supremacy on the ocean.

Nelson died on board the *Victory* before the firing ceased. The great work he had done for his
country was completed and his name was enshrined
forever among England's heroes.

CHAPTER XVIII
THE NORTH ATLANTIC PACKETS

THE NORTH ATLANTIC PACKETS

IN the reign of Queen Elizabeth there was begun by the English government a post-office service for foreign letters that was much used by the merchants; sailing ships were employed for this purpose and there were post-office packet stations at Dover for letters to be sent to France, at Harwich and Yarmouth for Holland and Hamburg, and at Holyhead and Milford for Ireland. Falmouth, which was situated at the western end of the English Channel and which had a fine harbor, became the main port for the foreign packet service, and especially for the transportation of mails and passengers to Spain and the West Indies. By 1702 Falmouth packets, which were usually of about two hundred tons and were well armed, were sailing regularly to Barbadoes, Jamaica, the southern ports of North America, and to Corunna in Spain, and by 1704 also to Lisbon. These ships were not owned by the post-office, but were hired by private contract, although the officers and sailors were post-office servants. Like the East Indiamen and all the merchant ships of that era the packets frequently had to fight enemy warships.

These ships, in spite of the many difficulties they

encountered, maintained an excellent service.   There was a rule that the packet should put to sea from Falmouth as soon as the mails were received on board, no matter what the weather or wind might be, provided the ship could carry a double-reefed topsail. Sixteen packets were employed regularly in 1798 in the run between Falmouth and the West Indies; and captains and sailors added to their wages by taking out secretly consignments of potatoes, cheese, boots, shoes and other goods to sell for English merchants and by smuggling into England on their return trips wines, brandy, lace and tobacco.

In 1808 Falmouth boasted thirty-nine packets, one sailed each week for Lisbon, one for a Spanish port, one for the West Indies, and at less frequent intervals others for the Mediterranean, Brazil, Halifax, and New York. Passengers were carried as well as letters, and the Falmouth ships conveyed between various ports from two thousand to three thousand passengers a year.

This business became very profitable, and in 1816 there was started the first regular service between Liverpool and New York by the famous Black Ball Line of New York packets, which consisted of four ships of about four hundred tons each, the *Amity, Courier, Pacific,* and *James Monroe.* These were full-rigged ships, and were distinguished from other vessels by a large black ball on the foretopsail. They averaged twenty-three days on the run from New York to Liverpool and forty days on the westward course, the difference being due to the prevailing winds of the route they took across the North Atlantic, which were from the southwest, and to the Gulf Stream, which aided them on the eastward run.

These Black Ball liners were commanded by captains who had sailed American privateers in the War of 1812. They carried passengers, mails and bullion. Between the foremast and the mainmast was the galley, and in the long-boat lashed amidships was a collection of sheep, pigs, geese and chickens to provide food for the ship's company. In a small house on the main hatch there would be a cow or two to furnish milk. The passengers' cabins were aft and were lighted by candles and whale-oil lamps.

The Black Ball Line soon had rivals; packets ran from New York to London and to Havre as well as to Liverpool. There were the Red Star, the Swallowtail and the Dramatic Lines, Cope's and Girard's ships from Philadelphia, and Enoch Train's from Boston. With the opening of the Erie Canal in 1825, which gave access to the Great Lakes, the New York shipping business boomed. Larger ships were built, and by 1836 there were many packets of one thousand tons.

The Dramatic Line ships had a diagonal cross reaching almost from corner to corner of the foretopsail, and the *Dreadnought* of the Red Cross Line carried an upright red cross on her canvas. The packet ships were mostly American owned and man-

aged, but there were few American-born sailors in
the crews; they were usually English, and frequently
of the class known as "Liverpool Irishmen," a rough
type, often jail-birds, who went by the pleasing name
of "packet rats."

The captains and mates, however, were able dis-
ciplinarians and kept the crews in order. The ships
sailed on schedule and made their twelve knots pretty
regularly, even through fog or storm, ice or snow.
Carrying plenty of sail, they often raced each other
for considerable wagers, and not infrequently made
the voyage to England in sixteen days.

One of the best known of the packet captains was
Samuel Samuels of the *Dreadnought,* who related
many of his adventures in the book "From the Forecastle to the Cabin." The *Dreadnought* was built
at Newburyport, Massachusetts, for the Red Cross
Line, which was owned and managed by a number of
New York merchants. She was of 1413 tons, and
sailed on her first voyage to Liverpool in December,
1853. She had been built specially for Captain Samuels and under his command she made in 1859 the
fastest run ever accomplished by a sailing packet,
thirteen days and eight hours. Her record voyage
from Liverpool to New York was nineteen days.

In his book Captain Samuels says: "On our first
voyage outward bound, we crossed Sandy Hook bar
with the then crack packet ship *Washington,* Captain Page. We landed in Liverpool, and took on
a cargo and two hundred immigrants, and met her

off the northwest lightship bound in as we were running out. On our way home we crossed the bar the day after the steamer *Canada* sailed for Boston, and when the news of her arrival reached New York, we were reported off the Highlands."

Captain Samuels writes of the crews: "The Liverpool packet sailors were not easily demoralized. They were the toughest class of men in all respects. They could stand the worst weather, food, and usage, and put up with less sleep, more rum, and harder knocks than any other sailors. They would not sail in any other trade. They had not the slightest idea of morality or honesty, and gratitude was not in them. The dread of the belaying pin and heaver kept them in subjection."

Oftentimes a captain had his hands full in controlling such crews, who would not stab and rob a veteran "packet rat," but did not hesitate to plunder a green sailor. Captain Samuels had his men searched for loot of this kind whenever his ship entered port. On a voyage in 1859 he shipped a crew that belonged to a gang known as the "Bloody Forties." A mate searched the forecastle and took the weapons from the crew, but a few days afterwards the men mutinied and refused to work unless one of their gang who had been put in irons for insolence to the captain was released. The officers and cabin-boys sailed the ship for several days until the commander with the help of some of the passengers beat the mutineers and starved them into obedience.

This ship, writes Captain Samuels, "was never passed in anything over a four-knot breeze. She was what might be termed a semi-clipper, and possessed the merit of being able to stand driving as long as her sails and spars would stand. By the sailors she was nicknamed the 'Wild Boat of the Atlantic,' while others called her the 'Flying Dutchman.' Twice she carried the latest news to Europe, slipping in between the steamers. The Collins, Cunard, and Inman Lines were the only ones at that time. There are merchants still (in 1887) doing business in New York who shipped goods by us which we guaranteed to deliver within a certain time or forfeit freight charges. For this guarantee we commanded freight rates midway between those of the steamers and those of the sailing packets."

The sailing packets carried the great stream of immigration from Europe to the United States. If the accommodations of the cabin passengers were meagre, those of the immigrants were immensely worse; these travelers were crowded into the steerage and had to provide and cook their own food, in storms the hatches were battened down, and if the voyage was a long one and many were seasick the immigrants were likely to starve.

On the larger packets the cabin passengers fared fairly well; they usually had fresh food, and their cabins, which were aft under a companion, were airy, trim and comfortable. The ships were well built and kept comparatively dry. They were smart looking vessels; the hulls were painted black, with the ports outlined in white, and the inside wood-work, which in the early packets was generally green, in later ships was yellow, gray and red.

Ralph Waldo Emerson made a passage on the packet ship *Washington Irving,* of seven hundred and fifty tons, in 1847. He wrote of the voyage: "Our good master keeps his kites up to the last moment, studding sails alow and aloft, and by incessant straight steering never loses a rod of the way. . . . Since the ship was built, it seems, the master never slept but in his day-clothes whilst on board. . . ."

Again he writes: "I find the sea-life an acquired taste, like that for tomatoes and olives. The confinement, cold, motion, noise and odour are not to be dispensed with. The floor of your room is sloped at an angle of twenty or thirty degrees, and I waked every morning with the belief that someone was tipping up my berth. Nobody likes being treated ignominiously, upset, shoved against the sides of the house, rolled over, suffocated with bilge, mephitis and stewing oil. We get used to these annoyances at last, but the dread of the sea remains longer. . . . Such discomfort and such danger as the narratives of the captain and mate disclose are bad enough as the costly fee we pay for entrance to Europe; but the wonder is always new that any sane man can be a sailor."

Yet the American sailing packet was famous, and found no English rivals. Charles Dickens wrote from New York in 1842: "Below here, by the waterside, where the bowsprits of ships stretch across the footway and almost thrust themselves into the windows, lie the noble American vessels which have made their packet service the finest in the world."

A new driving power for ships, however, was coming into use in the nineteenth century. Robert Fulton built the *Clermont* in New York in 1807, a small ship with a steam engine, and made the run from New York to Albany, about one hundred and fifty miles, in thirty-two hours. Then the *Phœnix,* a steamer built in 1809, was driven under her own power from Hoboken to Philadelphia. Thereafter several small ships were constructed with steam engines in their hulls, and sails on their masts, and in 1818 a full-rigged ship of three hundred and eighty tons, the *Savannah,* was built in New York and was equipped with paddle-wheels turned by a steam engine of seventy-two horse-power.

The *Savannah* crossed the Atlantic in 1819 from Savannah, Georgia, to Liverpool in twenty-five days. This voyage was not accomplished entirely by steam power, for the engines ran out of fuel, a circumstance that led critics to say that steamers would have to be convoyed by sailing ships to provide fuel for the engines.

In 1820 the General Steam Navigation Company was organized in England, and five years later the steamship *Enterprise* made the voyage from England to India around the Cape of Good Hope in one hundred and three days, during which on thirty-nine days she used only her sails. In 1838 the steamship *Sirius* made her first trip across the Atlantic, though she had used all her coal by the time she reached Sandy Hook and was obliged to burn resin and spare spars to get to her dock. Before 1840 the *Great Western,* a steamer, crossed the North Atlantic in fifteen days, which was considerably better time than any sailing ship had made.

Now began rivalry between the American sailing packets and the English steam-driven ships, for the American lines found steam unprofitable and the English championed it. American ports were placarded with signs headed: "Sails vs. Steam"; and all these advertisements pointed out the great superiority of the sailing ship over the steamship. In 1840 the English Cunard Line of steamers was started with an English mail contract guaranteeing $425,000 a year, to run between Liverpool and Boston, with a stop at Halifax. The American company which had built the Dramatic Liners responded to the challenge and built four fine steamships, but one was sunk in a collision, another was never heard from after leaving Liverpool for New York, and the company soon afterwards went out of business.

Passenger service was becoming more and more important and profitable and in the Eighteen-forties a division began to be made between ships that carried passengers and those that carried freight. The sailing packet was still a more aristocratic vessel than the steamship, but as steam engines were improved the latter type of vessel proved faster and more reliable than the former and consequently more popular with ocean-travelers.

The invention of the screw propeller was a long step forward in the history of the steamship, and another was the use of iron plates in the construction of the vessel. One of the earliest ships to demonstrate the advantage of iron over wood was the *Great Britain,* of 3600 tons, built in 1843, capable of carrying two hundred and sixty passengers and more than a thousand tons of freight, divided into watertight compartments and provided with bilge keels, which served to lessen the ship's rolling.

Up to the American Civil War the sailing packet fought the steamship for passenger traffic, then steam beat sails. The Cunard Line built the *Scotia,* a 3300-ton iron steamer driven by paddle-wheels, in 1862, and she crossed the Atlantic in eight days and twenty-two hours, a voyage that completely outclassed those of the sailing ships. The *Great Eastern* was another record-maker in point of size, of 18,900 tons, and driven both by paddle-wheels and screw propeller. She had six masts that could carry sails and five funnels. She was built to carry a large number of passengers and a great cargo from England to Australia without having to stop for coal on the voyage. She did not make the trip to Australia, however, but crossed the Atlantic, and was employed from 1865 to 1873 in laying the first Atlantic cable.

Competition between the American packet lines was now succeeded by rivalry among the English steamship companies. In 1870 the White Star Line launched the *Oceanic,* which in many respects was the first of the modern Atlantic greyhounds, built with an eye to the comfort of passengers. The Cunard Line in 1881 built the *Servia,* a steamship of 7300 tons, that lowered the transatlantic record to seven days, one hour and thirty-eight minutes.

Steam had driven sails from the ocean where comfort and speed were concerned; the clipper and the sailing packet disappeared, and the Atlantic became a highway over which gigantic liners raced with thousands of passengers. But the packet played a great part in the history of ships and provided during the pioneer years of the republic an invaluable bridge between Europe and America.

CHAPTER XIX
"OLD IRONSIDES":
THE FRIGATE *CONSTITUTION*

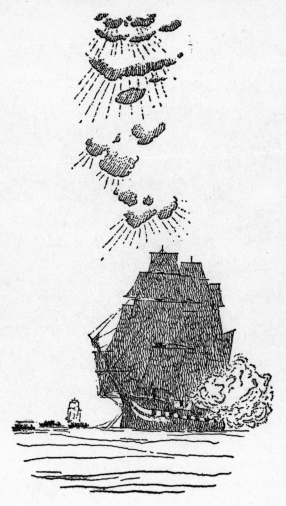

XIX

"OLD IRONSIDES": THE FRIGATE *CON-STITUTION*

OF all the ships that have ever flown the flag of the United States the frigate *Constitution,* nicknamed "Old Ironsides" because of her heavy timbers, is the most renowned. Launched at Boston in 1797, she was the largest and most heavily-armed frigate of her day and the pride of the American navy before the era of sails and wooden hulls gave place to that of steam and iron-clads.

At the end of the eighteenth century most great warships were known as line-of-battle ships. They were tremendously heavy and clumsy and capable of little speed. Their sides were high and below the main deck there were three gun-decks, each filled with cannon that fired through square ports in the vessel's side. Such a ship was the *Victory,* Lord Nelson's flagship at the battle of Trafalgar, an awkward, powerful giant constructed only for fighting, and generally engaging the enemy in fleet formation. Great was the difference between a line-of-battle ship such as the *Victory* and the new type of frigate like the *Constitution.*

The frigates were the cruisers of a century ago,

built for speed in order to enable them to prey on the enemy's commerce. Sometimes they sailed in fleets, but more frequently alone. They carried guns on the main deck and on one gun-deck below, and so needed little of the high superstructure that encumbered the earlier warships.

In planning the armament of the *Constitution* her builders improved on other frigates. She had thirty 24-pounders on her gun-deck, twenty-two 32-pound carronades on her quarter deck and forecastle deck, and in addition three long guns, called "bow chasers," to use when pursuing an enemy. With her fifty-five guns she outclassed most European frigates, which customarily carried from thirty-two to fifty guns, of lighter weight than those of the *Constitution*.

She was also built of heavier timbers than most foreign frigates. Of finer design than the line-of-battle ship, with lower sides and a lighter bow and stern, she could easily outsail the latter type of vessel while her heavy armament enabled her successfully to compete with its fire. What she could do in combat with an English frigate was a question, for the British navy had a long record of triumphs and that of the United States was practically untried.

The *Constitution*, having served as Captain Preble's flagship in the war with Tripoli in 1805, sailed from Boston on August 2, 1812, commanded by Captain Isaac Hull, who was eager to meet some of the widely-celebrated English frigates whose officers had frequently spoken derisively of "the fir-built Yankee frigates flying a piece of striped bunting at their mastheads."

North she cruised to the Bay of Fundy without meeting an enemy ship and then headed for the Gulf of St. Lawrence in hope of intercepting some English vessels bound for Quebec. Finding none in that vicinity Captain Hull stood out to sea, and on the morning of the fifteenth sighted five ships. Crowding on all sail the *Constitution* was overhauling them when, after setting fire to a brig, the strangers scattered. Hull chose the largest ship, and coming up with her found that she was an English merchant vessel in the hands of an American prize crew. As it happened, however, the *Constitution* had arrived at an opportune moment, for the prize had been about to fall into the clutches of the British ships which were now scurrying to leeward. Later that same day the *Constitution* sighted another ship, which she pursued and caught up with after a sharp chase. This proved to be the American brig *Adeline,* which had been captured by the English sloop of war *Avenger* and which was now in charge of an English prize crew. This crew surrendered to Captain Hull, who destroyed the brig and ordered the merchant vessel to proceed with its American crew and British prisoners to Boston. The *Constitution* then sailed south, with the intention of looking for enemy frigates in the waters off Bermuda.

On the night of August eighteenth a ship approached close to the *Constitution* before she was seen. When sighted, Captain Hull immediately chased the stranger, which fled away from him. After a long pursuit the *Constitution* overtook the other vessel and Hull sent an officer aboard her who learned that she was the American privateer *Decatur,* and that her captain had mistaken the *Constitution* for a British cruiser and had thrown overboard in his flight twelve of her fourteen guns in order to lighten her weight.

The commander of the *Decatur* informed Captain Hull that on the previous day he had sighted an English frigate sailing southward. In the hope of coming up with this ship Hull changed his course and at one o'clock on the next day, when he was about opposite the port of Halifax, he discovered a sail on the horizon, a ship on the starboard tack, close hauled and under easy canvas. Soon this ship was made out to be an English frigate and from her maneuvers it appeared that she was desirous of engaging the *Constitution,* for as the latter bore down the English ship shortened her topsails, foresail, jib and spanker and braced her main topsail to the mast, with the object of waiting for her opponent to come up.

When the frigates were about three miles apart Captain Hull sent down his royal yards, reefed his topsails, hauled up the courses, and ordered the *Constitution* cleared for action.

American tars, like American frigates, were not
veterans of many sea fights as were their English
rivals. But the men under Captain Hull were a
stalwart, determined crew; in their minds rankled
the memory of the arbitrary impressment of American sailors by British commanders, a practice that
had been one of the causes of the War of 1812; not
a few of them had felt the English lash on their own
backs; and some were the descendants of men who
had been in British prison ships during the Revolution. They were well disciplined, had been thoroughly drilled at the guns, and now were eager to
prove the Yankee frigate the peer of any fighting
ship on the seven seas.

About four in the afternoon the English frigate
hoisted four flags and fired a few shots at the *Constitution* to get the range. The two ships exchanged
broadsides, but the shots fell short. Then for some
time the English frigate maneuvered to obtain a rak-
ing position, but, finding that the American would
not allow that, she laid her main topsail to the mast
and ran with the wind on the quarter under topsails and jib.

Captain Hull, seeing that the enemy was willing
to engage in a yardarm fight, made sail to come
up with her. He had his colors flying, a jack at
each masthead and one at the mizzen peak. To
avoid being raked by the American guns the English frigate wore three or four times, discharging al-
ternate broadsides, which took little effect, however,

owing to the frigate's constant change of position and the resulting alteration in the level of her guns. For the same reason the fire of the *Constitution* was also ineffectual.

As these maneuvers kept the two frigates too widely separated for fighting, Captain Hull, at six o'clock, ordered the *Constitution* steered directly for the enemy and the main topgallant sail set. The English frigate then bore up gradually to almost the same course as the *Constitution,* but the latter's greater canvas allowed her to close upon her opponent's port quarter and beam, at about two hundred yards' distance, and then to approach still nearer.

The frigates were about to engage in an action at close quarters, so Hull ordered his men to cease firing and prepare to deliver their next broadside with the most telling effect. The guns were loaded with round shot and grape and the crews stood at attention. The ships were now only a short distance apart and the gun-crews could see each other distinctly through the open ports.

The English frigate continued her firing, but no command to return it came from the quarter-deck of the *Constitution*. A shot struck the American's bulwarks and sent splinters flying and wounded several men. The English crew cheered. A few moments later First Lieutenant Morris of the *Constitution* went to the quarter-deck where Captain Hull was pacing and said: "The enemy has opened fire and killed two of our men. Shall we return it?"

"Not yet, sir," was the answer.

Three times Lieutenant Morris asked if he might fire, and each time Captain Hull made the same reply, "Not yet, sir." At length, when he had gained a position about forty yards off the enemy's port quarter, Hull gave the order to fire. The *Constitution* belched forth a storm of shot from guns that were carefully aimed and discharged at short range. That first broadside ripped through the enemy's bulwarks, splintered wood in all directions and scattered the gun-crews.

Broadside now followed broadside. So rapid and so accurate was the American fire that within a few minutes the English frigate's main yard was shot away and her hull, rigging and sails badly slashed and cut. The *Constitution,* on her part, suffered no serious damage. Then a 24-pound shot crashed through the English ship's mizzenmast a few feet above the deck, and, the weight of the sails bringing it down, the mast fell over the quarter and knocked a large hole in the hull.

The wrecked mast acted like a rudder and brought the frigate up to the wind in spite of her helm. The *Constitution* turned to rake the enemy and sent in two broadsides. A moment later the jib boom of the English ship passed over the American's quarter-deck.

Now the cannonading stopped as each crew waited to see if the other would board. The English commander ordered his first lieutenant to send all the men up from the guns to the main deck; but when he saw the crew of the *Constitution* ready to repel boarders he hesitated to give the word to his men to leap to the other ship. With the crews of both frigates on deck the riflemen were now able to fire at close range and the men in the tops on both sides energetically renewed their shooting. So close by now had the two ships swung together that the English vessel's cutwater chafed against the side of the *Constitution,* her white and gold figurehead was within grasp of the American crew, and her bowsprit reached entirely across her opponent's quarter-deck and rose and fell over the heads of the Yankees with the motion of the waves.

This spar would afford the enemy an excellent means of boarding, and in order to see if they were preparing to make such an attempt Lieutenant Morris climbed up on the taffrail. From there he heard the English commander directing his crew, gathered on the forecastle, how to board the *Constitution.* Morris reported this to Captain Hull, and immediately sailors and marines were stationed on the quarter-deck, armed with pistols, muskets, cutlasses, and boarding-pikes, ready for the first Englishman who should thrust his head over the bulwarks.

Lieutenant Morris, intending to lash the two frigates together, seized a rope that dangled from the enemy's bowsprit and, climbing up by it, was taking a few turns of the main brace about that spar when a bullet from a sharpshooter in the English tops struck him and he fell to the deck.   It was now seen that the frigates would foul, and the first lieutenant of marines and another officer on the *Constitution* ran to the taffrail with their men to board the enemy. A shot from the main-top wounded an officer and the lieutenant of marines was killed as he mounted the rail.   Captain Hull leaped on an arms chest to lead the boarding-party, but was dragged back by a sailor who urged him not to climb the taffrail unless he took off the epaulets that indicated his rank.   The two ships were now so close that an American seaman, having fired his boarding pistol, and missed, threw the weapon and hit an English sailor.   The American flag at the main topgallant mast-head was shot away and a sailor climbed the rigging and lashed another flag in its place.   In each of the *Constitution's* tops were seven marines, six loading muskets while the seventh, the best marksman, did the firing, which from that height could rake the enemy's decks.

The ships were rolling so much that neither side found it practicable to board the other.   As she stood, the English frigate could not bring a single one of her broadside guns to bear on the *Constitution,* and as she was herself exposed to a heavy cannonade she was in peril of being speedily destroyed. At this crucial point, however, the ships fell somewhat apart and the English vessel, tearing her bowsprit loose from the *Constitution's* rigging, paid off a short distance and so was enabled to bring her guns into use.   Some of the burning wads from her cannon were blown into the after cabin of the *Constitution* and the ship was in danger of taking fire, but the crew put out the flames before they reached the decks or sails.

As she dropped astern the English frigate's bowsprit, hitting the *Constitution's* taffrail, slackened the forestays of the English ship, and as her fore shrouds on the port side had already been cut away the foremast now went by the starboard side, and so crossed the main stays. This wrench given the mainmast carried it along with the foremast, and the tremendous weight of masts, yards and rigging came down with a terrific crash, and left the English frigate without any masts standing.

The ship, shattered and hardly more than a hull, fell into the trough of the sea; her guns, entirely useless now, rolled in the water.

The American commander, seeing that his opponent could make no further resistance, drew off to repair the damage to his own rigging, since at any moment another British frigate or a squadron might appear and have him at a disadvantage.

About seven o'clock in the evening the *Constitution* returned and Captain Hull sent Third Lieutenant Read alongside the English ship to receive her surrender. The vessel was the 38-gun frigate *Guerrière,* commanded by Captain Dacres. When the American officer asked if the frigate had struck her colors Captain Dacres replied: "I don't know that it would be prudent to continue the engagement any longer."

"Do I understand you to say that you have struck?" demanded the American lieutenant.

Dacres hesitated; he had been one of those who had ridiculed the new American frigates and he hated to surrender to one of them. "Not precisely," he answered; "but I don't know that it will be worth while to fight any longer."

"If you cannot decide," said the Lieutenant, "I will return aboard my ship and we will resume the engagement."

"Why," cried the English captain, "I am pretty much *hors de combat* already! I have hardly men enough left to work a single gun, and my ship is in a sinking condition."

"I wish to know, sir," was the retort, "whether I am to consider you as a prisoner of war or an enemy. I have no time for further parley."

"I believe now there is no alternative," Dacres reluctantly answered. "If I could fight longer I would with pleasure; but I must surrender."

Captain Hull and Captain Dacres, like many of the American and English officers in the War of 1812, had frequently met before hostilities began between their two countries, and Dacres, according to report, had made a wager of a hat with Hull on the outcome of any engagement between their two frigates should they chance to encounter each other.

When Dacres, who had been wounded during the fighting, went up the ladder to the *Constitution's* deck to surrender his sword, Captain Hull said: "Dacres, give me your hand. I know you are hurt"; and helped him over the ship's side. Then when Dacres offered his sword Hull promptly responded: "No, no, I will not take a sword from one who knows so well how to use it; but I'll trouble you for that hat."

When he learned of the heavy casualties on the English frigate the American commander immediately sent his surgeon's mate to assist in tending the wounded.

Boats removed the prisoners from the *Guerrière* to the *Constitution* during the night, and when, early in the morning, a sail was sighted heading south Captain Hull at once cleared for action. The stranger ship stood off, however, and presently disappeared. Soon after daybreak the officers on the *Guerrière* shouted that the ship had four feet of water in the hold and was in danger of sinking. All the remaining British wounded and prisoners were then transferred to the *Constitution,* and as the *Guerrière* was too much of a wreck to be towed into port she was blown up.

The *Constitution* was twelve to fifteen feet longer than her opponent and had a trifle more beam. At the time of the battle she carried fifty-five guns and had a crew of four hundred and sixty-eight. The *Guerrière,* which had been captured from the French by the English frigate *Blanche* in 1806, had in her fight with the American ship forty-nine guns and two hundred and sixty-three to three hundred in her crew. The actual duration of the engagement had been forty minutes and the hull of the *Constitution* was scarcely touched, her injuries being mainly to the rigging, while the *Guerrière* had been rendered utterly unseaworthy and been practically demolished by the remarkable fire of the American gunners.

Until that encounter the small American navy had met with little success against England in the War of 1812. Great was the rejoicing therefore when on August thirtieth the *Constitution,* decked with bunting, appeared off Boston Lighthouse and amid the booming of cannon sailed up the harbor with news of her victory over the *Guerrière.*

That victory emboldened the American navy and gave Yankee crews confidence in their ability to meet the English on an even footing. The American-built frigate had been proven as good as any on the seas. The *Constitution* was victorious in many later engagements, but it was because "Old Ironsides" won such a signal triumph over the *Guerrière* that she became the idol of the American people and has always been given the place of honor in the American navy.

CHAPTER XX
SHIPS IN EASTERN SEAS

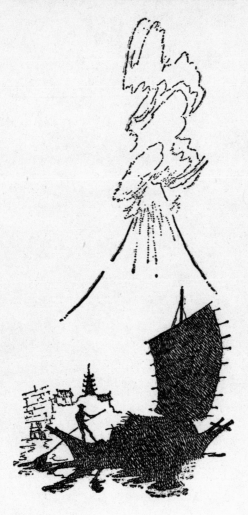

XX

SHIPS IN EASTERN SEAS

IN the legends of prehistoric Japan it is said that the mythical hero or demigod Susanoo carried with him quantities of tree seeds to be planted in the Land of the Eight Great Islands—the poetic name for Japan—which were to provide the material for "floating riches," or ships. In those times the boats of Japan, like those of so many other lands, were probably simply the hollowed-out trunks of trees and in these the fishermen poled along the shores and occasional adventurers paddled from island to island.

Later arrivals than Susanoo had more seaworthy vessels, for many invaders reached the Eight Great Islands. The names that were given these boats tell of their speed or of the material employed in their fashioning; the "bird-boat" one was called, the "pigeon-boat" another; a third was spoken of as the "rock-camphor boat."

But these Far Eastern people were not great boat-builders, as may appear from an imperial edict issued in the year 81 B.C. Therein it is stated: "Ships are of cardinal importance to the Empire. At present the people of the coast, not having ships, suffer grievously by land transport. Therefore let every province be caused to have ships built.''

A vessel called the *Karano,* one hundred feet in length, was built in the province of Izu in the year 274 A. D. and was used for twenty-six years. Then the Emperor made proclamation: ''The Government ship named *Karano* was sent as tribute by the Lord of Izu. It is rotten and unfit for use. It has, however, been in the Government use for a long time, and its services should not be forgotten. Shall we not keep the name of that ship from being lost and hand it down to after ages?''

The *Karano* was then demolished and her timbers used as firewood for roasting salt, which was given to the various provinces, each of which in return was directed to build ships for the nation; and from this there resulted a fleet of five hundred vessels.

When this fleet gathered at Hyōgo it was the wonder of Japan, for so many ships had never been seen in one place before. Unfortunately some of the vessels were destroyed almost immediately by a fire that broke out in the lodgings occupied by some envoys from Korea. The envoys were held responsible for the damage and their sovereign hastened to send a company of skillful shipbuilders to make atonement, and these organized themselves into a hereditary guild of marine architects.

Ships were frequently sent as tribute from the provinces to the Emperor or from a country in vassalage to Japan, but the people were not natural mariners, and the boats that were chiefly used were the small, sturdy craft of the fishermen, who plied their trade close ashore.

By the sixteenth century, however, the Japanese, impelled by the desire for commerce, had reached a high point in the art of shipbuilding, to judge from their pictures. These representations show vessels larger than those of Columbus, capable of great speed, and armed with cannon. Trade, either lawful or piratical, and the zeal for discovery sent these ships to India, Siam, Burmah, the Philippines and the Malay Archipelago, and in several of the seaports of these Eastern countries there is a Japanese "quarter" that was originally the trading-post of sailors from Nippon.

This intercourse with other countries resulted in the arrival of missionaries in Japan, and the efforts of these new-comers to introduce Christianity into the land of the Mikado proved so unpopular that the ruling class decided that the only way to secure their national safety was to isolate their country from the rest of the world. Therefore in 1638 the Japanese seaports were closed to all foreign vessels except those from China and Holland and an edict was issued forbidding the building of any ship of more than one hundred and fifty tons or intended for ocean navigation.

The sea then saw no Japanese ships of size and Far Eastern waters were largely navigated by the type of craft known as the junk, a flat-bottomed,

high-sterned vessel with square bows and masts that
carried lug-sails that were generally made of matting. In the rivers and along the coast the sampan
was used, a light boat propelled by a single scull
worked over the stern and with a screen of matting
covering the centre and after deck.

With the junk the people of Japan were satisfied
and for three centuries the Land of the Eight Great
Islands was a hermit nation, from which all foreigners were excluded and where the inhabitants
kept as aloof as possible from all outside influences.

One nation after another tried to break down this
wall that the rulers of Japan had built, but with
small success, and so strong was the prejudice against
foreigners that when a Japanese junk in 1831 was
driven by a storm to the mouth of the Columbia
River in North America and a ship of the United
States carried the shipwrecked crew back to Yeddo
the Japanese fired on the vessel and drove it away.

This action roused the United States government
to try to come to some amicable arrangement with
Japan and if possible to make a treaty permitting
commerce between the two countries. But all efforts in this direction were rebuffed and the American Commodore Biddle was turned away from
Yeddo when he came on a friendly mission.

With the discovery of gold in California in 1849
the Pacific Ocean, that had until that time been little
used for navigation, suddenly blossomed out with
ships and trade with the Far East began to seem

most desirable. Again the United States took up the project of securing a treaty with Japan and this time Commodore Matthew Calbraith Perry was selected to be the envoy.

Perry was instructed to sail in the *Mississippi* to Hong Kong, take command of the fleet of Commodore Aulick and proceed to Japan. He set out in October, 1852, arrived at Hong Kong the next April, and after stopping at Shanghai and Napa reached the Japanese coast off Uraga, a town twenty-seven miles from Yeddo, with the four United States ships, the *Mississippi, Saratoga, Plymouth,* and *Susquehanna.* These ships were propelled by steam as well as by sails, their guns were placed in similar positions to those of the earlier frigates, and this type of man-of-war was commonly called a "steam frigate," or sometimes still by the simple designation of "frigate."

The fleet, an impressive sight to eyes unaccustomed to such great vessels that belched smoke from their funnels, came to anchor in the wide bay in a line broadside to the shore. Gun-ports were opened and Perry ordered a salute of thirteen guns fired from the *Susquehanna* to announce—according to the grandiloquent language he adopted in order to impress the native people—that "the great commodore, the august ambassador of the President, upon whom no Japanese eye had yet been privileged to gaze," had arrived.

Amazed at such sights and sounds, the natives

swarmed out in their small boats; but none was allowed to come aboard the ships.   Then a state barge,
with the Vice-Governor of Uraga, was rowed out to
the *Mississippi* and the Japanese official asked to
see the commander of the fleet.   He was told that
only an officer of the very highest rank could see
Commodore Perry.   Surprised that the foreign sailors were not more dazzled by his gorgeous robes
and by the flag and spears his companions carried,
the Vice-Governor thereupon requested to speak with
some official of his own station.   Lieutenant Contee
met him and, explaining that the Americans had
come to Japan as friends, stated that Commodore
Perry had brought a letter from the President of
the United States to the Emperor of Japan and
wished an interview with a dignitary of the most
august position in order to deliver the letter.

To this the Vice-Governor answered that Nagasaki
was the only place where foreigners could present
themselves on business with the government.

Commodore Perry understood that the people of
this hermit country were easily impressed by lofty-
sounding titles and ceremonial observances, and also
appreciated that if he were to succeed in his mission
he must take a haughty position.   Acting according to Perry's plan therefore, Lieutenant Contee declared that the American ships had come to Uraga
because it was near Yeddo and that they would not
go to Nagasaki, but expected the letter to be received
where they were.

A few days later the Mayor of Uraga came out to the flagship, but Commodore Perry would not see him in person. The Mayor repeated that the strangers must go to Nagasaki; the answer that was made him was that if a proper officer of the highest rank was not appointed to receive the letter from President Millard Fillmore the Americans would land in force and deliver it themselves. At once the Mayor agreed to send a messenger to Yeddo for instructions.

Yeddo was the chief city of Japan. At the time of Perry's visit it was the residence of the Shogun Iyéyoshi, who was the real ruler of the country, although the nominal sovereign was the Emperor, or Mikado, whose palace was at Kioto.

And when word of the arrival of the American fleet at Uraga was brought to Yeddo the Shogun bestirred himself, called his wise men into council, bade his soldiers polish their armor and repair the fortifications, and made a great show of resentment at the intrusion of the ships of the "foreign devils."

Nevertheless the Shogun and his chieftains knew they could not oppose the frigates off their shore. Japan had no navy and little protection against bombardment from sea. It also occurred to Iyéyoshi that the American commander might insist on seeing the Mikado, and that would be a great blow to the Shogun's dignity. Therefore he finally appointed two daimios to receive the letter of President Fillmore and sent a message to Perry through the Mayor of Uraga.

Perry still kept himself from sight, assuming as much mysterious importance as the Shogun or the Mikado, but he permitted his officers to arrange with the daimios for a meeting at the little town of Kurihâma, near Uraga. When the daimios came aboard the American ship they were received most courteously, wines were presented to them and they were seated in great upholstered armchairs. The daimios regretted that they could not return the compliment of wines or chairs when the visitors should come on shore, but the Americans assured them they would be pleased to adopt Japanese customs.

On July thirteenth the foreigners landed and marched to Kurihâma, the band of the fleet regaling the delighted Japanese with music of cornets and drums, the officers wearing cocked hats and dress uniforms decorated with many brass buttons. Soldiers in lacquered armor and retainers in all the colors of feudal days lined the road, along which were stretched hundreds of yards of canvas adorned with the Shogun's emblems. Through crowds of wondering natives the ships' crews proceeded; there were sailors with the American flag, then two boys carrying a magnificent red box, then the haughty Commodore, flanked on either side by a man with a sabre.

A pavilion had been set up and there the daimios

received the envoy from the United States. The box was opened, then a scarlet cloth envelope and gold-hinged rosewood cases, and the President's letter was laid on a lacquered stand. A receipt for the document was presented to Commodore Perry, who announced that he would sail away but would return to Japan after allowing the Emperor sufficient time to consider an answer to the letter.

The fleet steamed out from Uraga and went to China, where Perry spent the autumn and part of the winter charting the coast and visiting ports where American merchants were established.

In Japan the letter of President Fillmore caused great excitement. A messenger was despatched to the Shinto priests at the shrines of Isé to offer prayers for the peace of the country and to urge that the barbarians be swept away. Some of the daimios wished to fight, some considered that it would be madness to oppose an enemy whose ships could capture all the Japanese junks and destroy the cities on the coast. The Mikado took little part in the discussion; the Shogun Iyéyoshi died, and his son the Shogun Iyésada took charge of the government. He hastened to build forts and turn out guns and ammunition, repealed the law prohibiting the construction of warships and commanded the rich daimios to set about making a navy.

In February, 1854 Perry was back at the anchorage off Uraga with the *Mississippi, Lexington, Vandalia, Macedonian, Susquehanna* and *Powhat-*

tan. By now the Shogun and his advisers had decided that the wisest course would be to make a treaty with the United States, so when the frigates dropped anchor the Governor and his interpreters went out to the flagship, presented the visitors with gifts, and suggested that there should be a meeting of envoys at a point twenty miles below Uraga.

The Commodore replied, through his captain, that the meeting place must be somewhere between his anchorage and Yeddo, and when the Governor had withdrawn Perry sailed in the *Mississippi* within sight of Yeddo, to impress the natives with the size of his ship and the smoke pouring from its funnels. The Shogun feared that the barbarians might actually enter the city, and to prevent such a national disgrace acceded to Perry's demand and appointed a place for the meeting opposite the fleet's anchorage.

On March 8, 1854 the American Commodore landed with five hundred men and three military bands. He was met by the Japanese envoys in a great reception building, elaborate courtesies were exchanged, many gifts were offered, and the terms of a treaty discussed. Other meetings were held; meantime the visitors delighted their hosts with the rifles, the clocks, the stoves, the sewing-machines, the model of a steam locomotive, the agricultural tools and the maps and charts Perry had brought the Mikado. The Americans set up telegraph poles and laid rails to show the working of the model locomotive. The Japanese opened their eyes at these many wonders and were inclined to believe that the barbarians from across the ocean could teach them some things.

At length the draft of a treaty was presented and signed on March thirty-first. This provided that the ports of Shimoda and Hakodate should be open to Americans for water, wood, provisions and coal, that shipwrecked sailors should be well treated, and that the gold and silver coins and goods of the United States might be exchanged for the coins and goods of Japan.

With that Perry was satisfied; he had made a good beginning for commerce and the hermit nation had learned something of the dignity and friendly disposition of his nation. He cruised from port to port, familiarizing the people with the sight of his "fire-vessels," and the sailors were well treated and the governors of the different provinces presented the Commodore with many beautiful specimens of Japanese art.

So the rulers of the Land of the Eight Great Islands looked out across the sea at the smoke rolling from Perry's steam frigates and, deciding that there would be profit in intercourse with other peoples, began to build ships and become a seafaring nation as they had been in the sixteenth century.

CHAPTER XXI
"THAR SHE BLOWS!"
THE WHALER

"THAR SHE BLOWS!" THE WHALER

THE New Englander, struggling to make a living on his rock-bound coast, trying to turn to profit everything that came to his hand ashore or afloat, was a hunter of whales; at first with the object of boiling out the oil from the blubber and using it for candles and lamps in the long Northern winters, and later to supply a worldwide market with sperm-oil and whalebone.

Fishermen of Cape Cod and the neighboring coasts, seeing whales spouting offshore, rowed out and captured them, and towed the carcasses to the beach where fires were built and the oil boiled out. Presently whales grew more wary and were not so frequently sighted, and then the fishermen had to make longer trips and use bigger and heavier boats for their hunting. Certain ports on the New England coast became the headquarters for whalers and with the beginning of a profitable commerce in oil and bone the whaling industry centered in a dozen or more harbors, notably those of New Bedford and New London, and on the little island of Nantucket, twenty-eight miles off the coast.

As the value of oil increased the hunt for whales covered greater and greater distances. From the

waters of New England the chase led north to the
ice-floes of the Arctic Ocean, south through the
Atlantic to Cape Horn, thence to the Pacific, to
Alaska and Japan, even to the Indian Ocean.
There were three varieties of whales that were
sought. Frequenting the ocean where the depths
were greatest was the deep-sea sperm whale that fed
upon the squid or octopus it found at the bottom and
which it cut up with its sharp-toothed lower jaw.
This whale was a huge fighting monster, but very
valuable for the fine quality of its oil and especially
for the wax-like spermaceti taken from its head and
used for making candles. The right whale, as another variety was called, furnished a less highly-
prized oil, but provided the whalebone, which makes
an immense sieve in the whale's mouth to catch the
mollusks and small fish on which it lives, the throat
of the whale being very small for so large a creature.
A third variety, the bowhead whale, was found off
the coast of Greenland and in far northern latitudes,
and supplied both oil and whalebone.

The early whalers were broad, sturdy little sloops
with square topsails trimmed by braces leading
forward to cleats on the bowsprit. The crew usually
consisted of thirteen men, six for each of the two
small boats that pursued the whale when it was
sighted and a cook who kept charge of the ship when
the boats were away. With the increased demand
for oil the dimensions of the whalers grew larger
until they averaged between three hundred and five

hundred tons; but the model remained much the same. Sailors on merchant ships spoke of them derisively as "spouters" or "blubber-boilers," and certainly they were built with an eye to cargo-carrying and seaworthiness rather than for speed or beauty.

The boats in which the whales were chased—the whaleboats, as they were called,—were the great pride of their crews. They were double-ended, about thirty feet long and six feet wide, propelled by oars and sometimes by a spritsail, and as strong as their builders could make them. They had need to be very sturdy and the steersman very skillful to prevent an upset in the sea when the man in the bow had sunk his harpoon in a giant sperm whale and the creature went tearing through the water, lashing its great tail and dragging the whaleboat after it at a furious pace.

When the whale was hunted in far distant reaches of the Pacific the whalers were vessels of consider-able size. Voyages often lasted three years, and the oil had to be boiled out on deck, frequent repairs made, and large supplies carried. The Pacific whalers were ships, barques and occasionally brigs, bluff in the bows and heavily timbered throughout. No other vessel could possibly be mistaken for one of these whalers when sighted at sea; the whaleboats, five in number on most of the deep-water fleet, were slung on wooden davits along the rail, at the mainmast-head were two heavy pulleys to hold the tackle needed in stripping the blubber from the whale, and high on the main royalmast was the crow's-nest, sometimes a barrel, sometimes merely an iron ring, used to support a sailor, who from that lofty perch kept watch over the ocean for the steam-like spouting of the game they sought.

For days the whaler might roll on the long Pacific swells before the lookout in the crow's-nest would sing out "Thar she blows!" At that shout there would be a scramble to the boats. In each whaleboat would go five oarsmen, pulling oars of different lengths, so arranged as to keep the boat balanced when the man who rowed in the bow, and who was also the harpooner, should stand up to hurl his iron. The sixth man in each whaleboat was the steersman, who guided the boat by a twenty-foot oar worked at the stern-post, and who also watched for the whale—which, being a mammal, had to rise to the surface from time to time for air—and directed his course so that if possible the boat should come up behind the monster.

The crew pull away from the ship. Presently there is a shout from the steersman: "Now! Stand up! Let him have it!" The bow-oarsman drops his oar, rises with his harpoon and flings it at his target. "Starn all!" cries the steersman, and the crew dig in with their sweeps to keep the boat away from the sudden wild thrashings of the wounded whale.

The man in the bow holds the harpoon-line and tries to maneuver so that the boat shall come in close to the lateral fin of the whale, which meanwhile is rushing through the water at full speed, dragging the whaleboat so viciously that the steersman has hard work to keep it from capsizing. Gradually, however, the whale tires and his speed slackens; then the crew pull up hand over hand on the harpoon-line and a well-aimed thrust from a ten-foot lance puts an end to the battle.

Not always, however, would the crew win the engagement. Many a fighting sperm whale destroyed his pursuers instead of their capturing him. Sometimes he would rise with open jaws directly under a whaleboat and shoot it twenty feet into the air, crushing its wooden sides and scattering the men widely over the water. There was adventure and to spare in hunting these deep sea monsters and many a whaleboat crew had hairbreadth escapes.

When the whale was killed the carcass was secured to the ship by a chain and the crew began the work of "cutting-in." An immense hook which swung from the tackle at the mainmast-head was fastened in the whale's gristle and as the men on deck swayed away at the fall the blubber was torn off, unwinding somewhat like a spiral. The lengths of blubber as fast as they were removed were lowered into the hold. The head, which was one-third the entire length of the whale, was then cut off, and from this was bailed out the spermaceti, the most valuable product. This spermaceti in a good-sized whale often filled more than twenty barrels.

Next the trying-out of the blubber began. A fire was kindled under kettles set in a brick structure amidships on the deck. In these kettles the sliced blubber was tried-out, as it was called, and the oil thus obtained was poured into barrels. A strange sight was presented at night on the ocean when the fires blazed up on the decks of a fleet of whalers after a good day's hunting among a shoal of sperm whale.

The owners of the whalers made large profits, but the pay of the crew was small and their treatment by the skipper and mates frequently so harsh that few Yankee sailors would ship on the long Pacific voyages. American seamen did ship as harpooners or boat-steerers, since men in these positions received a share in the profits that netted them a fair wage and moreover were better treated and had quarters separate from the crew. On the long voyages the whaling crews were generally made up of boys from farms eager to try the excitements of the sea, immigrants out of employment, the derelicts who swarm in every harbor, and to these there were added foreigners shipped aboard at various ports. Many of these latter came from the Azores and the Cape Verde Islands, and were known as "Porty-gees," and after whaling voyages so many of these dark-skinned aliens settled on Cape Cod and in the neighborhood of New Bedford that the Western Islanders and Bravas, as they were called, became a numerous element in the population.

The choice berths on the whalers generally went to sailors from Nantucket or New Bedford or near-by seaports, and boys in those towns practised hurling harpoons at floating logs along the water-front and cherished the ambition to wear the "chock-pin" through the upper buttonhole of their jacket, the greatly-prized badge of the man who had taken his whale.

Nantucketers always referred to the whaling-grounds in the Pacific as "the other side of the land," and many were the strange tales the whaling crews brought back of adventures in those distant waters, at their ports of call on the coast of South America, at the Galápagos Islands, where they some-times stopped for water and to catch the great turtles which furnished a delightful change in their menu of salt beef and hardtack, and on the beautiful shores of the Hawaiian Islands.

The little island of Nantucket, that had early been a whaling port of importance, lost half her fleet of forty-six whalers in the War of 1812. Resolutely, however, the people set to work to rebuild their shipping, and at the height of the island's pros-perity, in 1843, they owned eighty-eight whalers and marketed more refined oil and sperm candles than any other place in America. The harbor of Nan-tucket, however, was blocked by a bar, over which vessels had to be floated, and the islanders could not ship their oil by rail, as their rivals on the mainland were able to do when railroads presently were constructed, so the palm passed from Nantucket to New Bedford, which had a splendid harbor and a shrewd set of shipowners who turned every vessel they could lay their hands on into a whaler.

New Bedford became the chief whaling port of the world and her whale fleet numbered three hundred and thirty ships in 1857, more than all other American whale fleets combined. Edgartown and Provincetown and Fairhaven all had considerable fleets, but from 1850 New Bedford ruled the whale oil market until the introduction of petroleum and coal-gas replaced whale oil as a medium for lighting and the whaling industry declined. Yet as recently as 1920 a barque built in 1841 fitted out in New Bedford for a whaling voyage.

The whaler was not a smart vessel, like the California clipper; she was wall-sided and bluff-bowed; but she could weather all seas, and many a fortune she brought back to New England from her hunt for the great sperm whale.

CHAPTER XXII
THE DARLING OF THE SEAS:
THE CLIPPER SHIP

XXII

THE DARLING OF THE SEAS: THE CLIPPER SHIP

OF all the ships that have ever sailed the clipper ship was the most beautiful, the most like a great white-winged bird, fashioned for lightness and speed, a dream, a vision rising from the waves to delight the eyes of sailors and all who loved gallant ships. It was the cry that gold had been discovered in California in 1849 that brought the clippers to perfection; for a few years the ocean became a race-course, over which the great ships sailed with incredible speed; then, since it cost more to build and maintain them than their cargoes justified, they vanished from the sea while men were still fascinated by them.

A "ship," in the technical language of American sailors, always used to mean a three masted vessel, each mast carrying square sails. During the War of 1812 some schooners and brigs of Chesapeake Bay came to be called "Baltimore clippers." They were long, low vessels, so fast that they were very successful as privateers, and the term "clipper" was probably given them because of their speed. They were not real clipper ships, however. The first that deserved that name was the *Ann McKim,* of four hundred and ninety-three tons, built at Baltimore in 1832, a vessel considerably larger than the Chesapeake Bay privateers, but constructed on much the same lines.

The shipyards of New York had been building large vessels for the North Atlantic packet-service, but presently the merchants asked for speed as well as size. To meet this need John W. Griffiths, a designer of New York, drew plans for a new type that followed in some particulars the *Ann McKim.* His chief changes from earlier ships were in giving his model sharper bows and finer lines, moving the widest beam farther aft, and using "hollow" water lines; that is, he made the curve of the hull from the bow along the water line concave before it became convex, whereas in other ships it had been convex for its whole length. This last innovation he is said to have adapted from the model of a Singapore sampan. His ship was also more heavily sparred than her predecessors.

The first clipper ship built according to Griffiths' model was the *Rainbow,* of seven hundred and fifty tons, launched at New York in 1845. Critics said that the design of the *Rainbow* was freakish, that she would capsize from the weight of her spars, that she could not stand up in a boisterous sea, but her actual performances refuted all their objections. She made a remarkably fast run on her second trip out and back from Canton, China, and was generally regarded as the fastest ship afloat. Other New

York ships were built along her lines for merchants engaged in the China trade.

One of these ships was the *Sea Witch,* which set many new records.   And if these first of the clippers were wonderfully fine ships in themselves it should also be noted that they were handled by marvellous captains, who dared to carry royals and studding-sails when foreign vessels they met were wallowing about with two reefs in their topsails.   These skippers drove around Cape Horn and across to China with rackings on the topsail halyards and locks on the chainsheets, so that no timid seaman, frightened at the captain's seeming rashness, should tamper with the gear.   They cut in half the time required for voyages to China and Australia and by their masterly navigation skimmed the cream of the ocean freights of the world.

Then came the word that gold had been found in the streams of California and the rush of adventurers and cargoes from the Atlantic to the Pacific began.   The call for larger and speedier vessels roused the shipbuilders of Massachusetts, for the men of that state had always taken as naturally and eagerly to the sea as had their English brothers of Somerset and Devon.   The ocean was the main highway that led from the doors of Boston and Salem, Newburyport and New Bedford, Gloucester and a score of other ports on Cape Ann and Cape Cod.   If speed and size were wanted the men of Massachusetts would match themselves against the shipwrights of New York. In 1850 there were launched from the East Boston yard of Samuel Hall the first New England clippers, the *Surprise,* of 1261 tons, and the *Game-Cock,* of 1392 tons.

Samuel Hall was the leading shipbuilder of New England, and well did he justify his fame. When the *Surprise* was ready to glide into the water he gave a dinner to the mothers, wives and sweethearts of the men who had built the ship and afterwards a great crowd witnessed the remarkable spectacle of the new clipper launched, fully rigged and with her three skysail yards crossed. There were those who said no ship could carry such heavy top-rigging, others who loudly predicted that she would stick in the mud; but down the ways she glided, slid through the water with her sharp stern, poised lightly, caught her balance and rode easily in the harbor while thousands on the banks cheered.

The *Surprise* was commanded by Philip Dumaresq, a son of a long line of celebrated merchant-captains. Of a tonnage immense for her time, she was very powerful, with top-hamper that would have startled the mariners of earlier days. The great sails, borne on wooden spars, sustained by Russian hemp standing-rigging, carried a terrific strain as the clipper drove through the seas, but carried it successfully. On her maiden voyage to California the *Surprise* broke the record, reaching San Francisco in ninety-six days from Boston.

The next year the *Surprise* raced the *Sea Witch*

to San Francisco and won twenty thousand dollars for her backers; then, sailing to China she loaded tea for London, and earned for her owners $50,000 over her entire cost and the expense of the voyage.

In December of 1850 Donald McKay, the greatest of all clipper ship builders, who had made a reputation for constructing Liverpool sailing packets at East Boston, launched his first clipper, the pioneer of the new fifteen-hundred-ton class, the *Stag-Hound,* of 1534 tons. McKay later built faster ships, but the *Stag-Hound* still holds the record of thirteen days for a sailing-ship from Boston Light to the equator. This first venture proved so successful that he followed it with an even larger clipper, the *Flying Cloud,* which is said to have been the fastest ship on long voyages that has ever flown the American flag.

The *Flying Cloud,* a vision of great billowing sails with a winged angel blowing a trumpet for her figurehead, was commanded by Captain Josiah Perkins Cressy, of Marblehead, and on her first voyage she made the run from New York to San Francisco in eighty-nine days. From there she crossed to China for a cargo of tea and covered the two thousand miles from Canton to Java Head in six days, reducing by almost half the best previous record. Any of McKay's clippers could outsail the fastest racing yacht built to-day. There were the *Stag-Hound* and the *Mastiff,* powerful cargo-carriers, the *Flying Fish* and the *Westward Ho!*

made for the gold-seekers, *Lightning,* the swiftest
of all ships, and those wonders, admired around the
world, the *Romance of the Seas,* the *Sovereign of
the Seas,* the. *Glory of the Seas,* and the *Great
Republic.*

There are recorded twenty-two voyages made by
clippers from various Atlantic ports around Cape
Horn to San Francisco in less than one hundred
days, and of these seven were made by ships built
by Donald McKay. One-half of the twenty-two
voyages are credited to ships constructed in Massachusetts, and four of the other half were made by
vessels built in the other New England states and
the remaining seven by ships of New York. A clipper of medium size, the *Northern Light,* of 1021
tons, built by Edward and Henry O. Briggs, of
South Boston, completed the round trip voyage from
Boston to San Francisco in exactly seven months
and on this voyage set a record that has never been
broken for the eastward passage from the Golden
Gate to Massachusetts Bay of seventy-six days and
five hours. The prevailing westerly winds, however,
always favored the homebound rather than the out-
bound passages, and speedy as the *Northern Light*
was she could not equal the *Flying Cloud's* mark of
eighty-nine days for the westward voyage.

There was no skimping of labor or material in
building the clippers. Every man who worked on
them took pride in doing his best. The finest oak
and Southern pine were used; the ships were copper

fastened and sheathed with yellow metal, and mahogany and rosewood furnished the stanchions, rails and cabins.   Most of the clippers were painted black with a gold or crimson stripe about the hull.   The lower masts were white up to the tops, with the yards and bowsprits black.   With her high-tiered skysails and wide-winged stun's'ls the clipper was a creation of surpassing beauty, the supreme expression of the genius of the great race of Yankee shipbuilders.

The men who commanded these ocean greyhounds were most of them New Englanders bred to the sea from boyhood.   It took great skill in navigation to bring such ships through the seas off Cape Horn without loss of spars or rigging, and the clippers were driven at top speed.   The captain was an autocrat, tremendously admired on shore and implicitly obeyed when he stood on the quarterdeck. Sometimes he was part owner of the ship or the cargo; some captains received three thousand dollars for the voyage to San Francisco and two thousand additional if they arrived in less than one hundred days.

Occasionally a clipper captain took his wife with him on a voyage; Mrs. Cressy always sailed with her husband on the *Flying Cloud*.   It is related that when Captain Patten, of the *Neptune's Car*, fell ill during a storm off Cape Horn and the first mate was in irons for disobedience and the second mate proved inefficient the Captain's nineteen-year old wife, who had only made one previous voyage, took command of the clipper and brought her safely to San Francisco in fifty-two days.

Though the officers were almost always native Americans, this was not true of the crews. Yankee sailors had had a fine reputation, but by 1850 railroads and factories and Western emigration were providing more tempting occupations than life before the mast. Wages paid seamen were small compared with what could be earned ashore; an average pay for the voyage to California was eight to twelve dollars a month. When they could not get American sailors for such wages the shipowners filled up their crews with foreigners, generally of a poor type. Boarding-house keepers were bribed to induce drunken sailors to sign on for voyages, and shanghaiing was a common practice. Not only seamen, but landsmen as well, having taken a friendly drink with a stranger on the waterfront, would wake up the next morning to find themselves aboard a clipper well out at sea. Discipline was harsh, the food was poor; small wonder that a young fellow with any ambition preferred the land to the water.

Yet in spite of the difficulty of obtaining good crews the clippers were sailing marvels. Many a race was run on the course that reached down one side of South America, around the Horn, and up the other, a course that tested a ship in a great variety of seas and in many kinds of weather. In 1854 the McKay-built *Romance of the Seas,* leaving

Boston two days after the *David Brown* had sailed from New York, caught up with the latter off the coast of Brazil, and from there the two clippers raced, much of the time within sight of each other, to the harbor of San Francisco, which they reached on the same tide. There they discharged their cargoes, and sailed out together with all canvas spread, and without taking in sail crossed the Pacific to China, which they reached in forty-five days, the *Romance of the Seas* arriving at Hong Kong one hour before her rival.

Most of the American clippers were well known in the Far East, for there was little in the way of cargo for them to take aboard in California and, having unloaded there, they usually continued their voyage around the world. The English built many fine clippers for the China and Australia trade, but the Yankee ships proved so much faster than all others that British merchants preferred to send their teas to London in American bottoms rather than in their own East Indiamen.

Donald McKay was always building larger and faster clippers. When he constructed the *Sovereign of the Seas* he gave her a sharper bow and stern than any ship built and her lines were so much criticized that no firm of shipowners would finance her construction, which was paid for by McKay and his friends. When she was launched, however, she made such a splendid impression that she was immediately bought for $150,000, the highest price

offered for a clipper, and on her first round voyage
she reimbursed her owners almost the entire purchase price.

That maiden voyage of the *Sovereign* was a test
for any clipper. She was commanded by Lauchlan
McKay, a brother of the builder, and sailed in
August, which was considered an unfavorable season in the Atlantic. From the Falkland Islands to
the Horn she continually encountered southwest
gales, but she never wore nor missed stays in the
beat to windward. Rounding the Horn she ran into
a storm and lost her maintopmast, mizzen topgal-
lantmast, and foretopsail yard. Her captain had
the clipper under jury rig in thirty hours, and in
twelve days succeeded in putting her into almost as
perfect shape as when she had started. San Francisco was reached in one hundred and three days
after leaving New York, which was a record for a
clipper sailing in August.

In Honolulu the *Sovereign* took aboard a cargo
of oil and whalebone and spread her sails for home.
She was short-handed, and one of her foretopmasts
was sprung and a maintopmast needed replacing.
Lauchlan McKay, however, sailed her through a
part of the South Pacific that was rarely crossed by
clippers, and the northwest tradewinds blew her at
such a pace that she covered 5391 nautical miles, a
quarter of the distance around the world, in twenty-
two days. The *Sovereign* made many other remarkable voyages; once in a passage from New

York to Liverpool she outran for five successive days the steamship *Canada* of the Cunard line.

Donald McKay dreamed of yet mightier clippers, and in 1853 he built the *Great Republic*. The *Flying Cloud* had registered 1793 tons, the *Sovereign of the Seas* 2421 tons; the *Great Republic* was of 4556 tonnage! This new ship was fitted with double topsails, which were later universally used on all square-rigged vessels. Several sailing ships that have been subsequently built have surpassed the *Great Republic* in size, but no other ship has ever been designed with such gigantic spars, fashioned to carry such an enormous press of sail, for she spread more than 15,000 square yards of canvas.

Those sails were never tried out, however. The *Great Republic* was towed to New York, and there, as she was fitting out for her first voyage, she caught fire and had to be scuttled. When she was rebuilt her spars, sails and tonnage were much reduced; but even so she made the passage to San Francisco in ninety-two days.

McKay's greatest achievement in speed was the clipper *Lightning,* which he built in 1854 for the Australian Black Ball Line. On her maiden voyage to Liverpool she established herself as the fastest sailing vessel in the world by a run of 436 miles in twenty-four hours, the greatest day's run ever made by a sailing ship and one that was unequalled by any steamship for many years and that is not often surpassed even bv the transatlantic liners of to-day.

The clippers carried in five years thousands of adventurers to California, men who had left farms and shops and offices to hunt for gold and who sang to the tune of "Oh! Susannah!":

> "Oh! California,
> That's the land for me!
> I'm going to Sacramento
> With my washbowl on my knee!"

There were two routes to this land where fortunes were said to be found in every pan of gravel: one route was by the overland trails from St. Louis and other frontier cities, the other was around Cape Horn. Each was beset by dangers. The caravans that started across the plains had to brave hostile Indians, drought, blizzards in the Rocky Mountains. By the sea route there were storms, the chances of shipwreck in the Strait of Magellan, ship or typhus fever. Those adventurers who lived inland chose the overland journey by prairie-schooner, those who dwelt along the Atlantic seaboard embarked on the clipper ships.

A few of the Forty-niners did make fortunes in California, but most of the adventurers came home poorer than when they left. The owners of the clippers made a great deal of money and so did those men who were canny enough to prefer to sell supplies rather than hunt for gold. As the crowds poured in at the Golden Gate prices began to soar, and shortly a barrel of flour was bringing forty-four dollars, a bushel of potatoes sixteen, and a dozen eggs ten dollars. Those who found gold spent it recklessly.

In 1836 there were on the shores of San Francisco Bay a ruined Presidio, an almost empty Mission, and a small wooden shanty where a Yankee carried on trade with the Indians and the hide ships that occasionally anchored in the harbor. There was not a light-house, a beacon or a buoy on the entire coast of California, and the only charts were primitive surveys made by English, Russian and Mexican sailors.

By 1850 there had risen in this solitude a city of many thousands, scores of American vessels rode in the bay, and the cargoes they unloaded were bought and sold and bought again before they reached the warehouses. In one month of 1850 there sailed into the harbor seventeen ships from New York and sixteen from Boston. The average voyage of these vessels was one hundred and fifty-nine days. Then, on July twenty-fourth of that year there arrived the little clipper *Sea Witch,* which had taken only ninety-seven days from New York. At once the cry went up to send cargoes from the east by this new type of ship.

For five years the clipper ruled the ocean; then the rush to the goldfields diminished and owners found the clippers too expensive to maintain. Few new clippers were built. Steam made inroads on sails, and when the Suez Canal was opened in 1869 steamships could accomplish the voyage to the Far East through the Mediterranean and the Red Sea, where sailing ships could not go, in much less time than it took the clipper to round Cape Horn.

Previous to the clipper era ships had been built on the plan popularly called "the cod's head and mackerel tail." Abandoning this design, builders like Donald McKay gave their vessels a water line that was concave instead of convex at the bow and stern and such a vast stretch of canvas that their new creations were not only the fastest sailing but the most beautiful ships the world has even seen.

CHAPTER XXIII

WARRIORS OF THE DEEP

WARRIORS OF THE DEEP

THE earliest warships of which there are authentic accounts were those of the Egyptians, and the chief distinction between the vessels they used for commerce and those intended for combat consisted in the latter class of vessel being armed with a metal ram fastened to the prow. In the era when Rome had come to dominate the seas her battle-galleys were high, five-banked ships, provided with the great hinged gang-plank or *corvus* which was dropped on to the opponent's deck and across which the soldiers rushed to engage their enemies.

Then at the Battle of Actium in 31 B. C. the large galleys of Mark Antony were defeated by much lighter and swifter ships of two banks of oars, known as Liburnian biremes, and this type became the general pattern for the war-galleys of southern Europe during the Middle Ages, ships of long, heavy oars, with sometimes as many as seven rowers pulling a single sweep. Forecastles and sterncastles were added to the decks and these superstructures, elaborately carved and decorated, gave to the mediæval fighting-galley an imposing and vastly picturesque appearance.

The invention of gunpowder brought changes. On the caravels of Columbus's time the guns were small and were fastened on pivots in the rails. As larger guns were cast they were placed at the bow and stern, since the deck of many of the vessels was occupied by rowers. Then oars gradually gave way to sails and presently the ship driven entirely by canvas superseded the galley and the space that had been used by oarsmen was taken by cannon.

These cannon were at first fired over the side of the ships, but to allow for greater armament the sides were built higher and higher and guns were mounted below the main deck and fired through open ports. By the date of the Battle of Trafalgar the line-of-battle ships carried a hundred guns or so on three decks; these vessels, extremely clumsy and difficult to handle, were giants in close combat but capable of little speed.

The ships that could sail as well as fight were the frigates, with guns on the main deck and sometimes on one gun-deck below. They had finer lines than the line-of-battle ships and when it was found that the frigate could outfight as well as outsail her heavier rival of the older type the frigate became the popular warship. After the War of 1812, in which frigates played so large a part, experiments were made in two new directions; ships began to use steam as well as sails and builders to utilize iron as well as wood in construction. The new ships were called "steam frigates," and of this style was the *Hartford*, the flagship of Admiral Farragut at the Battle of Mobile Bay.

The old-fashioned solid round shot was being succeeded by shells that exploded and did tremendous
damage to wooden hulls. For protection armored
ships were constructed, and the steam frigates were
encased in strips of iron that stretched from below
the water line to the upper deck.

Then during the Civil War in America a new
warship appeared, a low, flat, armored vessel with
a turret, designed by John Ericsson and called the
Monitor. The Confederates described this peculiar-
looking craft as "a cheese-box on a raft." The deck
was only two feet above the water and was smooth
from bow to stern except for a small pilot house
forward and a round turret amidships. The turret
contained two guns.

The *Monitor's* first appearance was dramatic.
A Confederate ironclad with a ram at her bow had
done great injury to the wooden Union ships in
Hampton Roads. This ironclad, a converted frigate, the *Merrimac*, had sunk the *Cumberland* and
set fire to the *Congress*. The Union shells did her
no harm, and her crew were expecting to demolish
the enemy fleet when to their surprise they found
themselves confronted by a tiny new opponent.

In the fight that ensued between these two cham-
pions of a new order of warships the *Monitor's* revolving turret allowed her gun-crew to fire from
various positions and her armored deck was a perfect protection from the rain of shells poured on her
by the *Merrimac*. The *Merrimac* at last withdrew

and the timely arrival of the *Monitor* saved the Union frigates.

Iron had come to replace wood. Ironclad and then steelclad warships were built. The muzzle-loading guns of the Civil War gave place to breech-loading rifles. Meantime passenger ships were discarding sails and using engines, and battleships did likewise. A new type of warship was evolved, the torpedo-boat, small and very fast, and then, to offset this craft, there was constructed a vessel known as the torpedo-boat destroyer.

In no space of such brief duration in the history of the development of warships had there been such changes in construction as in the interval that elapsed between the Civil War in America and the war between the United States and Spain. In 1861 the battleship was the steam frigate with sails and wooden masts and little or no armor. In 1898 the battleship was a great steelclad vessel, with metal masts that carried guns instead of canvas, with sides that were armor plates, and with collections of turrets that were revolving turntables, thickly armored, and placed on circular steel bases through which shells and ammunition were hoisted.

The great engines that could drive this mass of metal at a speed of more than twenty knots an hour were protected by steel decks. The warship bore little resemblance to what had been known as a ship, smoke and boilers had taken the place of sails and spars; the vessel had become a gigantic floating battery capable of navigation.

The American battleship *Maine* was blown up in the harbor of Havana, Cuba, on February 15, 1898, and of her 350 officers and men 260 were killed or subsequently died of injuries received in the explosion. This catastrophe did not in itself lead to the war between the United States and Spain,—that was due to the belief in the United States that Spain was misgoverning Cuba,—but it served to inflame resentment. On April twentieth President McKinley demanded that Spain should "at once relinquish its authority and government in the Island of Cuba, and withdraw its land and naval forces from Cuba and Cuban waters." Spain severed diplomatic relations and war was declared.

Hostilities had been anticipated for some time and the United States Navy Department had been occupied with the problem of utilizing various warships that were in distant waters. In order to concentrate the fleet ships were ordered to stations in the North and South Atlantic, and among such ships was the first-class battleship *Oregon,* which made a remarkable run around South America.

On March first the *Oregon,* which was in dock at Bremerton, in the state of Washington, was directed to proceed to San Francisco immediately and take on ammunition. Reaching there on March ninth, she was ordered on the twelfth to go to Callao in

Peru. Captain Charles E. Clark took command, and sailing from San Francisco on March nineteenth the battleship arrived at Callao on April fourth, having accomplished an average speed of 10.7 knots an hour through the Pacific. Meantime the gunboat *Marietta* had been sent from Panama to Callao to purchase coal and have it ready for the *Oregon* by the time she reached the Peruvian seaport.

The *Oregon* took aboard eleven hundred tons of coal and left Callao on April seventh for the Strait of Magellan. Captain Clark had telegraphed the Navy Department: "On account of navigation of Magellan Strait, and reported movements Spanish torpedo-vessel near Montevideo, I should recommend *Marietta* to accompany this vessel. If required, I could touch Talcahuano, Chile, for orders six days after my sailing."

The Navy Department answered: "Proceed at once to Montevideo or Rio Janeiro. The Spanish torpedo-boat *Temerario* is in Montevideo. *Marietta* has been ordered to proceed to Sandy Point, Patagonia, to arrange for coal. How many tons of coal will you require? The *Marietta* and *Oregon* to proceed together. Keep secret your destination. Keep secret this message."

The Department also telegraphed the *Marietta,* which was at Valparaiso: "*Oregon* leaves to-day from Callao for Sandy Point, Patagonia. Go ahead and secure 600 tons of coal for her and accompany her to the north. The United States consulates in Cuba have closed. United States consul-general is coming home.''

The *Oregon* reached the western entrance to the Strait of Magellan on the afternoon of April sixteenth. A tremendous gale was blowing; the rain was so dense that the giant cliffs overhanging the narrow winding channel could not be seen; the wind whistled down through the ravines of the mountainous coast. The sailors could take no soundings. Captain Clark reported that ''just before dark the anchors were let go on a rocky shelf fringed by islets and reefs in thirty-eight and fifty-two fathoms of water, and they fortunately held through some of the most violent gusts I have ever experienced.''

The battleship worked her way through the tortuous passage, and reached Sandy Point on the following evening, April seventeenth. Her average speed from Callao had been 11.75 knots an hour. A little later the *Marietta* arrived, and the coal was taken on board from that port of Chile. The two ships left Sandy Point April twenty-first. The *Marietta* could not make as much speed as the *Oregon* and head winds and stormy seas prevented the vessels from reaching Rio de Janeiro until April thirtieth.

At this port Captain Clark received a message from the Navy Department: ''War has been declared between the United States and Spain from April 21. *Temerario* has left Montevideo, probably for Rio Janeiro. Await orders.''

The next day came this telegram to the *Oregon:* ''Four Spanish armored cruisers, heavy and fast, three torpedo-boat destroyers, sailed April 29 from Cape Verde to the west, destination unknown. Beware of and study carefully the situation. Must be left to your discretion entirely to avoid this fleet and to reach the United States by West Indies. You can go when and where you desire. *Nictheroy* and the *Marietta* subject to the orders of yourself.''

Captain Clark, thinking that the Spanish torpedo-boat *Temerario* might arrive at Rio, notified the Brazilian authorities that if she came into the harbor and approached his ship he would sink her. The Brazilian government answered that if the torpedo-boat appeared she would be conducted to an anchorage up the bay by a Brazilian man-of-war, and in order further to protect the American ships a cruiser was stationed at the harbor entrance to watch for the torpedo-boat.

On May fourth the *Oregon* and the *Marietta* left Rio and were joined the next evening by the *Nictheroy*. The two small vessels could not keep up with the battleship, so Captain Clark directed Captain Symonds of the *Marietta* to proceed north with his gunboat and the *Nictheroy* independently of the *Oregon* and to run ashore if he should meet the Spanish fleet.

The *Oregon* came to Bahia on May eighth and left next day for Barbados. There she arrived on May eighteenth, having made the run of 2500 miles from Bahia at an average speed of 11.73 knots an hour. Taking on coal, she laid her course to the east and north of the Bahamas and reached Jupiter Inlet, Florida, on May twenty-fourth and Key West on May twenty-sixth.

She had made the run from San Francisco to Key West in sixty-eight days. The voyage from the navy yard in Puget Sound had covered 14,700 knots, and this had been accomplished at an average speed of 11.6 knots an hour. On the run she had used 4100 tons of coal.

That voyage of the *Oregon* was a unique achievement in the history of battleships. Down one side of North and South America and up the other a great ironclad vessel had raced at a speed that was reminiscent of the days when the gallant clippers had rounded Cape Horn. Coal had taken the place of sails; indeed it seems a misnomer to use the word "sailed" in connection with the voyage of such a vessel; the glamour of great spars bending with the weight of wind-filled canvas is lacking to the picture; but the battleship's run, made in time of war and when it was not known where enemy ships might be cruising, roused the admiration of the people of the United States to a tremendous pitch. The *Oregon's* run became famous. No less deserving of praise was the voyage of the small gunboat *Marietta,* and another splendid accomplishment under difficult conditions was the voyage across the Pacific that was made by the American monitors *Monterey* and *Monadnock.*

Meantime other American battleships had been busy. The Asiatic Fleet was in charge of Commodore George Dewey, and he had received at Hong Kong on April 25, 1898, the following message from the Navy Department: "War has commenced between the United States and Spain. Proceed at once to the Philippine Islands. Commence operations at once, particularly against the Spanish fleet. You must capture vessels or destroy. Use utmost endeavors."

Dewey had been making preparations, supplying his fleet with coal, drilling his crews in gunnery, and on April nineteenth had ordered the sides of the battleships painted a dull gray instead of their usual sparkling white. He knew little concerning the location of the Spanish warships, but from the United States consul at Manila who came to report to him at Hong Kong on April twenty-seventh he learned the important news that the enemy fleet was lying in Manila Bay.

That same day the flagship *Olympia* gave the signal to the fleet to get under way. Manila was distant about 628 miles. Dewey's squadron consisted of his flagship and the *Boston, Baltimore, Concord, Petrel,* and *Hugh McCullough,* of which four were cruisers and two were gunboats, and the

Nanshan and *Zafiro,* which had been bought at Hong Kong and which were used as supply-ships. The ships were small and their total armament amounted to fifty-three guns.

At midnight on April thirtieth this squadron reached the entrance to Manila Bay, a wide expanse, protected by the islands of Corregidor and Caballo, both of which were fortified. On the eastern side of the bay, some twenty-five miles from the entrance, is the city of Manila, the capital of the Philippines. South of Manila extends a peninsula on which is Cavite, and it was off this point that the Spanish fleet of Admiral Montojo was lying when Dewey arrived.

The American fleet was cleared for action, and through the darkness the ships, their crews alert for mines or torpedo-boats, crept up the bay. The vessels had been darkened, but sparks from the funnel of one of the ships were seen and a Spanish gun broke the stillness. There was more firing, then quiet again. The fleet moved slowly forward.

At daybreak Manila was fourteen thousand yards by range ahead of the squadron. No Spanish warships were in sight, but they might be behind Cavite, and Dewey ordered his vessels to swing to the right. Batteries on shore were firing, but the Americans made no answer and kept their ammunition for later use.

At about five in the morning the Spanish warships were sighted at anchor off Cavite. The fleet

was made up of six cruisers and three gunboats, a
total of nine Spanish warships to six American.
Soon the Spanish flagship, the *Reina Christina,*
signaled "commence firing," and the guns began to
boom. On went Dewey's squadron, still without
firing. A mine exploded near the *Olympia,* and
shells whistled over her deck. Dewey waited until
the range was about six thousand yards, then, leaning over the bridge above the conning-tower, he said
to the *Olympia's* captain, "You may fire when you
are ready, Gridley."

From every American gun came a flash and a
roar and the line of Spanish ships was deluged with
shells. The cannonade continued hotly on both
sides; few direct hits were made on the American
vessels but presently smoke was seen rising from the
hatches of several of the Spanish cruisers and their
gun-fire slackened. The *Reina Christina* was in
flames.

Three-quarters of an hour after engaging the
enemy Dewey turned and swung back on the opposite course, keeping parallel to the Spaniards and
at closer range. At 7.35 in the morning it was reported to the Commodore that only fifteen rounds of
ammunition remained for each gun. This was
afterwards found to be an error, but Dewey gave the
order to "cease firing," and breakfast was served
the crews.

As the American ships drew out of range the
Spaniards cheered, thinking that the victory was

conceded to them. Dewey had no such intention, however. He directed the commanders of his ships to come aboard the *Olympia* and learned from them that not a vessel was injured, not a gun out of use, not a man seriously wounded.

Soon after eleven o'clock the Americans renewed the battle, and now the *Baltimore* sent such a devastating fire at the *Reina Christina* that Montojo's flagship was rendered useless and ran aground in flames. Next the Americans directed their guns on the *Don Juan de Austria,* which shortly blew up. Finally the only Spanish ship that was fighting was the *Don Antonio de Ulloa,* commanded by Robion. Of this ship an American observer wrote: "The flag-ship and the *Boston* were the executioners. Under their shells the *Ulloa* was soon burning in half a dozen places, but her fighting crew gave no sign of surrender. Shot after shot struck her upper works, but still there were no signs of surrender. The main-deck crew escaped, while the captain and his officers clung to the wreck. . . . Her commander nailed the Spanish ensign to what was left of the mast, and the *Don Antonio de Ulloa* went down, not only with her colors flying, but also with her lower guns still roaring defiance."

With the Spanish fleet put out of action Dewey turned to the land batteries, which were soon silenced; the forts surrendered and the Americans were in complete possession of Manila Bay. In the Pacific thenceforth American commerce had noth-

ing to fear and was as unmolested as in times of
peace.

While the Asiatic Fleet had been thus engaged the
American Rear-Admiral Sampson had led the North
Atlantic Fleet out from Key West on April twenty-
second to blockade the coast of Cuba, and a flying
squadron under Commander Schley was at New-
port News to guard against any attack on the mainland.

It was known that the Spanish Admiral Cervera
had left the Cape Verde Islands on April twenty-
ninth with the cruisers *Maria Teresa, Cristóbal
Colón, Vizcaya,* and *Almirante Oquendo* and the
torpedo-boat destroyers *Furor, Plutón,* and *Terror.*
His destination was supposed to be Porto Rico.
Thither therefore Sampson proceeded, but found no
enemy squadron there on May twelfth.

Then word came that Cervera was somewhere in
the southeastern Caribbean, and Sampson set out
to seek him, and presently concluded that the
Spaniards were making for Cuba. Sampson sent
an order to Schley: "You should establish a
blockade at Cienfuegos with the least possible delay."
So Schley sailed for Cienfuegos, which has a harbor
on the southern shore of Cuba almost opposite
Havana, and Sampson watched the north coast,
waiting for word that Cervera was caught at
Havana.

Instead of aiming at Havana the Spanish admiral
was steering for Santiago, on the southeastern coast

of Cuba, and when this was reported Sampson withdrew his patrol on May twenty-ninth and headed for the harbor where the Spaniards had arrived.

On the third of June Naval Constructor Hobson tried to block the channel at Santiago by sinking the collier *Merrimac,* and almost succeeded. Later in the month an American army of 16,000 men landed at Daiquiri, east of Santiago, and began to draw a net around Cervera's forces.

Caught in this trap, his men nearly starving, Cervera received orders on July second to leave the harbor of Santiago. He felt that he had no choice but to obey, and the next morning the Spanish ships left their anchorages to try to make their way out. That same morning, as it happened, Sampson in his flagship, the *New York,* sailed to the east to confer with General Shafter of the American army. Within an hour after his departure from one end of the American squadron to the other rang the cry, "The enemy are coming out!"

First came the *Maria Teresa,* then the *Vizcaya, Cristóbal Colón,* and *Almirante Oquendo.* When the *Maria Teresa* was out of the channel she ran at full speed west towards Havana. Captain Evans of the *Iowa* at once turned north opposite the enemy and opened fire at six thousand yards.

The blockading ships were at a disadvantage because shortage of coal had prevented them from keeping full steam up and the Spaniards were running with full pressure on their boilers. As the

American ships sent out clouds of thick smoke in their efforts to get more steam there resulted a low visibility that aided Cervera's vessels in flying from the blockaders' fire.

In spite of these handicaps the American ships poured a heavy bombardment on their opponents, which was vigorously returned by the Spaniards, but with less accurate aim. Soon the Spanish ships were badly battered. Cervera had had little expectation when he sailed out from Santiago of being able to fight his way through the blockaders. In his official report he wrote: "One of the first projectiles burst an auxiliary steam-pipe on board the *Infanta Maria Teresa*. A great deal of steam escaped, which made us lose the speed on which we had counted. About the same time another shell destroyed one of the fire-mains. Yet the ships made a valiant defense against galling hostile fire. Among the first wounded was our gallant commander, Captain Concas, who had to withdraw; and as we could not afford to lose a single moment, I myself took direct command, waiting for the executive officer to appear. Fire broke out aft and spread rapidly forward. It being impossible to flood the magazines, because of the smoke and flames, I beached the ship and surrendered."

The American squadron was picking up speed and the battleships *Iowa, Oregon, Indiana,* and *Texas,* and the cruiser *Brooklyn* were close on the heels of the Spaniards, while Admiral Sampson's flagship, the *New York,* was coming up from the east. The *Gloucester,* a converted yacht, which had been in the van of the fighting, was attacking the Spanish torpedo-boat destroyers, *Furor* and *Plutón,* as they brought up the Spanish rear.

Soon after Admiral Cervera beached his flaming flagship, the *Almirante Oquendo* ran ashore, also on fire. Next the *Vizcaya* was out of the combat. The *Cristóbal Colón* kept on, now six miles ahead of the *Brooklyn* and *Oregon.* The latter battleship continued the chase until she overhauled the *Cristóbal Colón,* when the Spanish commander struck his flag.

The battle of Santiago practically ended the war and peace was declared on August 12, 1898.

Long range guns and turrets and armor now distinguished the battleship. The English builders, seeing the error of arming a warship with guns of various sizes in the turrets, constructed in 1906 the *Dreadnaught,* an "all-big-gun" ship, equipped with only the heaviest type of naval guns and with small guns to use in repelling torpedo attacks. This ship was such an innovation that she gave her name to all the large modern battleships, and when even bigger ones were built they were called "super-dreadnaughts."

The *Dreadnaught* was of 17,900 tons, 490 feet long and 92 feet wide, with ten 12-inch guns mounted in five turrets; she could make twenty-one and a half knots an hour and could travel 5800 miles without renewing her coal supply.

In the World War England and Germany came to
grips on the sea in the Battle of Jutland, fought off
the coast of Jutland on May 30, 1916. The German
ships appeared from the direction of Helgoland
Bight in the afternoon and a squadron of English
battle cruisers, commanded by Admiral Beatty,
opened fire at a range of about twelve miles. The
Germans had the advantage of the light, and their
whole battle fleet was soon arrayed against Beatty
while the British Grand Fleet under Admiral Jellicoe was some distance away.

The superior speed of the English cruisers enabled
Beatty to take up a tactical position in advance of
the German line and so to prevent his ships from
being cut off from Jellicoe's fleet. The English battleships of the type known as Queen Elizabeths kept
up a steady fire at the flashes of the German guns,
which were the only targets visible to them in the
heavy mist.

By extreme skill in maneuvering the entire English fleet became concentrated across the head of the
German line and in a few minutes of good light Jellicoe destroyed the three foremost enemy vessels.
Then the mist blew down again and behind this
screen the German fleet was able to draw off to
shelter, though in ragged divisions.

The mist prevented the English from taking full
advantage of their superior position, but the Battle
of Jutland resulted in bottling up the German fleet,
which for the rest of the war did not again venture

forth from the protecting guns and mine fields around Helgoland; therefore the English navy was well justified in claiming that battle a victory for their fleet.

What a vast change had come about in naval engagements since the days of Nelson! The ship-of-the-line was now a first-class battleship and this battleship was itself only a part of the fighting fleet. Almost as important as the battleship were the armored cruisers and the destroyers; and in addition to these were the submarines and the seaplanes. A battle fleet had become a tremendously complex collection of many different kinds of units and the warship was hardly a ship at all from the standpoint of the eras of the Roman galley, the Spanish galleon, or the sailing frigate.

CHAPTER XXIV
SHIPS OF VARIOUS TYPES

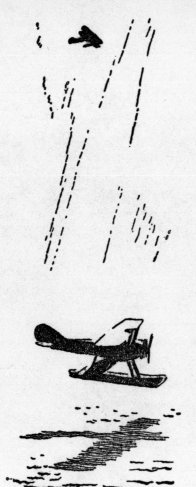

XXIV

SHIPS OF VARIOUS TYPES

EACH sea has produced its own ships, and there has been as great a variety among them as there were differences between the races of men who built and sailed them. The waters that were to be navigated, the winds to be encountered, the character of the people, the purpose to which the boat was to be put, all these have determined the types of ships. Oftentimes the same name is given to ships of different seas that actually bear little resemblance to each other and sometimes a ship with a certain name has altered so materially through the centuries that its latest form looks very little like its earliest model. There are some types that can be pictured fairly accurately, the galley, the galleon, the frigate, the sloop, the schooner; but there are many more to be encountered in the pages of history that have disappeared from the seas without leaving a clear picture of themselves or that have left pictures that vary in many details.

Yet some of these ships are interesting and deserve recording, if only because their names bring back something of the romance of ancient days on the sea. There is the carrack, for instance; the name that was used to designate some of the larger

379

ships of the fourteenth, the fifteenth, and part of the sixteenth centuries. The carrack was specially designed to carry large burdens, but was also frequently used for warfare. These ships usually had three, and occasionally four, masts, the mainmast being much larger than the others. A diminutive main-topmast also was carried on the carrack from an early date, but this appears to have been often little more than a flag-staff.

Another type of large ship that was popular during the early sixteenth century was the hulk, which had a round stern and a high poop and was rigged like the merchant vessels of that era. Great fleets of hulks are mentioned in history, the ships ranging in size from one hundred to eight hundred tons.

The cromster was a ship that was much used in England at the time of Queen Elizabeth and later in the Low Countries. This vessel took its name from the Dutch word "cromsteven," which meant a bent or crooked stem. Cromsters were frequently of one hundred and eighty tons or more, and had three masts, a fore staysail on a stay running from the masthead to the stem, a mainsail that was peaked up by means of a tackle, and a lateen mizzensail.

During the seventeenth century the hulk was replaced among the traders of northern and western Europe by a ship called the flute. This vessel had a stubby bow that extended into a curved beak, was curved along the sides, and the stern rounded in wide sweeps to a point as high as the top of the rudder. The flute was ship-rigged and often carried guns on a single deck. This type of ship was very popular in the Low Countries, where round-sterned vessels were always favorites, and probably many flutes crossed the Atlantic in the era when the Dutch were establishing their colony of New Netherland.

The lugger was a ship that sometimes had two masts, sometimes three, and carried lug sails. Being a very fast sailer, she was often used for privateering. Before the days of steam navigation luggers were the great supply-ships of the English fleets anchored in bad weather in the Channel ports. They were also celebrated as slave-ships and as wreckers.

A ship that was something like the buss, and of the round-sterned type, was the howker. She was used in the merchant trade, and was of fifty to two hundred tons.

Along the coasts of Brittany a popular ship was the bugalet. This vessel had two masts, the after one much larger than the other and carrying a large square sail surmounted by a topsail. The foremast had a square sail but no topsail. The bugalet also had a bowsprit set with one or two jibs.

To the family of the Mediterranean galley with its great lateen sails belonged the vessel known as the felucca. Feluccas were of many patterns, some of them had one mast and a triangular sail, some two masts with lateen sails, some of them were equipped with oars and some did without them. The masts usually inclined well forward. With its sails set upon opposite sides when running free before the wind the felucca was a very picturesque sight as it scudded through the blue Mediterranean waters.

The xebec was a ship of Far Eastern as well as of European seas. Its hull was much like that of a galley, but was rather narrow; it had a prominent beak and at the stern there was an outer platform composed of two wings. The three masts generally bore lateen sails, but there were many varieties of rigging on the xebec. Oars were used as a supplement to the xebec's sails.

Another Mediterranean ship was the tartane, which was of medium size with a large mainmast carrying a square sail and a small mizzenmast with a lateen. The hull was drawn in at the stern, so that the tartane was really a double-ender. In Southern Europe was also to be encountered the patache, a very slow sailing vessel, commonly used in the coasting trade, and a near relation to the brigantine.

In the thirteenth century the name "cat" was applied to a type of rowed vessel that had a beak like a galley, two steering oars, and that was propelled by a hundred sweeps, each pulled by two men. Afterwards the name was used for a three-masted merchant ship of the north of Europe with blunt bows and very full rounded quarters. This ship was designed to carry cargoes, and a small crew could handle it, as the yards and sails were so constructed that they could be lowered to the deck, thus doing away with the need of sending the sailors aloft to furl the sails.

There were many variations in the type of ship called the corvette, but in the early eighteenth century that name was commonly given to a ship that had two masts and a bowsprit with a spritsail. Later the corvette took the general build of a frigate and mounted from fourteen to thirty-two guns. This ship was popular in the French navy and corresponded in the class of smaller war vessels with the British and American sloop of war. It was distinguished by its comparatively low freeboard and the absence of a high quarterdeck.

The Dutch gave the name of barquentine to a ship with a square-rigged foremast and a mainmast that carried a fore and aft mainsail. The modern barquentine has three or more masts, is a close relation to the schooner, and is largely used in the Pacific Ocean. Among the larger sailing ships there are many variations of rigging between the brig and the schooner, and between the ship, the bark and the barquentine.

CHAPTER XXV
SHIPS OF THE MODERN WORLD

SHIPS OF THE MODERN WORLD

WHEN we speak of a ship we usually think of a vessel driven by sails and picture a caravel of the era of the great explorers, a sturdy ocean-voyager like the *Mayflower,* or a clipper like the *Flying Cloud,* her canvas bellied out by the wind, her bow cleaving the water, as she scuds across the seas. There are still sails on the ocean to delight the eye, but they no longer have the monopoly of the sea they enjoyed for many centuries; gradually they have given place to the reign of steam.

Man first used poles and oars for his barks, then sails, then engines; the galley of the Mediterranean was succeeded by the caravel that could cover great distances, the caravel by the frigate, the frigate by the clipper ship and that by the mighty ocean-liner and the armored battleship. Columbus struggled for weeks to cross the Atlantic Ocean from Spain to America, but men can now fly in a few hours across that expanse of water, and the voyage around the world, first made by Magellan's little ship *Victoria* through innumerable hardships, is now accomplished easily by luxurious steamers. Ships have searched

out all the ocean highways, and ships—if one may
use the word "ship" in reference to planes and submarines—have learned to navigate the air above and
the depths beneath the surface of the water.

There are still some men who go down to the sea
in small boats and keep up the traditions of the era
of sails. The fishermen of Gloucester go out to the
Grand Banks in their schooners and ride through
great storms in their stalwart wooden ships.
Frenchmen still fish off Newfoundland as they did a
century ago, and all over the world one may see the
sails, of many colors and many designs, of those who
make their livelihood from the denizens of the deep.

In modern times Captain Joshua Slocum sailed
alone around the world in the 37-foot yawl *Spray*
in three years and two months, and in 1911 Captain
Thomas Fleming Day and two companions voyaged
from Providence, Rhode Island, to Gibraltar in the
25-foot yawl *Seabird* in thirty-seven days, which in-
cluded a stop of five days at the Azores. Sails still
have their appeal for adventurous navigators and as
daring voyages are made in small sail-driven boats
as those attempted by prehistoric travelers in
hollowed-out canoes.

In place of the fighting frigate there is now the
first-class battleship or the cruiser capable of a speed
of from twenty-eight to thirty-five knots an hour.
The modern battle fleet consists of many units,
dreadnaughts, super-dreadnaughts, battle cruisers,
scout cruisers, destroyers, submarines, gunboats, col-

liers, supply-ships, hospital ships and airplane carriers, to name but the more important.

The small sailing packet that carried passengers across the ocean has become the gigantic liner, driven by screw propellers; in 1924 there were in the transatlantic service ten of these liners of more than 25,-000 tons. The most modern ones use oil instead of coal, and a new development—that of the motor-driven vessel—bids fair to put an end to the era of steam.

In addition to the large liners there are mail liners and "intermediate" liners that are of many sorts, carrying passengers to ports outside the general run of the biggest ships, loading cargoes in places far afield, the successors in commerce to the clippers that sailed in the China trade or around Cape Horn.

Then there are the tramp steamers, hard-working vessels that deserve a better name, the ships that carry the bulk of the world's trade. These have a raised section amidships, where is located the bridge, the funnel, and the quarters that contain the galley, or kitchen, the staterooms and the messroom. Below are the boiler and engine rooms. At the bow the deck rises to the forecastle, still called by the name that was given to the lofty structure that adorned the forepart of the ship of an earlier era. At the stern the deck also rises, as it did in the mediæval vessel, but the designation sterncastle was long since abandoned and the structure aft is known as the poop.

Such are some of the ships that now move upon the waters. Beneath the sea glide the submarines. Above it fly the airplanes; and of both the sea and the air are the hydro-airplanes, that mark a new chapter in the history of ships. Equally at home in water or air their uses are manifold; as scouts they can supply eyes and ears to a fleet; they are the nearest approach to the sea-gull that has yet been fashioned.

Birds of the sea, such are ships: what vision was ever more romantic or beautiful than the Dragon boat of the Vikings, the lofty galleon of the Mediterranean, or the many-sparred American clipper with the sunlight on her sails!